About the Editor

BILL FAWCETT is the author and editor of more than a dozen books, including *Oval Office Oddities, You Did What?, How to Lose a Battle,* and *You Said What?* He is also the packager and agent for several of our very successful military titles, such as *One Perfect Op* and many of our SEALs titles. Fawcett lives in Illinois.

Books Edited by Bill Fawcett

HUNTERS
&
SHOOTERS

An Oral History of the
U.S. Navy SEALs in Vietnam

Edited by BILL FAWCETT

HARPER

NEW YORK • LONDON • TORONTO • SYDNEY

HARPER

Written with the cooperation of the UDT/SEAL Museum and the UDT/
SEAL Association.

A hardcover edition of this book was published in 1995 by William Morrow
and Company.

HUNTERS & SHOOTERS. Copyright © 1995 by Bill Fawcett and Associates.
All rights reserved. Printed in the United States of America. No part of this
book may be used or reproduced in any manner whatsoever without written
permission except in the case of brief quotations embodied in critical
articles and reviews. For information address HarperCollins Publishers, 10
East 53rd Street, New York, NY 10022.

HarperCollins books may be purchased for educational, business, or sales
promotional use. For information please write: Special Markets Department,
HarperCollins Publishers, 10 East 53rd Street, New York, NY 10022.

FIRST HARPER PAPERBACK PUBLISHED 2008.

The Library of Congress has catalogued the previous edition as:

Hunters and shooters: an oral history of the U.S. Navy Seals in
Vietnam / edited by Bill Fawcett.
   p   cm.
1. Vietnamese Conflict, 1961-1975—Commando operations. 2. United
States. Navy. SEALs—History. 3. Vietnamese Conflict, 1961-1975—
Regimental histories—United States. 4. Vietnamese Conflict, 1961-1975—
Personal narratives, American. I. Fawcett, Bill.

DS55.92H86   1995   94-42764
959.704'345—dc20   CIP

ISBN: 978-0-06-137566-8 (pbk.)

   11 12   RRD   10 9 8 7 6 5 4 3

ACKNOWLEDGMENTS

I t was impossible to record more than a small number of the uncounted incidents of courage, loyalty, and devotion involving the SEALs in Vietnam alone. Before any other expressions of gratitude, I have to thank those SEALs who were willing to recount so many often emotionally traumatic memories. The modest, quiet courage of those we were privileged to interview never failed to impress those of us recording their tales.

It is also impossible to list everyone who contributed to this book. Among the many are James Watson, the curator of the UDT/SEAL Museum in Fort Pierce, Florida, and Linda, his lovely bride; Marge and Rudy Boesch; Harry Humphries; Captain Ryan McCombie; Captain Rick Woolard; Bob Shuman; Andy Andrews; Red Hart; Rick Marcinko; Mark Wertheimer; and Tom Colgan.

These men are, by the very nature of their methods of operating, very closemouthed about their accomplishments. Not only have their stories been largely untold until now, these quiet professionals are justifiably proud of their silence. To thank these men sufficiently for their openness and trust in telling the interviewers about their very personal experiences is as impossible as some of the operations they took.

The more we spoke with the SEALs, the more we came to understand the immense and often unseen contribution they made, and continue to make, to our country. So let this end with thanks to all SEALs for what they have done and continue to do for our security and freedom.

—BILL FAWCETT
Chicago, 1995

CONTENTS

INTRODUCTION

In 1943, at the height of World War Two, a specialized unit of men, the Navy Combat Demolition Units (NCDUs), was formed to complete a specific mission. The NCDUs were highly trained and physically fit demolition specialists, volunteers primarily from graduates of the bomb and mine disposal school, the Seabees, and the fleet Navy. The objective of these men was to blast the obstacles clear from the beaches of Europe where the Allied forces would land. Normandy was where the NCDUs performed their greatest mission.

For the island-hopping campaign in the Pacific, a new form of amphibious scout and demolition specialist was needed to chart and clear enemy-held beaches prior to invasion landings. The Navy already had a superbly fit and trained force in the NCDUs; further specialized training was all that was needed. Within weeks of arriving at Maui in the Pacific, men of the NCDUs completed further training in reconnaissance, charting, and surveying. Operating in the field by early 1944, the NCDUs were now known by a new name, Underwater Demolition Teams, or UDTs.

The UDTs expanded in size until, by the end of World War Two, they numbered almost 3,500 men divided into thirty Teams. These UDTs had led the way for almost every major amphibious landing of World War Two during 1944 and 1945. By the end of the war, the UDTs were setting their sights on the largest target of all, the invasion of mainland Japan.

Though a combat invasion of Japan never took place, the UDTs still were the first to land and take the surrender of mainland Japanese soil. Scouting beaches for the occupation forces put a small group of UDT men in the position of accepting the surrender of a small Japanese fort. But for all their accomplishments and the accolades they earned, after the final operations of World War Two were over, the UDTs were dismantled until only a small nucleus of trained men remained.

By the time of the Korean War only five years later, the UDTs had made a slight comeback in numbers. The war in Korea added to the UDTs' repertoire of skills. In addition to their roles in the water, charting beaches, attacking ships, clearing mines, and demolishing obstacles, the UDTs now had occasion to operate on dry land.

Missions now took place where the men of the UDTs attacked enemy structures well behind the lines, using their skills with explosives to bring down bridges and tunnels. Moving through and under the water helped make the UDT men almost invisible to a searching enemy. Further missions included inserting and extracting guerrilla forces to operate at the enemy's rear. Later UDT training, after the Korean War, included parachute jumping and the development of new forms of underwater breathing and swimming equipment.

By the first years of the 1960s, a new form of warfare was becoming more common in the world, and a new kind of warrior was needed to combat it. A new administration under the direction of President John F. Kennedy recognized the need. By Executive Order of the President of the United States, each arm of the U.S. military was to create a new counterguerrilla force. The Army had the Special Forces, commonly called the Green Berets for their distinctive headwear. The Navy looked to its UDTs as the source of manpower for its new unit.

The new Navy unit would be able to fight on land or sea and to infiltrate by air if required. Taking the first letters of the three environments they would operate in, the new units would be called the Navy SEALs, for SEa, Air, and Land. Men were chosen from the UDTs of the East and West coasts to fill out the ranks of the new units. Finally, fifty men and ten officers on each coast were chosen to make up the new SEAL Teams. On January 8, 1962, at 1300 hours, SEAL Team ONE was commissioned at Coronado, California, and SEAL Team TWO was commissioned at Little Creek, Virginia. The commissioning orders were backdated to January 1, 1962.

The men who made up the Teams were chosen for a variety of skills. Notably these men were all UDT operators, qualified to work underwater with a variety of equipment including open-circuit SCUBA, closed-circuit rebreathers, and mixed-gas systems, as well as being experienced parachutists. A few individuals trained in very specialized fields were added to the first SEALs, the "plankowners," to round out each Team's skills.

The training regimen all these men shared is considered one of the most difficult in the military. During basic UDT training, whether it is called BUD/S (Basic Underwater Demolition/SEAL), UDTB (Underwater Demolition Team Basic), or UDTR (Underwater Demolition Team Replacement), each man faces the hardest week of training there is. Officially named Motivation Week, those five days and nights of training are always referred to by the men who have completed them as Hell Week.

During that one week, UDT or SEAL volunteers undergo days of maximum physical output and minimum rest. Perhaps one or two hours a day might be scheduled for sleep. All of the other time is taken up by "evolutions," exercises that must be completed to pass. And a volunteer can end his training simply by saying, "I quit."

During training, and especially during Hell Week, the men learn the essence of being a UDT or SEAL operator—teamwork. Many of the evolutions cannot be completed by a single man—they can be accomplished only by a team's concerted effort. Beyond the value of teamwork, the men also learn that they are capable of ten times what they thought was their maximum output prior to training. And that philosophy traces its way back to those first days in 1943 and the beginning of the NCDUs.

RUDY BOESCH

One of the legendary names of the SEAL Teams is that of Rudy Boesch, who holds the distinction of having the longest time in service of any man ever in Naval Special Warfare. Long known as a steadying influence on the quarterdeck, Rudy, as he was called by his men, served with SEAL Team TWO from its first day in 1962 to the late 1980s.

World War Two was in its last year, though I didn't know it, when I joined the Navy. I was seventeen years, three months old in April 1945 when I enlisted. Boot camp for me was in Sampson, New York, not far from my home in Rochester, New York.

While I was in boot camp, the war in Germany ended. Now it looked as if the Pacific and Japanese would be where and who I would fight. Just after graduation while still at Sampson, the class was lined up for an announcement. What we were asked was if anybody wanted to volunteer for a special program. That was about all the information they gave us, a special program. Out of my class of about one hundred guys, I was the only one to put his hand up.

The next thing I knew, I was on a train heading for Fort Pierce, Florida, and the United States Naval Amphibious Training Base there. Arriving at the base, I still didn't know anything. The NCDUs were training there before going on to the Pacific and becoming UDTs, but the units were so secret that, as a lowly seaman apprentice, I knew nothing about them at the time. Arriving at the base on South Hutchinson Island, I was assigned to the Scouts and Raiders.

The mission of the Scouts and Raiders during the last phase of the war in the Pacific was to go into mainland China and prepare for the final invasion of Japan. As a seventeen-year-old, none of this meant a great deal to me—the big picture just went over my head. As it was, the big picture never happened.

In August, the class was out in Lake Okeechobee doing training in the swamps when the atomic bomb was dropped on Japan. We knew absolutely nothing about it until the instructors came out and got us. "Stop what you're doing," we were told. "The war is over. Everybody is going back to Fort Pierce."

When we got back to the base, our orders were simple—we were going to tear the base down. Within a week, the large naval base on South Hutchinson Island simply ceased to exist. Buildings were stripped out and returned to their former owners. Mostly what we had were tents, and those we just tore down and burned. The base was now gone, and so were we.

It was the longest train ride of my life, a troop train from Fort Pierce, Florida, on the Atlantic, to the West Coast and the Pacific. Five hundred men left Florida, and only about 250 arrived in California. The rest jumped off the train whenever it would stop—just went over the hill after the war had ended.

Still heading west, the Navy put me on a slow boat to China. I finally arrived in the harbor at Hong Kong in October 1945. One day while going out on the mail run to Kowloon, I and two other guys came back to a decommissioned ship. In the six hours that it took us to make the run, they had emptied the ship of personnel. Taking our orders from another Navy ship nearby, I and four others ended up spending eighteen months in the Far East, most of them guarding that empty ship.

The first year we all spent guarding that ship in Hong

Kong Harbor—breaking into the food lockers and fresh-water tanks, selling parts and fixtures for money to go ashore with, and holding off mobs of people on junks, first using rifles, pistols, and submachine guns and finally .22 pistols and flare guns when the ammunition ran low.

The U.S. Navy finally remembered us, and we spent some time going to Shanghai, then upriver to the Navy base. After drawing eighteen months back pay, we finally were returned to the United States. The Navy put me on a destroyer for two years, and then I pulled a stint of shore duty in London, England, for a good while.

By 1950, I had read in *All Hands* magazine about the UDTs and how they were coming back from their postwar cutbacks. The UDTs with their small numbers, camara-derie, and interesting assignments looked like what I wanted to do during my time in the Navy, so I put in my chit and volunteered.

In January of 1951 I first arrived at Little Creek to attend UDTR training. I had no idea that I wouldn't per-manently leave the base until 1988, and if someone had told me that, I wouldn't have believed him. I've spent more time at Little Creek than the post barbers, and in a military installation the barber is considered a permanent fixture.

As I came to understand it, after World War Two, the Navy had gathered all the UDTs in California for decom-missioning. With most of the men gone, two Teams were created, one for the West Coast and one for the East Coast. The East Coast Team was going to be stationed at Indian Head, Maryland, up the river from Norfolk and Little Creek. When the Team stopped off at Little Creek on their way upriver, they decided they liked the location. The Teams have been at the Creek ever since.

To join the Teams you had to go through UDTR (Un-derwater Demolition Team Replacement) training. With my class, Class 6, the training was almost all physical. As I remember, the amount of demolition training I received at the time I could teach to a soldier in about fifteen minutes. It was the physical training that was seriously emphasized. If you could hack the physical end of training you were in, and I wanted in.

Starting in January—I had a winter class—we finally graduated that April. Sixteen weeks of the hardest training in the military. Time has passed and made memories of training a blur. Time spent at Little Creek was cold, and the instructors made the most of the weather to make sure you felt the cold. When ice forms and floats on the sea, you know it's cold.

And the expression "colder than hell" took on a whole new meaning when my class pulled Hell Week at Little Creek. That week was tough. At the time, the instructors didn't have limitations put on the size of the charges they would fire during "So Solly" day, the last day of Hell Week. Without the buildup of houses and other construction that's all around the base today, the instructors didn't have to worry about breaking windows, just breaking us.

A twenty-pound charge of explosives going off near you can pick you right up off of the ground, and then slam you down with your teeth rattling and ears ringing. For myself, I had started the course and I was going to finish it. I was just too stubborn to quit and they weren't going to make me quit.

The instructors were able to make a lot of our class quit. After we had lost two-thirds of our people, the rest stabilized out. We graduated about twenty-five people, if I remember correctly.

We finally left the Creek and headed for St. Thomas in the Virgin Islands for the balance of our training. It was much easier not having to battle the elements every day. But the instructors kept things from being too relaxing, having us in the water for swims at five o'clock in the morning and pulling us out at about nine o'clock at night. All-day swims, long runs, and PT kept the physical end of training at a high level. But there was technical material for us to learn as well.

A lot of underwater work was given to us in St. Thomas. Hydrographic surveys with a lead line, beach charting, reconnaissance. All the duties of the UDT during World War Two and then some. It wasn't until after we had "graduated" UDTR that we really got into the underwater swimming end of training. We hadn't actually graduated—we didn't do that officially until we returned to the Creek—but we did take our diving training while in St. Thomas. We spent two weeks in the water with each type of 'lung we used. The LARU (Lambertson Amphibious Respiratory Unit), a closed-circuit, pure-oxygen rebreather, and the twin-hosed open-circuit SCUBA were the systems we trained on. The new Perelli closed-circuit system was just being tested by the Teams, and we trained on that system as well.

The Lambertson was referred to as the "Black Death" rig for quite a while. The system had been in use during World War Two for OSS sabotage swimmers. Coal miners had also used the system for breathing in contaminated mines, and some of our rigs still had the little lamps on them for use in the mines. Closed-circuit systems take a lot of training and attention if they aren't going to kill you when you use them.

The breath you put out would go into a flexible bag that had a CO_2 absorbent in it to scrub out the carbon dioxide you exhaled. The absorbent was baralyme, a caustic mixture of hydroxides that could cause a severe burn if it contacted the skin. And we breathed through this stuff underwater! A tank of oxygen would replace the oxygen you had used up while breathing and let you continue underwater for hours, without ever releasing a bubble into the water.

Money was tight at the time, and the instructors would have you use the same baralyme during each of a day's three dives. Many of the guys would flood out their 'lungs, let water into the system, so that they could throw out the old stuff and get issued new absorbent. After a while, we started running short of baralyme, so we had to spread out the wet baralyme on newspapers in the sun so that it could dry and we would use it again. A lot more dangerous than anything they do now. But the Teams know a great deal more about diving today than they did then. As it was, a number of guys almost drowned when they flooded out their rigs. Some of them passed out at the end of their dives. But we didn't lose anyone to a diving accident.

Returning to Little Creek, Class 6 graduated, and we were assigned to UDT 2. From 1951 to 1962 I spent my time with the UDTs, first Team 2 and then Team 21. Most of the time away from the Creek, we were on Med trips [Mediterranean cruises] with the fleet on exercises. It was on one of these trips about five years later that I was assigned to UDT 21. Not a big deal—everyone with me was assigned to the Team. We went out as UDT 2 and returned as UDT 21. Just a paperwork drill. Why they changed the numbers, I don't know.

Anybody who goes through UDTR training tends to hate PT after he graduates. After all, all you do in training is PT. And I wasn't any different. As a Boatswain's mate, I would hang out in the Bosun's locker when PT time rolled around. The Team held a pentathlon competition, running, swimming, exercises, stuff like that, and I won. That incident turned me around a little about PT and I started getting more involved with that training. I didn't start running the daily PT until after the SEAL Teams were commissioned in 1962. But after the pentathlon, I participated a lot more in the regular PT program.

Late in 1961, I was on detachment in the Med along with Lenny Waugh when a message came in for us. Lenny and I were to get back to Little Creek as soon as possible. We had been assigned to SEAL Team TWO. Neither one of us knew what a SEAL Team was, but off we went back to the States. The Navy detached us in Naples, Italy, with instructions to find our own way back to Norfolk. Lenny and I started bumming rides on any planes headed in the right direction. We did make it back in time for the commissioning date, but by New Year's Eve, when Lenny and I were in Casablanca, Morocco, it was looking like a close race.

On commissioning day for Team TWO, I was standing in the formation at UDT 21. As the names were called out for men to report, I was the only Chief present among the men chosen for SEAL Team TWO. Two other Chiefs, Doc Stone, a corpsman, and Hoot Andrews, a Storekeeper

Chief, didn't arrive at the Team until at least a week had gone by, so for a while I was the highest-ranking NCO at Team TWO.

It didn't matter much that some of the guys weren't at the formation that first day—they were still among the plankowners of Team TWO. Even our CO, Callahan, wasn't able to report in at the Creek for several weeks. He was tied up in Washington, D.C., at meetings about what the Navy was going to do with this new group they had created. Roy Boehm, who had been one of the driving forces behind the new SEAL Team concept, was the acting CO and officer in charge of the Team until Callahan was able to arrive.

Roy Boehm had been the primary chooser for who would be in the new SEAL Team. The reason I was picked, as near as I could tell, was that I was the only Chief in UDT 21 who was airborne-qualified at the time. Back in 1958, I had been one of the few men from UDT 21 who had attended jump training down at Fort Benning. At the time, it was strictly voluntary for frogmen to go to jump school. When Roy needed a Chief for Team TWO, I was it, and that resulted in me being the Chief of the boat at Team TWO for quite a while.

When the SEALs were first commissioned, we didn't really have a specific job to do yet. Vietnam was just starting up—we sent a small contingent of guys over there within a few months of our commissioning date. But that was nothing compared to what was waiting down the road for us. Cuba was the big problem at the time, but even it hadn't really peaked yet. The missile crisis wasn't going to happen until the fall of 1962.

It was actually a good thing that the SEALs didn't have an immediate, pressing mission to accomplish right after our commissioning, because we didn't have anything to do the job with. There were very few weapons in the Team and little or no equipment. Almost everything we needed was still coming in through channels. But channels were not something Roy Boehm was known for waiting on when there was a need.

While Cuba was heating up, one of the missions the

SEALs might have to do involved going into Cuba to perform guerrilla operations. No gear meant no operations, but that situation wasn't allowed to last long. Roy had an open purchase from the Navy to buy materials and equipment on the civilian market, and he used it. One night after nine o'clock, a number of the guys with Roy in the lead went to Sears and Ward's and had the managers open the places up. The Team's first small arms, mostly pistols, came right out of the stores' showcases. The materials were needed, we had the money to buy them, and we wanted them now!

Watches, uniforms, police holsters and ammunition holders, all kinds of gear was bought on the open market. While gearing up for possible operations in Cuba, men came in from Team ONE on the West Coast as well as men who would form the Special Boat Units. All of us were living in this one small dumpy place the Team had. Men were sleeping on the deck, and piles of gear were all around.

As the men came in, we issued what we had. Watches, pistols, and other gear were given out. Then when Cuba calmed down, the additional men went back to their parent units, and a lot of our gear went with them. One of the items we had before anyone else in the Navy was the AR-15 rifle. Roy Boehm bought 136 of the weapons from a supplier in Baltimore. Half of the weapons went to the West Coast and SEAL Team ONE, with the remainder staying with us. Those were the first rifles of their kind in the Navy and were later adopted by the military as the M16. We had them first because we needed them.

After the Cuba thing calmed down, the Team went back to a normal day-to-day routine. In the beginning, the Team had been going to all sorts of Army and Marine schools in order to learn what we needed to know to operate. Schools such as kitchen demolitions, survival, and others were all tried. Some we stayed with and others we dropped as unnecessary. Eventually, the Team all got back to Little Creek only to find ourselves with nothing to do.

Nothing to do really meant that we didn't have an immediate mission to perform or train up for. But the physical fitness level of everyone in the Team had to be kept up. PT is something that you just can't do all the time and keep the levels up. Sports competitions are a good way to exercise and blow off a little steam at the same time. For SEAL Team TWO, our sport was soccer.

With the running and kicking involved with soccer, the legs of the players stayed built up for the long swims with fins that we might be called upon to do. Instead of the normal eleven guys on a side for the game, we would get the entire Team involved, with thirty-two guys on a side. Kicking that ball around wasn't the safest way for us to exercise, either—the Team had three broken legs in one week. And six hours a day of soccer, every day, would either build you up or break you down. By Friday, my legs would be hurting so much I could barely walk.

PT was still something we did often, a SEAL way to start the day. During the Cuba excitement, we did PT three times a day, with Joe DiMartino leading us, as I remember. Eventually, PT became something of an obsession with me. I would lead the Team in its daily exercises and became known as a real hard charger for physical fitness. Some members of the Team even had a special set of dog tags made for me that they gave to me during Quarters one morning. In the space for ''religion'' they had put ''PT.''

Every morning during the week, I would lead the Team in PT. And every morning, about 10 percent of the guys would manage to sneak out of at least some of it. It would really burn me up that I couldn't catch these guys. Every morning it was a little different. The XO would stand in front of the Team formation at Quarters in the morning, about seven-thirty a.m., and make his talk for the day. Right after the XO was finished, ten guys would go off to the head, two guys would go another way, and four more would go somewhere else. And none of them would make it back in time for PT.

Finally I tried something else. Immediately after Quarters, the Team would be called to attention. With the order ''Right face,'' I would turn the Team and the formation would be off for the morning run. That technique managed to catch most of my escapees. Other teammates would have excuses or be ill. Another trick minimized those people going off to sick bay.

"All right," I would call out to the formation, "who's going to sick bay?"

Say five or so hands would go up. "Stand out here and tell us why you're going to sick bay," I would tell them.

One guy would stand in front of everybody and say something like "My head hurts." The catcalls he would get from his Teammates indicated their level of sympathy. The embarrassment and peer pressure would usually cure whatever ailed most of my sick SEALs. But even that slowed down and stopped working after a while. It was a constant battle to catch these guys and get them to do their PT.

Even if I got the guys to do their PT, they would try to get out of the long beach runs afterwards. The bushes near Beach 7 were a favorite place for a quick leap into hiding. When the run formation came back along our usual route, any guys hiding in the bushes would just come back out and join into the back of the formation.

Of course, if I saw anyone jump out of the formation and into the bushes, we wouldn't come back that way at the end of the run. While we were sitting back in the building with a cup of coffee, those guys would still be waiting in the bushes, looking for the formation.

Those sorts of games also helped keep the morale up. My catching the "skippers" and their getting away with it were all part of being in the Team. MacEvoy was particularly good at playing those games with me, as well as being the most consistent at getting away with it. None of the guys really liked the runs—I didn't like them myself. But somebody had to get in front of the formation and put the pressure on to keep up the fitness level. And as the Chief of the boat, I had the job.

One time, while Gormly was the CO [September 1972 to July 1974], being the PT leader backfired on me a little bit. That morning's endurance exercise was a two-mile swim. The water was pretty rough, and after about a quarter mile of swimming, I started to feel ill. When I headed in to the beach, most of the formation followed me in. Only Gormly and about six guys, who were the really good swimmers, were far out past the breaker line and going strong. I got out of the water and about ninety guys followed me onto the beach. "What are you guys doing?" I said. "I don't feel good—that's the reason I'm getting out."

"Well, we don't feel good either," was their answer.

Ninety guys followed me back to the Team building, walking across the sand dunes. Far out in the water, Gormly stopped and looked back at my little parade on the beach. About an hour later, after he had completed the swim, Gormly wanted to know what had been going on.

"Why did everybody stop?" he asked me.

"I got sick," I answered. "When I got out of the water, all the guys just followed me. They just wanted an excuse to get out of PT."

"I tell you what, Rudy," Gormly said. "Tell them all to follow you Friday afternoon when liberty has gone down and they do that swim again."

When liberty goes down, that's normally the end of the working day. Friday liberty is especially important, because that's when the weekend starts. That one Friday, the weekend started a little late. I took the Team out and we did a two-mile swim in the afternoon. Not even I could get out of PT, it seemed.

All kinds of excuses would be used to get liberty time—that is, time off for personal business. "My wife is sick" and "I need to take my dog to the vet" were among them. The single guys didn't have those reasons, but they soon came up with some of their own.

The first time one particular excuse was used was during the very first few months of the Team. We had all been on alert in case of action in Cuba for some time, and the strain was beginning to show. One morning a stack of chits came in, all with the same reason, all wanting liberty.

Each man's reason for wanting liberty was to go out and get drunk with his buddy, and almost everyone in the

Team filled out a request chit. I signed the chits and filled out one for myself. Callahan wasn't at the Team, and Roy Boehm saw the requests and filled out one for himself. I didn't have to sign Roy's. The reason held, and the whole Team, less one guy to pull watch duty, took a day off. Things like that could happen and help ease the strain that can build up during a long alert.

The whole Team was pretty small during the early 1960s, less than a hundred guys for the most part. We didn't have a Command Master Chief or Senior Enlisted Advisor slot at that time. The duty I pulled was as the Team Master at Arms from 1962 to 1988. During my long watch on the quarterdeck, I saw a lot of men go by, over a dozen COs, a large number of junior officers, and hundreds of enlisted men.

For example, I remember Rick Marcinko as an enthusiastic free-fall parachute jumper. While Rick was in UDT 21, Team TWO was doing a lot of parachute jumping, and he would come over and ask if he could jump with us. None of us had any objections as long as he could get the time off and had his own gear. There would be plenty of room on our aircraft, but jumping gear was in short supply. In the Team, we would go to Air Force and Navy supply dumps and pick up salvage chutes for our own use.

Lieutenant (jg) Chuck Le Moyne was over in 21 with Rick at that time, and he also liked to jump with us. Later on, Le Moyne would become an admiral and Rick would be the CO of Team TWO, but then they were just a couple of frogs who liked to jump.

I didn't know Rick that well, as I was a Chief in the Team and Rick was a second class over in UDT. But later on, Rick got his commission and came over to Team TWO as an ensign and made quite a name for himself. By July 1974, Lieutenant Commander Richard Marcinko came onto the quarterdeck at SEAL Team TWO as the eighth commanding officer since the Team's commissioning. And I was there to work for him.

When the Team started, we had been broken up into assault groups for assignments and operations. Shortly before the Vietnam War commitment started, we changed the names of the assault groups to platoons. Each platoon was ten enlisted men and two officers, the platoon leader and his assistant. There would be at least two noncommissioned officers in the platoon, either a platoon chief or leading petty officer and his assistant, one of which would go with each squad when the platoon broke down into its two squads of five enlisted men and an officer. Later, during the war, the makeup of a platoon would be changed slightly, with twelve enlisted men to two officers.

I was the platoon chief of Tenth Platoon—we only had ten—when Team TWO received orders to start sending platoons to Vietnam. The orders were received in mid-1966, and by January 1967, we had sent our first two platoons to war. Within a year, Team TWO would have three platoons in Vietnam at any given month with an additional two platoons in transit, one coming from and one going to Vietnam.

There was enthusiasm on the part of almost all the men at the idea of going to Vietnam. After all, this was what we had been training for. When things really got rolling, many of the men at the Creek would check the message board to see if there was a need for replacements in any of the deployed platoons. If somebody was wounded over in Nam, we would send a replacement that day if at all possible. Some men just lived for going to Vietnam. Jim Finley is one name that immediately jumps to mind.

Finley spent most of his career in the Teams over in Vietnam. Not just on deployments with platoons, but as a replacement for injured men. I think Finley spent two and a half years total in Vietnam during the five years that Team TWO had men in combat.

As for myself, my platoon was called up to go to Vietnam in 1968. Even though I was the Master at Arms for the Team, I was also a platoon chief, and when my platoon's turn came up, I would certainly go with them. Tenth Platoon climbed aboard a Navy RD-5, a DC-6, and headed to Southeast Asia. Those planes were slow, 180 knots with a good tailwind, and the trip across the Pacific was a long one.

In April of 1968, I arrived in Vietnam with my platoon.

My first impression of the place was that it was certainly
different. But I didn't spend a long time looking around.
My platoon had to get ready to operate quickly. The Tet
offensive had finished up just a short while before the
platoon arrived in Vietnam, and the country was still
stirred up.

Each SEAL platoon in Vietnam did things a little differently from the other platoons. But every incoming platoon was introduced into its operational area by members
of the platoon that had just been relieved. This way the
lessons learned by the preceding platoon could be immediately picked up by the incoming SEALs. Tenth Platoon relieved Seventh Platoon, who had been operating
out of My Tho. I remember that one of the two men Seventh left behind for us was Mike Boynton, who had really
seen some action with Bob Gallagher and the Seventh.
Mike and the other SEAL taught us for about a week,
how they did this and that, as well as taking the platoon
out for several small operations, before they headed back
to the Creek.

Now it was time for the Tenth Platoon to start operating
on its own and learning which techniques worked best for
us. The platoons would all know well in advance when
they would be leaving for Vietnam. That extra time was
for predeployment training to prepare for the upcoming
missions. The added advantage of getting introduced to
the operational area by the men who had just been there
gave us an additional edge.

And that edge was used. The platoon went into operations hard and fast. Everything was quick—we would do
up to three operations a night. Intelligence, and its timely
use, was the main reason we were able to get away with
doing so many operations against the enemy.

Going out one day, we might capture a guy. We would
turn the captive over to Intelligence, and they would in-
terrogate the man. As soon as the next night, we could be
going out again on an op based on that intel. And if Intel
turned him, we would be guided to our target by the man
we had captured.

And we made sure that our guide knew that he would

be the first man going through the target's door. If he was leading us into a trap, he would be the first one hit. Once those procedures got set up and running well, we were able to do operations almost whenever we wanted. And the operations were pretty safe, with our guides knowing the situation and not having a weapon.

Our primary operations were snatch-and-grab ops with the intention being to gather intelligence. We would go into a hooch—just a large grass-and-bamboo hut, really a bullet would go right through the whole thing—and grab who we wanted. Operating in darkness, we would slip into the hooch. The guide who took us in would point out who was the target we were after. Using flashlights at the last moment, we could see the targeted individual, say some guy sleeping in a hammock with his rifle on the floor. Snatching up the weapon, we would wake the guy as we bundled him out of the area.

Usually, coming awake only to look down the barrels of at least four weapons being held by camouflage-faced SEALs, festooned with ordnance, was enough to prevent any resistance on the part of the target. Once we brought the target in, he would be interrogated and might be leading us out the next night on another op.

The huts were flimsily made by our standards, with the door, if there was one, being held by a simple hook. When we approached a target, one man would be sent around to the back window or door in case the target tried to run. If they woke up and heard us, some of the targets would run right through the wall of the shack to get away.

In general, once our procedures got into place and started to work, the operations were pretty safe. The big thing we really had to worry about was booby traps on the trails. The VC would come through an area and tell the farmers to set up a booby trap on the dike at say six o'clock every day. The next morning, the farmer would take the booby trap down at six o'clock. And if the farmer didn't do what the VC told him, they would kill him.

While on patrol, if we tripped a booby trap, we would immediately hose down the area with firepower. After all, the booby trap might be the start of an ambush. The farmer's house would usually be nearby, and he could easily get hit during the incident. That would put the farmer square in the middle between two forces. If he didn't do what the VC told him, he would be killed. If he did what the VC told him and we came along, he would probably get killed. The locals were really between a rock and a hard place. Talking to them sometimes, they would tell us about the situation, even maybe show us the booby trap. But there was little we could do to help them except clear the VC out of the area.

On our operations, we worked alone mostly or with the PRUs [Provincial Reconnaissance Units]. The South Vietnamese police—the White Mice—and the CIA would assist us with intel and interpreters. But that tour, we didn't work with any Army or Marine units. The Navy would support us with the PBRs [Patrol Boats, River], but my platoon didn't have the Seawolves supporting us much. When we had helicopter support it was usually an Army bird, either a slick for transport or a gunship for fire support.

Rarely, we would operate alongside a larger unit. The PRUs would sometimes have intelligence on an operation that was too big for them to hit without additional support. A SEAL platoon could supply that support. The PRUs were large forces of maybe one hundred men who were led by an American advisor, and they were paid and supplied through the CIA. Advisors could be Army, Marine, or CIA personnel, but some of the most successful PRU operations were conducted by units that were led by SEAL advisors. On this trip, Tenth Platoon hadn't supplied a PRU advisor, but we would still be willing to support any PRU SEAL who asked for our help.

We were so busy during my tour that I didn't have a chance to take any leave or R&R. The platoon would take liberty in My Tho, and we could easily get a beer or whatever we wanted without having to go far. Most of the time, we were on operations, and the operating was going good.

While I was in Vietnam, I ran into Roy Boehm, the man who had picked me for SEAL Team TWO. Roy had gotten out of the Teams by now and was in Vietnam for other duties when I met him. Roy asked if he could go out with the platoon on an op we had coming up. There was no problem with Roy coming along, and he asked me for a 9mm pistol as a weapon. Roy liked going light, and we did have some shots fired that night, but it was pretty much an easy op.

Choice of weapons was left as much as possible up to the tastes of the individual SEAL. The squad had to carry a balance of firepower, but that wasn't any problem to accomplish. For myself, I had taken a liking to the Harrington & Richardson T223 rifle. The H&R T223 was an imported version of the German Heckler & Koch HK33. The weapon had been available for a few years, and the Team was evaluating it in combat.

We had a lot of experimental weapons at the Team, and when I went over it was suggested that I take the T223 over and see what I thought about it. Though the weapon is slightly heavier than an M16, it fires the same ammunition, so ammo supply wouldn't be a problem. The Team had been using the AR-15/M16 rifles since its first days, but we only had the twenty-round magazines. There were some thirty-round magazines around, but they were few in number and hard to come by. One thing that immediately made the T223 appeal to me was the fact that it came with forty-round magazines.

I liked the weapon. It was a lot easier to clean and maintain than the M16 and worked well in the jungle environment. While the other men of the platoon would be just starting to clean their weapons after an op, I would already be done and moving on to something else. The T223 [HK33] was good but it was a foreign [German] weapon and suffered from the "not made here" school of thought. Later on, after Vietnam, the Teams would find it easier to obtain the weapons they liked best, and the HK33's little brother, the 9mm MP5, became commonplace with the SEALs.

My H&R came with four 40-round magazines, which I carried in the leg pockets on my cammies for a while. The magazines tended to rattle around and make too much noise on patrol but were too long to fit in an American ammunition pouch. I solved my problem by getting one of the Chicom AK-47 chest-type magazine pouches and carrying my ammo in that. The big cargo pockets on our field trousers were usually filled with a UDT inflatable life vest, so after I got the chest pack, my vest went back in my pocket. The vests were used if we had to cross a stream or other body of water when on patrol. In addition, if we really got into trouble, the SEALs were taught to get into the water for escape and concealment. It's pretty dangerous to climb into the water when you're carrying thirty or forty pounds of weapons and ammunition, but the life vest could help you swim with all your gear.

A special cloth vest with pockets for ammunition, grenades, and equipment was available in limited numbers. In addition to the pockets, the vest had a built-in inflatable bladder for flotation. But I found the vest too bulky and hot for constant wear. It was okay if you spent a long time in the water, like on an ambush. But for general patrolling, I liked to carry a UDT vest rolled up in my pocket.

There was one op that really stands out in my mind during my first tour in Vietnam. It was an ambush operation against an eight-man VC group with a Chieu Hoi [Open Arms; a turned VC] leading us in. The heavily armored Mike boat took us to within walking distance of our target. Traveling the river in the Mike boat made you feel pretty safe. The Mike boat was a converted LCM landing craft [LCM Mark 6] that sat real low in the water from all the weapons and armor that were mounted on it. Besides the M60s and .50 calibers along the sides of the boat, there was a 7.62mm minigun in a bow tub and a 106mm recoilless rifle on top of the overhead. Along with all of that, there was an 81mm mortar in the bow of the boat. That much firepower is a nice thing to have on your side.

We had heard everything the Chieu Hoi was telling us before. Many of the captured men would tell us about these important targets, but when they would take us in to them, nothing would be there. But you treat each one as if it's the real thing.

Walking in about a mile from the insertion point where the Mike boat let us off, we came up to a paddy dike with a trail along the top of it. Having brought three claymore mines with us, we set them up facing diagonally across the dike with their fields of fire overlapping. If eight guys did show up and they were walking fairly close together, we could get them all with the claymores. After crawling around in the eight-inch-deep water of the paddy setting up the claymores, we settled in about fifteen meters away from the four-foot-tall dike to wait for our targets to enter the kill zone.

The Chieu Hoi was armed with an AK-47—he had worked for us before and we trusted him with a loaded weapon. Our officer in charge was going to initiate the ambush. When the OIC started firing, that was the signal to fire the claymores and open up. The Chieu Hoi knew the plan and was ready.

The platoon had been on dozens of ambushes before, and not ten minutes would pass before some of the guys would be too comfortable and nod off asleep. Within twenty minutes of our settling in for the ambush, our targets walked onto the scene.

I had been nodding off myself, but the quiet sound of Vietnamese talking quickly woke me up. It sounded like a guy arguing with his wife, and it wasn't long before we could see who was talking.

One lone VC walked into the kill zone silhouetted against the sky, carrying his AK-47 across his shoulder by the barrel in the common Asian manner. About fifteen yards behind this guy was coming the main body of men. There were more than the eight VC we had been expecting, but that wasn't going to be a problem. Letting the point man go through, we waited for the main body of VC to enter the kill zone of the ambush. The point man only went a little farther when he stopped and called back to the others.

Suddenly, our Chieu Hoi opened fire with his AK, nailing the point man. Our officer had been supposed to initiate the ambush, but with that first burst of fire, we all opened up. With the flash and thunder of the claymores, you could see enemy bodies flying through the air on the dike. After the initial burst of fire was over, we quickly went over to search the bodies.

In that quick few seconds of fire, we had killed nine of the enemy. The point man was hit by the Chieu Hoi's AK, and the rest were killed by the claymores. One guy looked as if a Greyhound bus had hit him, he had spun around so. Rushing out, we picked up the weapons and made sure of the enemy. The claymores had done such a complete job that our firing wasn't really necessary, but it insured the situation.

While we were bent over the bodies, we started taking more fire. It was just a few shots to start with and we could see the muzzle flashes in the darkness, but there was only a single squad of seven of us and we couldn't sustain a fight. It was time to get out of there.

We started running back towards the river with the enemy in pursuit. I didn't know how many of the VC were there, but the incoming fire was picking up. When we got into range of the Mike boat, we put an earlier-arranged fire support plan into operation.

While we ran, the Mike boat would fire mortar rounds over our heads behind us. As we jogged along, we would call over the radio and tell the boat to "drop fifty." The next round would come in fifty yards closer to our rear. It worked well, and the rounds walked in behind us. I had been rear security and just called out, "follow me," and led the run back to the boat. Vietnam or the Creek, Rudy leads the runs.

Actually, the plan went pretty well, with the Mike boat's mortar laying fire behind us. The high lob of an 81mm mortar would put the rounds well over our heads, and when we got in close to the boat, there were other weapons that could be used. When we got in to the Mike boat, we were low enough that the direct-fire weapons could shoot over our heads. At our direction, the boat's minigun opened up, and that was all she wrote.

That minigun just hosed down the countryside, chopping down small trees and cutting grass like a lawnmower. When there was no more firing coming our way, we quickly scrabbled aboard the Mike boat and were safe.

Traveling back to the base along the river, we had time to relax. Now we could find out what had happened. The officer turned to the Chieu Hoi and asked, "Why did you shoot?"

"When that first man stopped and turned around," the Chieu Hoi said, "he called out to the other man that he knew somebody was around. He had seen the trails we left in the rice paddy while setting up the ambush. That's why I shot him."

He was right, and there wasn't anything to argue about. Besides, it had been a good ambush. People say that the only way to break out of an ambush is to charge the firers. In a properly conducted ambush, there's no time to charge anyone, it's over that quick.

During my first tour in Vietnam, I was the senior Navy enlisted man in the Delta at the time. That led to an interesting meeting that helped me in some later career decisions. There was now a Master Chief of the Navy, Delbert Black was his name, and he came over to Vietnam in 1968. I was assigned as Black's escort while he went around to various Navy stations in the Mekong Delta.

What Black wanted to do was go around to all of the little Chiefs and EM clubs around the Delta and tell people who he was, what he did in the Navy, and find out what they might want done. We went to this club and that and fielded some of the dumbest questions I ever heard asked. "Master Chief," someone would ask, "why do we have to pay ten cents a beer when that club over there only charges five cents?"

I would sit over by the bar and wonder what was the big deal when you're only paying a dime a beer anyways. Sitting there, I would hear that Chief field questions like that at every club we went to. And he had to answer them. He couldn't say "Shut up!" like I could. That day I made up my mind that I never wanted that job.

In fact, Joe DiMartino had put my name in against Black's for the job the year before. I had put a stop to that idea as soon as I found out about it, and I was glad I did. I didn't even know what the Master Chief of the Navy's job would be. No one did—Black was the first one. But I did know I didn't want the job, and I was right.

Black, of course, knew I was a SEAL and what the SEALs were doing in Vietnam. In fact, he wanted to go along as a tag-along on an op with us. After we had completed his touring of the base, we were sitting down relaxing back in my area. Black asked, "Can I go out with you guys tonight?"

We had an op going out about nine that night, and there was room for another man. "As far as I'm concerned," I answered, "I don't care. If you want to slop around in the mud out there with the rest of us, that's okay. But I have to ask the officer in charge if it's okay."

Finding the OIC, Lieutenant Quist, I told him, "The Master Chief of the Navy wants to go out with us tonight."

"Do you object?" Quist asked me.

"No," I answered. "It's all right with me."

"Well then, bring him along."

Getting back to Black, I told him the situation. "Before I go," Black said, "I have to call Saigon and make sure they say it's okay."

The answer from Saigon came back fast and clear. "No," they said to Black, "you will not operate with the SEALs." He was disappointed, but I guess things turned out for the best. The operation got a little hairy that night and the bullets were flying.

Finally, on October 22, 1968, my first tour in Vietnam ended. Fifth Platoon had arrived a week earlier and was conducting its own operations now. Tenth Platoon headed back to the Creek.

Things had changed for the Team by the time I got back to Little Creek. The Team had moved from the first building we had been quartered in. Things were going hot and heavy, with our Vietnam commitment reaching its peak. There always seemed to be at least one platoon on the move to or from Vietnam.

In fact, the turnover of people was so fast that you

could easily lose track of who was in the Team. With the platoons doing six-month tours in Nam, a guy could be in the Team almost two years before I even saw him. If I was away on deployment, a new Teammate could arrive while I was gone, get assigned to a platoon, and be deployed himself while I was on my way back. With the nine-platoon rotation list—we did not have a First Platoon—a given platoon could expect to deploy at about one-year intervals.

Some people in the Team everyone knew. Bob Gallagher had made a real reputation for himself as a hunter. Bob seemed to just not have any fear and would instill confidence in anyone who followed him.

Mostly, the Team stayed the same, only we were in a new building and more people had come aboard. COs would change, and with a new officer would come different SOPs [Standard Operating Procedures]. New COs always knew what to expect from me—I tried to always do the same thing and keep the same standards.

Things like haircuts and making sure the men kept their personal grooming up was something I kept a steady hand on. Slightly different handling was needed when it was a junior officer who needed, say, a haircut. But I usually found a way of dealing with the situation without bothering the CO or XO. I would tell the Exec that some of the officers needed haircuts, without naming anyone specific. If that didn't work, peer pressure could be brought into use. During Quarters, I would point out that some of the men—there was always at least one—needed a haircut. "Get that taken care of," I would say. "The next thing you know, you're going to look as bad as Ensign Jones there." After everyone in the formation looked at Ensign Jones, he would usually show up the next day with a fresh haircut.

My first tour in Vietnam, I received the Bronze Star. It wasn't any big deal—almost everyone got one. The officers would specify incidents that a man was involved in, and the proper paperwork, with the right wording, would get submitted. The highest award received by my platoon while in Nam was the Bronze Star. Others had different situations. The platoon we had relieved, Seventh Platoon, had Bob Gallagher receive the Navy Cross and Mike Boynton the Silver Star for the same operation they were involved in, a really hairy one. Medals weren't terribly important to most of us in the Team, though. We just looked at the missions as doing our jobs. The Team did seem to end up having an award ceremony almost every week. Purple Hearts, Bronze Stars, and Commendation Medals were given out often. And if anyone earned those medals, the SEALs did.

A new job came up in late 1969 that kept me from going back to Vietnam with Tenth Platoon when their rotation came up. One day during Quarters an announcement was made to the formation: "The Navy needs a couple of people to slide on their bobsled team. Does anybody out there know what a bobsled is?"

Two of us, myself and Bob Coulson, did so we raised our hands. "Okay, you two have volunteered."

The Navy had been running a bobsled team in the national, international, and Olympic competitions. The team was run by Commander Lamey, and he had his Navy people at Floyd Bennett Field up in New York. Overnight, it seemed, this Commander lost a number of his people, and with winter coming up, he needed replacements fast. Somebody told him that the best place to get people was the SEAL Teams, since we were always in shape.

Since I was the Team's Command Master Chief, it wasn't the easiest thing for me to leave. I had to get a relief. Ev Barrett had the rank and more than enough experience, so he stood in for me. "Don't worry," Ev told me before I left. "I'll keep things straight and get that building painted for you."

We had moved into the new building, but there was still a lot of fixing up to do before the place became shipshape. While I was gone, Ev made more than a few people unhappy with the amount of work he got out of them. By the time I got back three months later, the building was all painted and a number of improvements were in place.

My wife, Marge, came up to New York with me and got to ride the bobsled. The duty was really different and more than a little fun. The bobsled team wasn't being supported the same way that the European teams were. We had some older bobsleds, and we spent time polishing up the runners and Simonizing the bodies to cut down on friction. But the European teams make a science out of bobsledding, and whole nations get behind their teams. But all in all, we did pretty well. I have a number of plaques on my wall from some of the events we won.

Duties at the Team called me back, and I wasn't able to compete with the team at the Olympics. Al Ashton relieved me and went in my place. The idea of the Teams supplying men for the Olympic team worked pretty well, and the SEALs competed a number of times. Fred Frisch made the bobsled team for a later Olympics, I think the Japanese games. Fred had a great way of practicing for the event. He would get his wife up every morning and she would ride in the family Volkswagen around the block. She would be doing the steering and braking if it was necessary but didn't bother with the accelerator. The car's engine wasn't running—Fred was behind the Bug pushing it at a hard run.

We arrived in Vietnam in December of 1970 with Vietnamization starting to go full swing. The war was changing hands, with the American forces turning over all operations to the South Vietnamese forces. Only four of us had come over—there wasn't enough action for the whole platoon. We reported in at Saigon to an old friend of mine, Captain Schaible.

Schaible was the senior SEAL in Vietnam at the time, and it turned out to be a good thing that I knew him. Turning to the other three men with me, Schaible said, "You three are going to report to SOLID ANCHOR. You," he said, indicating me, "are going to Cam Ranh Bay."

SOLID ANCHOR was a base in the Delta that was surrounded by a whole lot of nothing, a real miserable place to be stationed. "Why can't I stay with these guys?" I asked. "We trained together for three months before coming over here."

"Never mind," Schaible said. "You're going to Cam Ranh and these guys are going south."

Not much choice in arguing about that, so I later boarded a plane for Cam Ranh Bay for duty with Detachment Echo and the LDNNs [Lien Doc Nguoi Nhia, "soldiers who fight under the sea"—the South Vietnamese equivalent of the SEALS]. Flying in to Cam Ranh Bay, I looked down from the plane and wondered what this place was. It looked like Miami Beach down there. Long stretches of clean beaches bordering blue ocean waters. I had gotten used to the muddy waters of the Delta and had a hard time believing that this was in the same country.

Later, I realized what Captain Schaible had been doing. He had done me a favor by picking me as the man to go to Cam Ranh Bay, just looking out for an old Teammate. A month later, my Teammates came up from the Delta for a visit and they didn't want to go back. They stayed for nearly a month, and then a phone call came in telling them to get back down to the Delta.

"Sorry, guys," I said, "but I'm not going down there with you. I'm staying right here."

The duty wasn't too bad—just do liaison with the LDNNs. There weren't any ops to pull. In fact, even the LDNNs didn't want to go out. The place was a training center for the LDNNs, much like our center at Coronado. And the base at Cam Ranh Bay itself was huge. It was so big that the base supported fifteen NCO clubs. Everyone was using one or another part of the base at Cam Ranh. The Americans, Koreans, and Vietnamese all had their own sections they operated from. There were even small native villages that had been absorbed by the base as it expanded over the years. Now these villages were still intact, inside the perimeter of Cam Ranh Bay.

We were down at the Navy end of the base, near the water. The ammunition piers that jutted into the water had an unusual security system—dolphins trained to act as guard animals. The Navy EOD [Explosive Ordnance Disposal] unit were the people actually responsible for the dolphins, and I didn't work directly with them much.

The U.S. Navy base had a fence around it as a simple security device. The LDNNs had been causing so much friction between themselves and the Navy personnel that they were finally asked to move outside of the fence. The LDNNs had been working in the black market and were basically bandits by our Western way of thinking. They could be good fighters, but they were not to be trusted among all of the base's stores.

When the LDNNs moved off the base, we did as well. Since the SEALs were acting as the LDNNs' advisors, we would stay with our men. The funny thing was that the base commander, an American Navy commander, would come out of the gate at night and spend time with us, outside of the fence.

"Captain," I asked him—he was the captain of the base—"why do you stay out here with us? Why don't you stay inside of the base where you're guarded?"

"I feel safer out here with you guys," he answered, "because you guys are SEALs."

"If that's the way you feel," I said, and went back to drinking my beer. It was a nice compliment to us, but there were only two SEALs in the detachment at the time, George Doran, the OIC, and myself. We were armed, guns were all over the place, but our security wasn't anything special.

Guns were easily available to us. One SEAL who was going back to San Diego was getting rid of his AK-47. "Do you want this?" he asked.

I was never much for souvenirs. "Not really," I answered.

So he just left it in the corner of the building, and I mostly forgot about it. About two months later, there was a Navy guy standing guard nearby and I remembered that AK. Walking up to him, I asked, "Hey, would you like to trade that carbine for an AK-47?"

He jumped at the chance, and we swapped guns. An AK-47 was something of a status symbol among the troops, and most of the sailors never had a chance to get hold of one.

Hearing that Joe DiMartino was on duty in Saigon, I

went up there one day to see him. Joe D had been the XO of Team TWO for a number of years just after we had been commissioned and had been the CO of the Team for a short while back in 1966. I pulled into his office area in Saigon and asked a lieutenant where he was. "That's his desk over there," the lieutenant answered, "but I haven't seen him for three months." Nice to know that some things don't change.

Joe ended up down in my neck of the woods at Cam Ranh Bay for a while. He had been put in charge of the guard-dolphin program for Vietnam and wanted to see the dolphins in action for himself.

But neither Joe nor I ever did see the dolphins in action. The only enemy swimmer who showed up while we were in Cam Ranh Bay was stopped by a Navy guard. There was a river feeding into Cam Ranh Bay, and this one VC was swimming in underwater. What he had was a weight belt to hold him down, the inflatable bladder from a basketball or a soccer ball, a clothespin on his nose, and about four pounds of C4 explosive. He would fill the bladder up with air and then travel underwater breathing the air from the bladder. The air didn't last very long and the swimmer had to come up about midriver to reinflate the bladder.

An alert guard on one of the bridges over the river spotted the swimmer when he came up to refill his rig. The guard managed to wound the swimmer and force him to surrender without killing the man. We were called in as experts in underwater breathing apparatus to identify the man's rig. It didn't take us long to explain what the setup was. Primitive as his system was, if there hadn't been an alert guard, that swimmer might have gotten into the base and caused some real damage.

During interrogation, the swimmer was asked where he came from. Pointing up into the mountains, the man indicated "up there." Then he explained how it had taken him four days to get within range of the base. His objective was to blow up one of the large fuel storage tanks that were on the base.

That swimmer was an example of how dedicated an

enemy we were fighting in Vietnam. The VC did a tremendous amount of damage with very little in the way of support. The NVA was better equipped than the VC and was able to do even more. But the backbone of the enemy forces in Vietnam was the individual soldier. The guys that we fought, and shot, would have maybe a little parcel of rice wrapped in a cloth handkerchief. Their black pajamas were a simple cloth uniform, and their field gear not much more than a net hammock to keep the sleeper off of the ground. The average VC would have a rifle and perhaps four bullets with which to fight us.

The VC lasted over ten years fighting with such equipment. If the South Vietnamese had been equipped the same as the VC, they wouldn't have lasted a day. On the other hand, if the VC had the equipment available that we had, we would still be fighting that war. The VC were good, dedicated fighters, anything but the dumb slopes that some soldiers called them.

The South Vietnamese weren't always the way they were in the last years of the war. We caused a lot of their problems by just being the kind of people we are. We are a materialistic military that drowns an enemy in equipment. Besides just overwhelming the Vietnamese with our culture, we tried to drag them into the twentieth century all at once, instead of taking the natural course over time.

Our servicemen were paid much more than the pay the ARVNs received. And this caused the prices to rise in the marketplace to the point where the native people couldn't afford the products we took for granted. Our men would go out into the field and do the ARVNs' fighting for them. They were more than happy to let us go out and get shot at rather than them. A lot of friction developed between our forces and theirs because of these things.

The entire running of the war was to be turned over to the ARVN forces during my last tour. None of us were supposed to go out into the field for operations. The Vietnamese were to do everything. First, we would show them how to do the maintenance, order the parts and so on. Then they would have to get their hands dirty fixing what was needed and filling out the paperwork. That was something they didn't like very much. Especially after years of us doing it all for them.

We had left our mess halls open to the South Vietnamese forces while I was there. The men became used to eating steak and ice cream, a lot different than their native fish heads and rice. Then in April the orders came down to close the mess halls to the Vietnamese. I remember saying to myself it was going to be a bad day when we closed the mess halls. The Vietnamese outnumbered us by a wide margin at Cam Ranh Bay by that time. In fact, many of the American base personnel were prepared to do battle that day with our ARVN allies. But the rebellion never came and the Vietnamese went back to their normal diet. All in all, the transition went pretty smooth.

But the war had lost public support back in the States. Nixon had tried to do the right thing by taking the war to the North. Bombing North Vietnam made a lot more sense than trying to hit the evasive VC in the South from a B-52. Vietnamization was an idea that came too late to do enough good. We had been running the LDNN school for some time now, but the time came to go home and the school was shut down behind us.

There were changes coming in the Team after I came back. A number of men left the Team looking for better things to do. The peacetime Teams didn't have the level of action that a lot of the guys had become used to. Money also became tight. Where before it was no big deal to attend a specialized school offered by the Army or Marines, now you practically had to pay your own way. Say if five guys wanted to go to Army tracker school, the Team would issue them a military vehicle and they could drive down to Georgia. Before the cutbacks, they would have been flown down.

Once at the school, the men would have to buy their own meals at the mess hall. We just didn't have the money. If the guys didn't want to do that for the schools, they stayed here at the Creek. If you wanted the school, wanted it in your record, you paid your own way. It was as simple as that. The Army, especially the Special Forces, was in much the same situation.

Everything slowed down and the excitement ended. It seemed for a while that we were going to go back to playing soccer every day. As the years went by, things started picking back up again. This country is always involved in some rinky-dink operations somewhere. And the people in charge were learning that you can't always send the heavy forces in. Instead of a hammer, you need a scalpel. And the SEALs can be that precise scalpel.

Now the Teams have expanded. Instead of two Teams, there are seven SEAL Teams and two SDV [SEAL Delivery Vehicle] Teams. The Teams are a great life and adventure. It is different and exciting. I can go home to Rochester, New York, today and meet old buddies of mine who stood behind a lathe all their lives and made twenty or thirty bucks an hour. But they did the same basic thing day after day, week after week. In the SEALs, it's different all the time. You never know what you are going to do today or tomorrow.

People coming in the Teams today are smarter and in better shape than we were back then. I personally know that they're better physically—I've run them through PT.

I spent forty-five years and three months in the Navy, most of that time in Naval Special Warfare. I wish I was seventeen so that I could enlist and do it all over again. I wouldn't do anything different than I did.

As the Teams developed as an operating unit, new skills, many of them unfamiliar to Navy men, had to be learned. Schools and training programs offered by all of the other services were examined and tried out. The Marine escape and evasion course at Pickle Meadows was one of these. The E&E course was a notorious training regimen that gave men a very good idea of what they could expect if ever captured by the enemy. Though it was considered good training, it was not thought of fondly by any man who took it.

Other schools won varying degrees of acceptance. Army Ranger school, Special Forces kitchen demolitions, Air Force judo school, Army jumpmaster and rigger school—all were tried and some were accepted as standard in the SEALs' training program.

Even civilian courses of instruction were taken, such as the Colt Firearms armorer school, as well as other manufacturers' equipment repair and maintenance courses. Navy schools and training were not ignored either. From the very exotic nuclear weapons training course to the much more prosaic ship-loading procedures course, they all became part of the skill pool to be found in the Teams.

Not all of the courses were physically demanding. Some were straightforward schoolwork taught in a classroom. Others were hands-on training in a shop environment. Even some of the more tedious classroom work was done with a proper SEAL attitude; "They aren't starving us or beating us, so pay attention" was an accepted SEAL comment.

JAMES D. WATSON III

USN (RET.)

Jim Watson is one of the enlisted plankowners of SEAL Team TWO. As one of the Team's first men, Jim had the opportunity to try out many of the schools that were being considered. Later, Jim went to Vietnam with the first Team TWO platoons to be deployed to the war. He retired from the Navy after three tours in Vietnam. Jim Watson is currently the curator of the UDT/SEAL Museum in Fort Pierce, Florida.

During the summer of 1962, I spent my time at the Team helping develop a standard day-to-day schedule. The Team had grown to near its assigned strength of sixty-six men. While trying to figure out what training would be needed to make SEALs fully capable of completing our mission, somebody came up with the best class the SEALs ever took, or at least the one that was the most fun. In August, SEAL Team TWO reported to Annapolis, Maryland, to take training in sailboat operation at the U.S. Naval Academy. We were all going to sailboat school!

Someone in the command structure decided that it would be a good idea if all the SEALs knew how to sail a boat. "What the hell are you talking about?" was the general question raised when these orders came down.

"Look," Roy Boehm said, "the way you guys are going to operate, if you get in a situation where the only way out is in a sailboat, you had better know how to make the thing giddy-up and go.''

This made a certain amount of sense to us, and besides, we didn't have a choice. So the whole Team packed up and moved out to the hallowed grounds of our Naval Academy. The first surprise we found at the Academy was the living quarters they had for us. An APL [Auxiliary Personnel, Living] barge was anchored in the Chesapeake, just off the Academy. We were to live on the barge while we were at the Academy. Enlisted men were not allowed to be berthed on the Academy grounds. It seemed that the original land grant that resulted in the Academy being placed where it was had a provision that no enlisted men would ever be housed on the property.

The APL is nothing more than a large barge broken down into different rooms and bays where the stewards and other working enlisted men of the Academy stay. Since this was our Naval Academy, we would obey the rules and not cause any trouble, or at least not much trouble. One night coming back off of liberty a group of us decided we weren't going all the way back to the APL. Finding a nice, grassy spot in the middle of the grinder, the parade field, we just laid down and went to sleep. Well, the walls didn't come crashing down because (gasp!) enlisted men slept on the hallowed grounds of the Academy. Getting up the next morning before anyone else did, we continued on to the APL. That was about the most messing with the Academy we did while we were there.

The sailing was a real blast. The boats we were using were twenty-six-foot knockabouts with a lead keel and six-foot draft. Working with only a mainsail and a jib, we soon learned how to control these craft under the watchful eyes of our instructors. And our instructors were a real piece of work. The retired Chief Bosun's mates who were teaching us had been in the Navy since Hector was a pup. These men had actually sailed whaleboats back when engines just weren't found on all Navy craft. Nice old guys who were *real* sailors and knew their stuff inside and out. Anyone can put a key in an ignition or holler down to an engine room to give you more steam. But when you can hoist sails up against the wind and get that boat where you want it when you want it, that's a real sailor.

After a number of days training us, the Bosun's mates felt we had been checked out enough that we could take the knockabouts out ourselves. Up until then, an instructor had been on each boat with a small crew of three SEALs anytime we went out. The knockabouts were tied up on the seawall facing the Chesapeake. Directly across the water from the Academy was a small yacht club and a bar.

As the Bosun's mates took us to our boats they said, "All right. Take the boats out and run them around. Be back by sixteen hundred hours."

We all put what was called a "close haul" on the boats, pulling the sails in tight and heeling far over, and went straight across the water towards the yacht club. The retired Chiefs were running up and down the seawall shouting, "You can't go over there with Academy boats!"

"Sorry, Chief, we can't hear you."

But our fun was short-lived. The people from the club were waiting on the shore for us to tell us we couldn't land and to turn us around. It seemed that the whole town of Annapolis had it in for anyone who even looked like they might be a middie from the Academy. If they thought you were a middie, they wouldn't serve you or wait on you in most of the restaurants and bars. Since we were in Rome we did as the Romans did. As Navy men, we represented the Academy as well as the Navy. We behaved and didn't cause any trouble in town. But those townies never knew how close they came to seeing real action when they messed around with a bunch of SEALs.

There was no one outside of the Team in this sailing class, and we were all having a great time competing with each other as boat crews. The Bosun's mates competed among themselves to see who could train green crews like us the fastest and the best.

We spent some time just sailing around the Chesapeake getting experience handling the boats. Jessie, Brozak, and I were in one knockabout just sailing along. Chuck Jessie is an Airdale—works on the flight deck of an aircraft carrier—so he and Brozak were acting as the crew. As a

Quartermaster, I could read charts and was acting as the coxswain. We were really moving, heeling hard over from the wind, and generally having a great time. The boat was a few hundred yards off the beach and I was wondering how much water was under us.

"Hey, Chuck," I called out, "pull that chart out and see how much water there is five hundred yards off the beach."

The Bosun's mates had shown us where the charts were kept in a small drawer in the bow of the boat.

Being a good Airdale, Chuck pulled out the chart, checked the depth, and threw the chart back in its hole.

"We're all right, Jim," Chuck called back.

"How's that?"

"You've got three fathoms [eighteen feet]."

"What?"

"It says '3 FT.' "

"That's feet, bud. There aren't fathoms in inland waters."

About then the wind changed. Ka-bunk, we hit bottom.

Our boat needed six feet of water to float when she was standing still. Since we had been heeled over, the boat drew less water and we were clearing the bottom by inches. As soon as the wind stopped, the boat straightened out and the keel hit bottom.

There we were, canted partway on our side and aground. All the instructors had been watching us and saw our predicament. "Oh shit," they were thinking. "Now we have to get a small-draft boat and go help them."

Being the senior man in the boat and acting skipper—she was my first command—I put the other two men in the water. Grabbing hold of the boat, Jessie and Brozak turned it so the sails were again facing against the wind. The wind now heeled the boat over and she was free of the bottom. I controlled her so Jessie and Brozak could climb back aboard, and we sailed right out of there to the cheers of the Chiefs.

Frogmen are used to working in the water, and we have our own ways of solving problems.

In general, Team TWO had a great time learning to

sail. The Chiefs put us on everything that could float and put sheets against the wind. We even sailed the old tall ship the Navy raced, the *America*. That was really fun. When you lay a big craft like that over and have her running fast, you feel a kinship with your naval forebears unlike anything else there is.

They had three large sailing craft at the Academy, and the Chiefs had us crew all of them in a big race. I can't remember who won, but it really didn't matter. When we finally left there, those Chiefs really loved us, and we had the world of respect for them.

Getting along with the people at the Academy was another story. Nobody knew who we were—SEALs were still classified, and no information had been released about us. When we went to watch the Navy football team practice, they threw us off the field! In our green fatigue uniforms, we didn't look like normal Navy personnel, and we couldn't convince the officials that we were Underwater Demolition Team personnel. No UDT men would have any business at the Academy, they thought, so we must be Army spies checking out the football team!

But it was still our service's Academy, and we were not going to cause any trouble. We left quietly and returned to Little Creek. I think our SEAL football team could have taken those middies anyway.

The mission of the SEALs, as well as their very existence, was highly classified even before their first days as commissioned Teams. It was soon realized that the original fifty-man Teams needed to be larger to accomplish all that was expected of them. As the SEALs' success grew, so did their numbers. The primary source of manpower for the Teams was the parent UDTs. During the first years of the Teams, individuals would be approached and asked if they would be interested in volunteering for the new unit.

The SEALs always seemed to be going somewhere and doing something, usually something fairly exotic. Volunteers were not hard to find—in fact, one of the problems was simply getting the parent unit to release the man for duty in the SEALs. The

SEALs wanted only the best, and UDT commanders found it difficult to release their best men to another unit, even if it was one of their own.

The general opinion among the operators was that if you liked to shoot weapons, blow things up, and jump out of the sky, the SEAL Teams were the place to be.

Lieutenant Commander

FRANK F. THORNTON, JR.

USN (Ret.)

*Frank Thornton entered SEAL Team TWO within a
year of the Team's commissioning date. He spent
twenty years in the Navy, most of them as an operator
with the SEALs. After his time in Vietnam, Thornton
took his commission and moved to SEAL Team ONE
on the West Coast. While there, he acted as the intelligence officer, among other duties. He assisted in setting up the first contingency platoon, the forerunner
to SEAL Team SIX. Though he is quick to point out
that he is not the most highly decorated SEAL, his
Silver Star, five Bronze Stars, two Navy Commenda-
tions, numerous other decorations, and eighteen Vietnamese combat awards make Frank Thornton the most
decorated SEAL of the Vietnam War.*

Being from Boston, Massachusetts, I've spent a good part
of my life around the sea. So in 1961, it seemed natural
for me to go into the Navy when I was looking at a military career. Boston struck me as having cold winters, it
being in the northern United States, but my first ship in
the Navy was the AGB 2 EDISTO, an icebreaker. Ice-
breakers travel in very cold waters, like the Arctic and
Antarctica.

My first major cruise was an Antarctic cruise with stop-
overs along the way. Short layovers in places like Panama, Hawaii, and New Zealand were all it took to confirm

that the Navy was where I wanted to be. But I wanted even more adventure, if it was available. One day I was reading a copy of *All Hands* magazine and there was this article that told about the UDTs and what they did. What I didn't know at the time was that on the cover of the magazine was Jim Watson jumping out of a Navy helicopter in the waters off of Greenland. The EDISTO was the ship that took Jim and his teammates from Greenland back to the States.

I was an impressionable kid only recently out of high school, and the UDT looked like what I wanted to do. When I discussed my request with the captain, he approved my chit and sent it along. After a few weeks in Boston, our home port, I went down to Little Creek to begin training with the next class.

Training wasn't quite the shock it could have been for me. Aboard the EDISTO there had been a Bosun's mate who had taken UDTR training some years earlier and had flunked out. He told me some stories about training, and I read as much as I could find on the subject. My captain had also helped me by having some of the pre-screening tests done before I officially volunteered. One of the Chiefs took me over to a pool and tested my swimming. Now the captain signed and forwarded my chit, after he was sure I could do the basics.

I was in Class 26 along with Dick Marcinko, Whitey Weir, Derwood White, and others. We started training with 118 guys and graduated 23. To this day, I'm not really sure what got me through training, unless it was just putting my mind in neutral. You didn't know what to expect from day to day, and if you didn't dwell on what was coming, you could get through the next day just like you had the last. We also had good instructors who knew their jobs well, even if those jobs seemed to be how to make us quit.

Hell Week was a strange and unique experience. You just had to dig a little deeper into yourself to get through the day. And every day you dug deeper than the day before. The guys I was close to in the class, almost from day one, were the same group I was with during Hell

Week. That kind of peer support can help you a lot when it comes time to drag that last little bit of energy up out of yourself. There's different kinds of friendships, and the ones we developed during training were tight. We ran around together, snuck off the base by climbing the fence together, and avoided the instructors together. That kind of group can support you through almost anything.

Part of the concept of training is to develop that mutual support, the teamwork that it takes to complete the course. No loners or individuals can get through the course. You are, of course, an individual and accountable to yourself, but you are also responsible for your Teammates.

After graduation, I was assigned to UDT 21. After making a deployment with 21, I was sent over to help fill out UDT 22. While with 22, I made several deployments, including a ten-month tour in the Caribbean. After getting back from the Caribbean, I was sitting up at a place called Brinn's Inn, a local Team hangout. While relaxing and having a drink, I struck up a conversation with Roy Boehm, who was spending some time in the bar. Roy asked me what I thought of the Navy and my duties with the UDT. I told him that I liked it and was thinking of making it a career. After all, the Navy was paying me to do all these exotic and crazy things and I really enjoyed my work.

It was only about six months into 1962, and the SEAL Teams had been commissioned on the first of the year. Roy had been one of the movers and shakers of the SEAL concept, but I didn't know that at the time. "So," he said to me in that gravelly voice of his, "you want to do something really different. We'll have to see what we can do about that."

By the end of the year, I had orders to report to SEAL Team TWO. Roy was right—the duties were different and unique. During this early period I met a number of people who worked for various government agencies. I received a job offer from one of these agencies that would allow me to work for them on one year's detached service from the Navy. I found the offer tempting and accepted.

From January of 1964 to January of 1965, I found myself conducting training in southern Florida and the Caribbean. When the year was up, I was back at Team TWO. That was the last time I left Team TWO until 1974.

Prior to Seal Team TWO receiving a Vietnam commitment for combat troops in 1967, we had sent several teams of different sizes to Vietnam on deployments. In 1966, I was able to volunteer for one of these deployments that put me in Vietnam well ahead of my Teammates. An MTT [Mobile Training Team] led by George Doran had been in Vietnam back in late 1962. The MTT had helped set up the South Vietnamese equivalent of the SEALs, the LDNNs.

With Lieutenant Joe DiMartino as the officer in charge, I was able to go to Vietnam on a thirteen-month tour of duty under COMNAV–V [Commander Naval Forces–Vietnam] late in 1966. Joe and I were the first two advisors of what became Detachment Echo, SEAL advisors to the LDNN. Our assignment was to bring up the LDNN training to include SEAL Team tactics and land warfare more than the diving side of their mission. We were also to integrate the LDNNs into SEAL platoons. Joe spent so much time in and around Saigon that he soon became known as the unofficial mayor of the city by all the U.S. forces stationed there.

When the Team TWO platoons started arriving in Vietnam early in 1967, I was able to spend most of my time operating with them in the Delta. I would spend a few days with one group and then a couple more days with another group, evaluating and observing what they did and finding out what was going on in the field. A call might come in about some hot intel that one group had received. ''We've got a good one coming up next Tuesday'' would come in on the radio, and off I would go to join the operation.

It was probably the best duty in the Teams at the time. I could operate with whomever I wanted and wasn't really accountable to anyone. Joe D would ask me to come back up to Saigon every couple of months. But I think all Joe wanted to do was physically see me and make sure I was still alive. Over my long tour in Vietnam, I had the chance to work with a large number of people. With Rick Marcinko and Eighth Platoon, I joined in the fierce house-to-house fighting during the Tet offensive in Chau Doc. When the Australians sent in a detachment of their SAS [Special Air Service], I went into the field with them to see how they operated.

My time with the LDNNs was like a whole bunch of tours compressed. I was able to travel all over the place and go out on the best ops. The experience was tremendous, and I was constantly learning.

In general, I had mixed feelings about the LDNNs. I had seen what had to be done, but the action was hard to come by. The LDNNs were a very political group, and, like everyone, there were good ones and bad ones. The LDNN COs had very little control over their men. It seemed there was always somebody above the CO who wanted them to do something besides operate. The LDNNs acted as bodyguards for the President of South Vietnam and held other high-profile roles. The Vietnamese had an expression: "Lien Doc Nguoi Nhia can piss anywhere." They had the status of special police and even had cards they only had to show to get out of jail. I had one of these "Get out of jail free" cards myself, but you would only use one of those sparingly if at all. After all, you can't do your job if you're in jail, or even just being hassled by the police. And standing out too much is a good way to make yourself a target.

There were LDNNs who were as good as our guys, and others who were just political appointees. But for the most part, I couldn't have asked for better duty, or a better guy to work for than Joe D, but I finally had to leave Vietnam and go back to Little Creek.

Before I had left for Vietnam, I had attended a new school in Coronado intended to train advisors. After I was back in the States for a while, I went back out to what was now the PRU advisor school taught by Team ONE. With my experience in Vietnam, I was one of the people who would evaluate the school for Team TWO. The school was good, with a number of great instructors who were very intel-oriented. I had learned the value of intelligence a long time ago, and a good op only came from good intel. You made your own luck by carefully examining the available intel and planning your ops accordingly. The difficulty is that not all of the SEALs are intel-oriented. It took time to sift through all of the agents' reports and combine them into an overall picture. Some of the guys were hot operators who primarily wanted to shoot. Nothing wrong with that, I was a bit that way myself.

After I was back from the school, I was looking for a slot to become available. Ninth Platoon was going to Vietnam, and I was going to be able to go along as an extra man. It was in June of 1969 that I returned to Vietnam, this time to act as a PRU advisor with the Phoenix program.

The PRUs, Provincial Reconnaissance Units, were groups of Vietnamese, Hmongs (Montagnards), Chinese, and even Chieu Hoi VC and NVA. Armed and paid by the CIA through the Phoenix program, the PRUs were military action groups led by an American advisor. Though the CIA ran the show, the advisors came out of the U.S. military, the SEALs included. In the field, the advisors were in charge.

The Agency people I worked with were interested in results. I only saw them about three times during my whole tour. They didn't want to know what I was doing or where I was, only that I was accomplishing the mission. When I arrived in Vietnam, I was sent up to Saigon along with a couple of other SEALs who were also going to be PRU advisors. We met with our CIA contact men and were briefed on the situation. After I agreed to pick up the Nha Be PRU, they called down to the Army guys there and pulled them out. "It's all yours," the agent told me. "Tell me what you need." And with that, I was on my way to the Nha Be PRU.

Nha Be is a small town just on the outskirts of the Rung Sat Special Zone, southwest of Saigon. The PRU at Nha Be was made up mostly of hard-core former VC, Hoi Chanhs. There was also a good number of draft-dodging Vietnamese who would rather go into the PRUs than be forced into the ARVN forces and just be cannon fodder. There were also some ethnic Chinese who entered the unit rather than be drafted.

I wasn't carried on the official Detachment Bravo rolls in Saigon. Though SpecWar knew where I was, not being on the Bravo list gave me more freedom to operate with my PRU. Det Bravo was the SEAL detachment in Vietnam that was to supply all of the "official" PRU advisors. With the Nha Be PRU being so close to Saigon, it was the one most often looked at. Getting results was what mattered most to my Agency people. As long as I did that and didn't allow any excesses with my men, I could operate as I wished.

The PRU commander was Mr. Ai, a former VC who had rallied to the South's side in the early 1960s. Mr. Ai was very hard-core with his men—he ran the PRU strictly with an iron hand. But he knew the enemy—after all he had been one. It took three months before Mr. Ai would involve me with his best, and most sensitive, intelligence. Once the SEAL platoon, and I, had proved ourselves by supporting him, Mr. Ai gave us full access to the intel network he had developed over time.

The layout was ideal for a SEAL to operate with this PRU. The PRU base was just outside of the gate of the SEAL compound. Working hard in cooperation with the PRU, I quickly started integrating their intelligence with our SEAL operations. Just about every day, I would come back to the platoon and brief Doug Ellis, our platoon leader, and Herb Ruth, the assistant platoon leader, on what the intel was that the PRUs had gathered. After the briefing, we would decide what ops the SEALs would do based on the intel.

If the operation the SEALs would go on was more than a regular ambush, I would have a couple of PRUs go along with the guide and he would take the squad in. That way the squad could concentrate on the area around them and the PRUs would watch the guide. If it turned out the intel was bad and the guide was leading us into a trap, he would be the first one to go. Hard as this system is, it cut way down on bad intel and bogus guides.

The squads were usually doing two ops a day, and I tried to go out on every good op that I could. Sometimes we would run the ops strictly from the PRU side of the house. When the PRUs would go out on a big op, I would get a few volunteers from Doug's platoon to go along as additional help, usually Mike Naus and Jim Glasscock.

The SEALs I would take along were usually big guys who carried big guns. These guys would carry an M60 machine gun and four to six hundred rounds of ammunition. This was nice, as these guys could stand up and cut trees down. You could also stand behind them if you wanted to. These guys would carry an M60 machine gun along with an assortment of other lethal toys. For myself, I preferred the CAR-15, the short submachine gun version of the M16. Using the CAR, I would rarely extend the stock, as most of our fighting was done close in with instinctive firing from the hip being the norm.

In Nha Be, Doug Ellis, myself, and a few other SEALs who were intel-oriented set up a SEAL intel net separate from the PRUs to support our operations. We would meet with agents in out-of-the-way places in Nha Be and provided really good intel to the platoon. The net was funded from Saigon through Lieutenant Commander John Ferruggiaro for SpecWar. The funds were supplied to pay our agents, helping us to secure the net. Now we had two sources of intel to plan operations. A good source of intel was needed to plan ops, and now we had two of them. That situation is part of what led to the very successful tour of Ninth Platoon and also to some of the successes of the PRUs.

The situation was a good solid meshing of two forces. One, the PRUs, was made up of good operators who knew the area and its people. The other, the SEALs, was made up of highly trained, top-level operators who had access to a good deal of support. All the SEALs needed was to be given the leadership and pointed in the right direction. With two groups like that working to a common goal, you can't lose.

It was almost a unique combination of units. The PRUs were able to supply good intel, some of the best of the war. On our side, we had a quick-response unit with access to all the material riches of the U.S. forces, the SEALs. We could supply helicopters, fire support, gunships, and highly trained, motivated individual operators. Before we became involved with the PRUs, they could react to maybe one target, even though they might have intel on five. Now with the SEALs involved, we could hit three or four targets at once. And with the medevac and other support we gave the PRUs, they could hit some of the harder and more dangerous targets, and still expect to come home.

Independent duty with the PRUs was most likely the best duty of the war for an operator. Here I was, an E-6 in the Navy in full command of a hundred highly trained indigenous operators, with unlimited support, able to go anywhere at any time and kick ass.

The PRUs were the action arm of the Phoenix program. Besides supporting the Provincial Reconnaissance Units, Phoenix was an all-encompassing program that included CORDS [Civil Operations and Revolutionary Development Support], Census/Grievance Committees, and other organizations under its umbrella. CORDS was the major organization that set up a chain of command that included the CIA and gave direct access to the U.S. military commander in Vietnam.

The Phoenix program and CORDS showed that the U.S. military and intelligence community recognized that there was more needed to solve the Vietnam conflict than just a conventional military force. The target of the organization was to locate the infrastructure of the Viet Cong, their command and control people, in South Vietnam and attack them specifically. If we eliminated the commanders, the local VC would quickly disintegrate and no longer be a viable military force.

The Census/Grievance Committees were another way of locating the VC and targeting individuals. Going around to the different hamlets and villages, the committees would run a head count of the people as well as listen to their bitches and what they wanted from the government. Besides trying to help get the people what they needed, the committees, by getting an accurate idea of the population of an area, could point out when new people started showing up. These strangers could be investigated more closely to see if they weren't VC units on the move.

The committees would also be recruiting agents and getting intel on an area without having the people they talked to stand out. They would set up their Grievance Committee in a single hut, and the locals could be called in one at a time. Since a census was also being conducted, everyone would be expected to show up. This gave the people a chance to be interviewed in private without anyone else knowing what was said. A lot of good agents and intel came out of this idea.

But once the intel was available, someone had to act on it. This is where the PRUs came in. The actions of the PRUs are what gave the Phoenix program such a bad image back in the States. The idea that the PRUs were "assassins" made the news very quickly back in the U.S.

As with any law enforcement or paramilitary organization in the world, only a few elements would have to start working independently and the entire organization would quickly receive a black reputation. Some of the PRUs did act as assassins—they had come from a violent background, and it was very difficult to cut them completely free of their earlier methods. In some areas it was the provincial chiefs who would direct the PRUs to take actions against individuals who were not legitimately VC but political rivals of the men in charge.

Personally, I am aware of a few situations where it was almost impossible to tell if the targeted individual was a VC sympathizer or had gotten on the bad side of the province chief's cousin. There were safeguards in the program to prevent abuses. And the safeguards were used on occasion to stop the actions of some individuals. But for by far the most part, the PRU and Phoenix program was the best program for eliminating the VC infrastructure as a functioning organization in South Vietnam.

The most common misconception of the Phoenix program was that it was intended to eliminate the VC infrastructure by just killing off people. The old adage "Dead men tell no tales" applies very well here. The idea was to capture targeted individuals and use the intelligence gathered from them to "move up the ladder," what law enforcement today calls "playing tag." That system just feeds itself and gradually eliminates the highest levels of command in an area.

The primary operation for the PRUs as well as the SEALs was the snatch. Jumping off the skids of a helicopter onto a hooch rooftop doesn't give the people inside much time to react. Sneaking into a building in the middle of the night, shining a penlight into an individual's face to identify him, and then silently snatching him up and extracting quickly builds a reputation among the people left behind.

By being able to bring in an agent and having him positively identify the snatch target, you keep yourself from grabbing the wrong person. Soon it becomes known that if you're a VC sympathizer or part of the chain of command, you will be found out and disappear. Among a superstitious people, almost mystical powers are attributed to the men who conduct these operations.

Once the target was snatched, field intelligence people would question him. In some situations, the PRUs would run the interrogations. But in all of my experience, I saw very little, if any, of what could be called torture, even by Western standards. Abuse would happen, but in the almost two years I spent in Vietnam, I saw no outright torture. Most of the time, the information could be extracted by just talking to the individual. A simple deal would be offered. "You help us out or you're going to jail." The VC operated as terrorists within South Vietnam, and that was simply against the law, just as it would be here in the West.

Some stories just seemed to perpetuate themselves, like the "chopper toss" method of interrogation. I personally never knew of this to happen or of anyone who even saw it done. The idea of taking a prisoner, or prisoners, up into a helicopter and tossing one out the door just doesn't make any sense. How could you tell which one knew the information you wanted? If you threw the wrong one out, he would be real hard to question later. And the guy who was left would tell you anything you wanted to hear anyway.

The Vietnamese didn't have a lot of time to perform field interrogations. And it wasn't the United States—they didn't spend time reading a prisoner his rights. Actions could be taking place out in the field that would remove any value from what a prisoner could tell us. So very often, a prisoner might find himself facedown in the mud until he wanted to talk. But I never saw an interrogation continue to the point of death, or even real torture.

What stories did get back to the States were usually badly distorted in the telling and retelling. For the SEALs, it was often enough just to threaten to turn the prisoner over to the Vietnamese. That, combined with our reputation, could quickly turn a man over to our side. In the same night, we could be back out on an op with the prisoner leading us in.

The "silent pistol shot to the head," a favorite story of the anti-Phoenix people, did take place. But the target of the shot was usually a noisy village dog that could alert people that we were there. On different ops, we would carry a hush puppy [suppressed pistol] in the squad. Often, the point man would carry the weapon, as he would be the first to make contact where a silent shot might be needed. Not many of the weapons were available, so what we had would be rotated around the squads.

There would have been times that having a hush puppy for each man on an op would have been great. You can't call 911 when in the bush, and the element of surprise was everything sometimes. Silent rounds snapping out in an ambush could eliminate a following enemy group without drawing attention from a larger force nearby.

As a PRU advisor, I ended up pulling a longer tour of duty in Vietnam than the Ninth Platoon. When the platoon rotated back to the States, I had to stay with my PRUs. The advisor who was going to relieve me, Curtis Ashton, was killed on an operation, so I stayed on an additional month until another replacement was available. When I arrived in Nha Be, the advisors I relieved were two Army guys. Some time earlier, Jim Watson had been a PRU advisor in Nha Be, probably with the same men I was leading in 1969.

Watson had been injured by an exploding mine while working with his PRU. For myself, I wasn't injured badly enough at any time to be relieved and sent home. But that doesn't mean some of the operations don't stand out.

There was one op I was on that is memorable just for when it took place. I was on an ambush when Moon River, our main communications station, broke radio silence. There was a great big full moon looking down at us as we waited to wax some VC. "Look up at the moon" was what came over the radio. At that exact moment, man was walking on the moon for the first time in human history. We did end up ambushing a couple of sampans later that night, killing three or four guards and capturing a number of weapons. There was a strange feeling of unreality about the situation, with our waiting on a mud bank, ready to do what man has done for centuries, kill his fellow man, and far above us, with no connection whatsoever, this high-tech event taking place that had never happened before.

There were a lot of good operations with the PRUs that I was a part of. What made them good was the success of the op, as well as the adrenaline factor. Seeing green [Communist] tracers go between yourself and the guy next to you let you know that you had cheated death one more time. I only did two tours in Vietnam, but they added up to twenty months in combat.

Orders came down from Saigon that PRU advisors would no longer be allowed to go out in the field with their men. Normally, this would have been a bad situation for me and my PRU. You cannot expect men to follow a leader who only sits back at camp, especially not the kind of men who made up the PRUs. But I wasn't on the official Det Bravo rolls. Without my name to work with, the orders were never sent to me. I think that situation resulted in my being the last SEAL to operate in the field with the PRUs. The time was late 1969 to early 1970. Ninth Platoon went back to the States in December of

1969. Finally, my PRU replacement arrived and it was my turn to go back to Little Creek.

Within a few years of their commission, it was evident that the SEALs were the next logical step in the evolution of the UDT. Many older and experienced UDT operators gradually moved to the SEALs for either a tour of duty or the balance of their career in Navy Special Warfare.

These seasoned UDT veterans brought a good deal of their own experience and expertise into the new Teams and were a strong influence on how the Teams operated. This was especially true on the East Coast, where the pool of veteran UDT men was larger and more established than on the West Coast. This situation resulted in SEAL Team TWO's having a higher average rank than SEAL Team ONE, as well as Team TWO's having a higher percentage of married SEALs with families. The older, experienced nature of Team TWO's men made their methods of operating in Vietnam different from those of the SEALs in Team ONE.

The SEAL Teams had retained the numbering system used by the UDTs. Even-numbered Teams were on the East Coast at Norfolk, and odd-numbered Teams were on the West Coast at Coronado. Many men, especially officers, would find themselves serving on both coasts during their careers in Navy Special Warfare. This became even more common after the Vietnam War had ended. This action helped spread the pool of experienced men throughout the Teams.

WILBUR "PAT" PATTERSON

Pat Patterson was a SEAL officer whose men respected him and would follow anywhere he would lead. As an officer from the older UDT Teams, with experience as both an enlisted man and an officer in the Teams, he had an outlook that few others shared.

I'm originally from Birmingham, Alabama. We lived on a rock farm there. In 1946 we moved to Florida, and I joined the Navy there in 1950. I was a student, going to high school. I joined the Navy just to go someplace, I guess. I quit school. I had finished eleventh grade when I went in the Navy and I finished high school with a GED in 1953. I just liked the Navy and I stayed with it.

My first two years I was in Panama City, Florida. There I worked as a crane operator on a YSD [seaplane wrecking derrick] for about six, seven months. Then I transferred to a torpedo shop and worked on torpedoes for about a year. From there I went to torpedo school in Newport, Rhode Island.

That was in August of '52. I graduated there in January and went to a tin can [destroyer], the USS MULLANY DD528, in January of '53. She was in the yards in Boston. We left the yards and went to the Mediterranean. We had some engine difficulties, so we came back to Brooklyn Navy Yard. While this ship was in Brooklyn I met Alicia [Mrs. Patterson] there.

Before getting to Brooklyn, when I was in the Med, they had asked for volunteers for UDT. So I took all the tests in Trieste, Italy. When we got back to Brooklyn I left the ship and came here [Virginia Beach, Virginia] for training.

That was in July. I came to training, and I guess I was like everybody else. It wasn't the easiest thing I've ever done. But I managed to survive it.

We didn't have half, or a third, of the equipment that they have now. We were right at the bottom of the totem pole as far as the Navy was concerned, to tell you the truth. They almost had done away with UDT at one time, sometime between 1945 and '49. Most of the main Teams still were in California up until '49. Then they split the Teams and kept some of them on the West Coast.

As far as the Teams of that time were concerned, fiscally they were pretty well strapped most of the time. We did a lot of living out of salvage in those days. We'd go to salvage to get a lot of things. There were types of tools and machinery we could pick up for nothing.

I worked with the boats, mostly. I traded swim fins for coffee and coffee for diesel engines. That was standard, that's standard practice. It was cumshaw, as they call it.

Even playing sports, we didn't have any uniforms. We played in shorts or bathing suits or greens, whatever we had at the time. Some of them had holes in them.

To get back to training, we had a fine little group. I didn't see any reason to quit once I got there. I didn't see any reason not to finish it. I'd have just gone someplace else. I had appendicitis at one point, but they took care of that. I had my health, so I just stayed there. And I stayed, really, for twenty years.

We used to go to the Caribbean in January, and we'd be there till some time in March for advanced underwater training. That's when we did all of our training which is now handled by BUD/S, or Basic Underwater Demolition/SEAL Team. In training now, they have a thing up to a point, and then when they go to the Teams more training is added on.

They're never finished with training. Initial training was

about twenty-six weeks [sixteen weeks at UDTR, six weeks of Swim school, and three weeks at UMP school]. They get a whole lot to stack up on that once they get to the Teams.

Back then the deployments were in our area of operation, and we were really limited. Our main operation, the biggest one that we had, was six months in the Med. And then we had training with the amphibious force. We were reconnaissance teams for the amphibious operations.

So back then, that was about it. We had one three-month deployment, I think, one platoon in the Caribbean and one in the Mediterranean. So a six-month deployment then was a long time, up until the Vietnam War. Then things started picking up some.

Now they have deployments quite a few places. Now the SEALs' area of operation is the whole world.

I went originally to Team 4. I was with Team 4 from '53 to 1956. Then it was changed to Team 22. Team 22 was decommissioned in . . . let me get the dates. It was Team 4 from 1953 to '55, then they redesignated it as Team 22. From '55 to '56 it was 22. They decommissioned it in '56 and we all transferred to Team 21. I was there from '56 to '62, and I received my commission in January of 1962.

I went to Newport, Rhode Island, to knife-and-fork [Officer Candidate] school. I came back to 22. I was there from 1962 to '63.

I had a good rapport with the people there [those with whom he had served as an enlisted man]. I attribute my future promotions to the fact that they did work well with me. And anything I had to do, they more than willingly backed me right on up. No, I had no problem at all.

Then in 1963 they commissioned a staff. Before, when they had the two Teams, and even when they had the one, what they had was a COMUDU. The senior Team commander, the skipper, was designated as Commander of Underwater Demolition Units. In 1963 they commissioned a staff to take care of the staff functions for the Teams. The Teams were starting to grow. It was the Commander of Naval Operations Support Group, I believe.

Anyway, I went to the staff in '63 and I stayed with the staff in Research and Development for two years.

I went to SEAL Team TWO in 1965 and was there until 1967. In January 1967 I went to California for Vietnamese language school in San Diego and then to Da Nang for one year as advisor to the Vietnamese SEALs.

There are a lot of opinions floating around about Vietnam. It was a job. I went over there to do a job and I did what I was sent there to do. I had been trained for that job and that's all I can say.

It was a pretty country and it's just a shame that it was in such a mess at that time.

Outside of that, just being there and doing my job and coming home, I can't say too much about the job because it was classified top secret. I doubt that it has been or ever will be declassified. I just can't say much about it.

We did a lot of things, but it was all in conjunction with the people who were in an advisory capacity to the people we were training. Like I say, it was all classified.

We were in Dong Tam, operating in Dong Tam down the Mekong by My Tho, and there was a detachment of SEALs in My Tho. I would have liked to have operated with them but I couldn't. They [the authorities] wouldn't let me. We could have done some good operating together. I was forbidden to do so.

I would rather have been [operating with a SEAL platoon]. Up until I went to Vietnam for that year, I had a platoon. We were the next platoon to deploy when they reassigned me and sent me over there for a year. I relieved another lieutenant in Da Nang. It was kind of a letdown, not being able to be out in the woods with these guys. But, like I say, I was sent to do a job and I did it. And I came home.

It was hard to tell just who the enemy was. I mean, you could go into a village and pick up the VC and you had no way of knowing. They were peasants, just peasants. There was no distinction, no military distinction, like uniforms or anything like that. There were as many VC in the pacified villages as they had out in the countryside. They were good guerrilla fighters. Of course, they had

Chinese there helping them, but they were good guerrilla fighters.

Except for one instance, the Vietnamese officers I worked with were all top-notch people. They were dedicated to what they had to do. I only had the one bad experience.

And I think . . . there's a lot of opinions of how the war should have been carried out. It shouldn't have lasted as long as it did, but it did. Anyway, it's not my business to condemn or condone. I was there to do a job, I did it, and I came home.

Anyway, that's one side of it.

So many units over there, they had their little clubs. We had one in Da Nang. They had one in Can Tho, My Tho, and Dong Tam. They were places you could go, enjoy people, and have a few drinks. As far as anything outside the bases you knew, I wouldn't say you could go to anything.

You never knew when a native satchel carrier would be coming in the door. They did that with impunity and they didn't care who was in there. They thought they could get some military in instances like that. We had to screen all the windows on the buses, so they started throwing live satchel charges in the backs of jeeps.

I knew a first class Bosun's mate who got it with a hand grenade a kid handed him wrapped like a birthday present. He opened it and that was it. So this eight-year-old kid could kill a man.

In Tet '68, what the VC used then was the children in Da Nang that they had built up and just gave them a grenade and told them to go get it. That's the way they were. They didn't care. Orphanages, they'd go in and kill everybody, children, nuns, didn't matter.

But none of that was put in the news here. The media only went after stories that were sensational. That was not sensationalism.

There were some places where the Army chopper pilots refused to go. We relied a lot on the chopper pilots for insertion and retraction. The Navy Seawolves were the most aggressive pilots we had over there. They'd go in to anywhere, anytime. But we have been refused by the Army. When the Seawolves weren't available, service had been refused. Working with the riverine staff, that was a good experience, working with the riverine patrol.

That was the Army riverine patrol. Our Army operated in the Delta quite a bit. And I was in their area of operations, so I had to liaison closely with them. They were pretty top-notch too.

It was all a completely new war for the Army to be in amphibious warfare, but that's what they had down there. It was kind of a backwards thing when the Marines had the land in the North and the Army had the water in the South. It was kind of a switch.

I got to meet General Westmoreland and talked with him one time. He came down to visit the riverine force and I happened to be aboard the USS BENEWAH at the time. We were standing around the deck talking, just general things, but it was interesting to talk to him. He was a good man. He was a gentleman's gentleman, and he was a good general.

All in all, we had good relations with the other services. Overall I have no complaints.

I had a lot of other different deployments, Mediterranean, Caribbean, Panama, and Norway, surveying the beaches and things like that for possible amphibious landing. There wasn't anything special or anything special happening in any of them. It all went pretty much regulation. We didn't have any riots or anything like that to put up with.

As far as any outstanding deployment, well, I've been in hot, been in cold. Been in Labrador, Thule, Greenland. As far as anything outstanding, they just were normal operations.

As part of the intramural sports on the base we played softball and touch football, mainly. We weren't too much involved in basketball. Our main rival was the Marines, and that was all the time. We always had a tough time with them. We could beat them, but . . . we had a tough time. Football especially.

I pitched softball for about seventeen years. We had a

second baseman named Jerry Todd. When we'd play the Marines he'd come and sit down by the mound next to me. And that would tear them all up. They'd always try to hit past the second baseman. Then we'd sing little ditties to them, tell them to buy some Visine to get the red out.

We almost had a riot when we played in football. It was for the league championship. And they were singing to them, up in the stands. They had a little song there, "From the halls of Montezuma to the shores of Tripoli, we will fight our country's battles in the wake of UDT." That used to get them.

We were base champions for many, many years. I guess we still are. They still have the Admiral's Trophy. They didn't have it when we were there, but they have the Admiral's Trophy now, I think.

Out in California they stole my cleats and bronzed them. We were thirteen for fourteen out there. I wondered how they got into the car. She [Mrs. Patterson] gave them the key. And I thought, "How did they get in there in my car and take my spikes and not break a window?"

I can't say I would have enjoyed the Navy any other way. I really wouldn't. I just say I was fortunate to have been able to operate in the team. With the kind of people we had, very fortunate.

I can't say we ever had a bad commanding officer, or a bad officer anywhere. You might find somebody who says, "This guy's this and this guy's that," but we didn't have that. We were really tight-knit. You just can't find people like that anywhere.

I was with the Teams up until '71, when they decommissioned Team THIRTEEN. I was Executive Officer of Team THIRTEEN. They decommissioned her in '71 and then I went to the staff through '73. Then I went to be director of diving school in San Diego. I retired in '74. So I had a pretty well-rounded career.

I was with the sea mammals program for about two years before I went to the dive school. In the sea lions program, they were trained to recover the exercise missiles. The missiles were built for transfer and recovery.

Just to work with those animals and see how intelligent they are, it's an experience. I was fortunate again in being able to do that for almost two years. I was with the staff then, in San Diego.

The SEALs didn't have them [the sea mammals]. The staff controlled them. The sea mammals were really just a research project. I don't know that they were ever approved for service use. I couldn't tell you if they're still doing research with them or not, if they still have some kind of research going.

A lot of people say the dolphins are misused or abused, but they weren't. They had the best handlers in the world. They treated them just like children.

Then again, the intelligence of a sea mammal is just unbelievable. It goes beyond imagination. Until you actually have worked with them in the water, then there are no limits to what you can teach them. Those things are smarter than a lot a people I know. They get grouchy just like anybody else, and you'd give them a fish and it would quiet them right down.

You put a muzzle on a marine mammal and send him over the side of a boat to do a job, and he'll go and do that job. The sea lions would put this clamp around a piece of machinery and then come right back up to the boat without taking off after fish or whatever. These little things never seemed to tire of going in the water. Of course, it's their habitat. They're a lot of fun to work with.

I retired at lieutenant commander. I had a real good career. I can't say that I have any regrets at all.

After I left the Navy I worked fourteen years at Old Dominion University, in the Public Safety Department over there.

Most of the people I operated with, they're still around. I see them. If they don't live around here I see them at the reunions every year.

My old buddy Frank Scollice is the most unusual person I knew, I guess. There's an instance, now that I recall. Frank was something else. He was an Engineman but he was a pretty good cook on top of that. He was working as an advisor to one of the Vietnamese units down in the Delta. And he came aboard ship.

Frank could grow a full growth of beard, just about, in two days. He came on board the BENEWAH, which was a converted LST [Landing Ship Tank] and was the command ship of the riverine forces down there. And he was muddy from here to across his feet, barefooted, a beard, a burst-out beard, and he had been in the bush for about a week. On those ships they kept the passageways dark, with just red lights, a darkened ship, for whatever reason.

He was going down a passageway and he scared a few people and they had the MPs out all looking for Frank. They didn't know who he was or where he was. Anyway, he went into the operations office on board and told them he was Colonel Frank Scollice and he needed a boat. They let him have the skipper's boat and Frank went ashore. That's about the best thing I can come up with.

He cooked steak in motor oil because he ran out of vegetable oil one time. Nobody knew the difference anyway.

Frank was something else. He was a good man.

Frank is deceased now. He's gone about ten years, close to. He was putting a water line in his yard and he had a heart attack.

We had the best equipment there was available at the time. As a matter of fact, we had weapons that had yet to be approved for service use. We, in the nature of our jobs, were able to take and use those weapons. We had everything we needed; we had the best we could get at the time, with no problems.

As soon as something new came out we were able to get that, too. So we had no complaints as far as equipment. It was all state-of-the-art at the time, or would be state-of-the-art shortly.

And to the men of the Teams, God bless all who went before and all who will come after me.

When ground forces started to be sent to Vietnam early in the war, the actions there were considered to be primarily a SEAL

Team ONE concern. Since Team ONE covered the Pacific, it was only natural that it send the first combat platoons to Vietnam. Men from SEAL Team TWO had been in Vietnam since 1962, but their numbers were limited and they acted primarily as instructors and advisors as part of SEAL MTTs (Mobile Training Teams). When the first SEAL direct action platoon was sent to Vietnam early in 1966, it was ALFA Platoon from Team ONE. Team ONE platoons were identified alphabetically from ALFA to ZULU and the squads numerically, two to a platoon. SEAL Team TWO's platoons are identified by number, Second through Tenth, with the squads identified as A or B.

Very quickly, it became obvious that there were more duties for the SEALs in Vietnam than could be adequately completed by a single Team. In the latter half of 1966, Team TWO platoons began training for duty in Vietnam, and the first platoons arrived in-country in January 1967. The strain of a SEAL platoon's actions was considered so great that a platoon's tour of duty in Vietnam was limited to six months. Some men would find the action in Vietnam much to their liking and jump from platoon to platoon in order to spend as much time as possible in-country.

Combat veterans in the SEALs were very few in number for those first direct action platoons. Training held true, and the SEALs quickly learned the ins and outs of combat. But mistakes were common for the first year of combat until experience was gathered and spread out among the platoons.

MIKE BOYNTON

USN (Ret.)

Mike Boynton, though an easy-spoken man with a ready laugh, is one of the foundations that the SEALs' reputation was built on. Boynton shaped many would-be Frogmen and SEALs while an instructor for UDTR at Little Creek. Mike also earned a reputation for toughness and an unswerving determination to get the job done in Vietnam that many later SEALs would admire and try to emulate.

My birthday isn't too hard to miss, 8 December 1941, just the day after Pearl Harbor. Though as a small kid in Dallas, Texas, you barely recognize that there's a world out there, let alone a world war. Shortly after the war ended, my family moved to Hawaii, not a bad place for a kid to spend five or six years. It was in Hawaii that I learned how to swim and developed my love for the water. My dad worked in the civil service at service clubs, so we did a bit of traveling during my early childhood. After Hawaii, we moved to Guam for two years. I loved it, more water, more swimming, more this and more that. As a kid in junior high school, I was having a great time.

Then the bottom kind of dropped out as my parents separated. Eventually, my family made its way back to Texas, where I had started. While in high school, I joined the swim team, as I still loved the water. After graduation it was time to look at other things to do with my life, and the Navy looked like a good prospect. Besides, the Navy worked on the water and I didn't want to be a Marine, or be in the Army, or be a bus driver in the Air Force. So in August 1960 I enlisted in the U.S. Navy.

Training wasn't bad. I ended up in Jacksonville, Florida, to attend AOA, aircraft ordnance, school. Now I was an Airdale, a BB stacker, qualified to shove bombs and bullets into planes. After a short time on a forgettable ship, I was assigned to the new USS CONSTELLATION. As a plankowner of the *Connie*, I was there just in time for the major fire she had in her engine room. Not the sort of thing that makes you want to stay on the crew.

Weeks after the fire, during a formation, we were told about the UDT and UDTR. After a short explanation of what was going on, we were told that any volunteers could report to the YMCA for the qualification tests. Man, I want to do this, I thought. I had seen the Richard Widmark movie *The Frogmen* several times. This sounded good. I had been swimming since I was a kid and still loved the water. It wasn't that I just wanted to get off the ship, it was that what was being offered sounded better than what I was doing right now.

I didn't know whether I could pass the tests or not. But I did know that if I was accepted for training, I was going to make it through the course. And I did have a good idea of how hard the course was going to be, I wasn't going in completely ignorant of the situation.

Fifty-seven guys showed up for the physical screening test. We had been checked for scores on our Navy tests—a lower score was acceptable then, unlike now. In the Brooklyn YMCA, we all showed up for the physical portion of the tests, to be administered by a brand-new ensign. Fresh out of EOD school, this man had no idea how to interpret what was asked for on the test. In place of the required thirty two-count squat-thrusts within one minute, he decided to make us do four-count thrusts. So instead of doing thirty exercises, we had to do sixty. In one minute.

Out of fifty-seven guys, I was the only one to get a set of orders to UDTR. I passed the test, but my legs were so sore I couldn't even walk the next day. Swimming had been no problem, and I had been doing push-ups and other exercises to keep a little in shape. But those squat-thrusts had been a killer. And I didn't even make the sixty—I think I did about fifty-seven. The ensign noted that I was a little weak in that area. I had doubled the required amount. That ensign is one person I will never forget. I wanted to kill him for the entire two weeks that I was hobbling around on my sore legs.

My orders came in, and it was off to Little Creek. January 1962, Class 27, a winter UDTR class. And the class was a big one, something like 148 students started and forty-eight graduated. A small amount considering how many began training. And they were dropping like flies from almost the first day.

Hell Week was stunning. It was the fifth week of training, and they had built us up during pretraining and the weeks earlier. But nothing can really prepare you for that long week. I knew it was going to be hard, but part of my driving force was that I didn't want to go back aboard a ship. Secondly, I told myself that I knew I could make it, I just had to not go to sleep. And I wanted to sleep.

When we did the Around the World evolution, dragging ourselves and an inflated rubber boat all over the base, the instructors drove us hard. Running around with these goddam rubber boats on our heads was difficult, but all I wanted to do was sleep. And I was colder than hell, which added to the misery.

Pointing us at the sand dunes one day, they told us we had to hide. Hide? In the open? Just burrow into the sand, huh? And here came the instructors in the jeeps. "So solly, you shitbag," would sound out as they spotted us. We couldn't hide. They could walk right up to us and piss on our helmets if they wanted to. How were we going to hide? They knew exactly where we were. And this was only the third day.

All that would go through my mind, whatever part of it was still working, was the desire to sleep. And then somebody would get up and quit. Shit, I thought, if he's going to quit I'm not. I know I'm better than him. And I would press on. I only thought seriously of quitting once while in training.

Every time I get close to even thinking about quitting, somebody would bomb out. What a jerk, I would think, and that would lift my spirits. And I would say something inane and uplifting, like "Yeah, okay, come on, let's go," and we would stumble on. Guys were getting closer together as the week went on, especially boat crews, where you needed to work as a team to just get through.

And guys were bombing out left and right. The group just got visibly smaller and smaller. Then the end of the week was on us, and we had condensed down to a hard-core nucleus. Now they had the Team members out to help work on us, and that was okay too. We were wasted, just stumbling zombies. And that was how I got through Hell Week.

My body didn't take any real damage. A slight problem with my left knee was about it, and that went away over time. No big-time problems with torn muscles or anything, just tired. And when Friday was over, Hell Week had ended, poof, everybody was gone. The barracks was empty. For the whole weekend, I had the place to myself. After cleaning up my gear Friday, I slept on the floor in a sleeping bag. Can't really say why, I just slept on the floor that Friday night and spent the weekend taking it easy.

Monday morning shined for us—Hell Week was over and we thought we had it made. We didn't have shit made. The instructors stuck it to us, calling us out of the barracks, blowing their whistles, and giving us an impromptu inspection. Nothing was good enough. Boots wouldn't be right or your belt buckle would be off. Everybody had something wrong, whether it was or not.

"Okay," the instructor said, "you guys think you're such hot shit right now. Okay, we're going to go for a little run."

So what? we thought, we had just gotten through Hell Week and that was supposed to be the hardest time, wasn't it?

So off we went for a run, right down to those miserable

mudflats. It was colder than it had been the week before. And here we were back in the mud. The duty instructor, Herb Clements, had his regular greens on, and he jogged along, leading us right into the mud. But Hell Week is over, isn't it? we thought.

And God was it cold. Froze so bad it felt like pieces of our bodies were going to fall off. We were supposed to have finished Hell Week and here we were rolling around in the freezing mud, again!

I think somebody quit right there. But looking over at the instructor, I thought, if he can do it, I can. And so I just toughed it out. To this day, I believe the reason they did that was to see if anyone would bomb out. We had gotten through Hell Week, so they knew we could take it. But could we take the possibility of there being more of the same?

It just so happened that night I was on the duty section. A small group of us had to go around and pull details like cleaning up the instructors' hut, fire watch, things like that. I was cleaning the instructors' hut and scrubbing out the head. What did I see hanging up in the shower but a dry suit. Holy shit, that guy had a dry suit on, I thought. He wasn't cold, he wore it under his greens. But psychologically, it looked like the cold wasn't bothering him.

That was good, I thought after the shock had worn off. Here I was, freezing my ass off and toughing it out because the instructor was just as cold as we were. And he wasn't. Was that cool or what?

Later on, we went down to Puerto Rico and continued training. There was one student we had, a black man who had graduated college, whose attitude changed drastically after we got down to Puerto Rico. He had gotten through Hell Week and was able to do all the physical stuff well. But he just wouldn't work with the group anymore. The instructors dropped him four weeks before the end of the class. It just showed that it took more than just brains and brawn to get through training. If you didn't work with the Team, you were gone.

At the end of our training in Puerto Rico, we thought we were going to fly back to Little Creek and be done.

Don't have to wear that damned red helmet anymore, I thought. All of the students wore a red-painted helmet liner to make sure everyone knew who was going by. By the end of training, I hated that red helmet. Surprise! We had to wear that red helmet the whole weekend after we got back to the Creek. The following week, we flew down to Fort Benning, Georgia, for airborne school. Then on to Key West, Florida, for five weeks of diving school.

Airborne school was a farce to me. We had just gotten finished with the hardest physical training in the military and these guys were making us run around. That was a joke, and we had fun with it. The jumping didn't bother me. I didn't have my eyes closed during my first jump, though I know some other Frogs who can't say the same thing. But I never developed a liking for jumping. To me it was just part of the job and I did it when I had to. There wasn't any problem with jumping, at least not the actual leaving the plane and stepping off into the air. HALO [High Altitude, Low Opening] school, free falling, water and night jumps, I did them all. But I never got used to the plane ride—that made me nervous. Which was okay in itself. Nervousness keeps you sharp.

On the other hand, diving school was great. All that time underwater, both during the day and at night. Beautiful waters and a nice area. We were all in the best shape of our lives, and the babes came around. No car, but then you didn't need one in Key West. Off-duty time was all right. Coming back from Key West, we graduated and I was assigned to UDT 21.

Some of the guys from our class were chosen to go directly to SEAL Team TWO. They helped commission the Team. But I wasn't one of them. I spent the next several years in UDT 21 until I finally made it to Team TWO in July of 1964.

Team TWO did everything it could to get me to come over to the Team earlier than I did. But Lieutenant Commander Kirby just didn't want to let me go from UDT 21. I thought that UDT was fine, but that the SEALs were better.

They just didn't stand still. It was fifty-five guys, and

when they wanted something, they just bought fifty-five of them. Everybody was always going to school, to Fort Bragg, to wherever. The first guys were great. Not to say that the guys now aren't every bit as good or better. But the first guys were tight in a way that just can't be anymore.

When I finally made it to the SEALs, I became one of the guys. And we would back each other up big-time. All of us. And there were individuals who stood out. Rudy Boesch, Hoss Kucinski, Pierre Birtz, Bob Gallagher, Jim Watson, Lump Lump, even Hoot Andrews was there for a while. These were the men who laid the groundwork for what the Teams would become. And I loved every one of them. The early days of the Team was the best time to be there. Everything was new, and we learned things all the time. When Vietnam came along, that was like a war designed for the SEALs.

Lieutenant Commander William Earley, good old Squirrely Earley, was the CO of the Team when we finally got a commitment to Vietnam. I think Earley was one of the men who pushed for Team TWO to get involved with the war. The Vietnam War had been strictly a West Coast gig as far as the SEALs were concerned. Later on, of course, everybody in the world got involved in the war, but for the Navy, only SEAL Team ONE was seeing any real action.

At the time, I was just a second class who didn't know anything. Whatever they wanted me to do, I did. I just followed my orders. There weren't many men in the Team who were junior to me at the time, maybe one or two, we were pretty rate-heavy. But we did have class.

Now, about 1966, they announced that the Team was going to break up into platoons. How they determined who went where, I don't know. I figure they had a ouija board in the wardroom, that and a little input from the senior chiefs. What I did know was that I was pissed because I wasn't in the first platoon picked to go.

Somebody had to go next, and next, and next. Not everyone could go first. A regular rotation of platoons was set up. But I felt that perhaps I just wasn't good enough in some way to be with the first. I was in the Seventh Platoon and it would be some time before I would be going to Vietnam.

That wasn't quite how my wife felt about the situation when I got home and told her the news. The rotation was being established and I knew roughly when I would be leaving. She didn't like the thought of me going at all. "Hey," I said, "nothing's going to happen to me." Certainly not to me, I thought, and that was the way I really felt. It would be a while before my own mortality would catch up to my ego.

Seventh Platoon wasn't scheduled to deploy until October of 1967. Long enough for the first guys who deployed to come back. And not everything had gone well for those platoons.

First of all, they weren't allowed to do anything. The Army and their Rangers or whoever didn't want the SEALs to operate the way they were trained. And it wasn't just the Army. Our own Navy officers didn't know how to utilize us. Maybe they thought we were going to get hurt. I don't know, I wasn't there, and those stories were all secondhand.

What I could see was the award ceremony they put on for those first platoons. Purple Hearts and Bronze Stars were the order of the day. All those decorations looked neat. Before then, having just two or three ribbons on your uniform meant you had been around. Now there were guys with two and three rows of ribbons.

Seventh Platoon was still filling up, and Bob Gallagher came over to us. This was great—now we had somebody with some Vietnam combat experience to show us the way. For the most part, we were just getting our feet wet. There was a lot for us to learn.

The training went on. We would go to Camp Pickett and practice with our weapons. Back into the mudflats at Little Creek, where we learned how to move on patrol without having our boots make a loud sucking sound with each step. Stealth, concealment, and surprise were the lessons we studied. Exercises went on all the time where we would further practice what we learned against each other.

And cross-training was done so that each man would know the other man's job in the squad. Formal schools were attended, such as field medicine school at Camp Lejeune.

Finally, we had our tactics, signs, and signals down. We felt good about what we knew and what we were going to do. There had been an accident on the ambush range where Chuck Newell caught a piece of shrapnel. His time in the hospital didn't go well, though he did recover eventually. The upshot of this was that Seventh Platoon had received its first casualty, and we hadn't left the country yet.

Gene Fraley and I took some training on a new weapon that we were going to take with us. The minigun is a six-barreled 7.62mm machine gun that could fire at very high rates of fire. A manufacturer's rep from General Electric showed us the weapon and made sure Gene and I knew how to take care of it. Changing the motor would give us different rates of fire, either six thousand or three thousand rounds a minute, as I remember. Taking it out to the bay, we fired the minigun at some floating oil drums in the water. Didn't hit anything, but it sure looked impressive. The plan was to mount the weapon on the Mike boat working out of My Tho. The minigun's firepower would do well for covering our withdrawals.

Along with the new gun, we took Rinnie with us. Rinnie was a German shepherd trained to operate with us as a scout dog. Along with the dog, we packed nine hundred pounds of dog food for him. For ourselves, we mostly packed beans and bullets on board the plane.

The plane we rode in was slow. It seemed to take us nine years to get over there, puddle-jumping across the Pacific. Hawaii, Wake, Guam, every chunk of dirt with an airstrip, we set down on and refueled. And no real time was spent on any of the islands. Guam, a place I remembered well, I was only on long enough to grab a bite to eat and then back on that slow plane to the Far East.

Finally, we were over Vietnam heading in to Tan Son Nhut airport near Saigon. It was 24 October 1967 and our six-month tour of Vietnam was just starting. Out of the window, the ground appeared covered in these large pock-marks, bomb craters from our planes. The first jap [Viet-namese] I saw was out in a field, wearing the straw hat and black pajamas we would later come to know so well. He was a farmer just planting rice like his people had been doing for centuries.

When the plane landed and the doors opened up, I had my first impression of Vietnam. This place is hotter than shit, I thought. We were not acclimatized, having come from autumn in Virginia to tropical heat. But there were things to do, and we ignored the heat. First we had our briefings on being in-country, exchanged our money, and otherwise fiddled about. Now we had to take our nine yards of dog food, beans, that stupid dog Rinnie, the min-igun packed up in its own box, and all our personal stuff, stick it on a truck, and drive down to Vinh Long.

Sixth Platoon was in Vinh Long, and we spent the night with them. I didn't really think much about what was going on or who we were facing.

Things were a little easier than we had thought they would be. This was a combat zone, and we had been pretty hyped on the plane. When the ramp had gone down, we all wanted to break out the weapons and lock and load. Cooler heads prevailed, especially Bob Gallagher's. He said what to do and we did it. Nobody was going to argue with Bob.

We didn't need the guns right away, of course. We did break them out once we were on the road. The thought of an ambush or something else happening was right in the front of our minds. But nothing did happen, and I ended my first day in Vietnam with a shower and down time, same as I would have at home.

Everything was new, even the Ba Muoi Ba beer, though we had some beer from the States as well. Sitting around, we just talked with the guys who had been there awhile. Mostly they talked and I listened. Few of us knew what was going on, and though I wasn't in awe of these combat vets, I was trying to get all the information I could. So in my own subtle way, I talked little and listened much, not trying to appear stupid.

I figured the other guys would eventually get drunk and start telling war stories. Not so, we got up and headed into town. Drank a little of this and ate a little of that. Played tourist and visited all the little places around. After that, we all just went back to the base.

The next day, all our gear was taken off the trucks and piled on a Mike boat. The rest of our trip would be done on the water. Traveling down the Mekong River to My Tho was a bit different than our truck convoy the day before. This time we broke out the weapons and locked and loaded for real. Being ambushed on the river was a possibility, even though the American forces owned the rivers during daylight.

Arriving at My Tho without incident, we moved into the compound and started to put away all of our stuff. A place was found for Rinnie at the PBR base, and then we headed for our hotel. It was funny in a way. Here we were, in the middle of a war, living in a hotel, with our PBR compound just a short distance away. My Tho is real small, so everything was a short distance away. Some lieutenant commander was in charge of the whole mess as CTF [Commander, Task Force] 116, whatever the hell that was. [It was Game Warden, the Navy task force operating against the VC in the Mekong Delta and Rung Sat.]

The boat people had their setup in one hotel. We were in another hotel across the street. Down that same street, by the water, was the PBR base. On the base they had the TOC [Tactical Operations Center], NILO [Naval Intelligence liaison officer], and all the other alphabet soup the Navy needs to operate. Up the road a short way was the Army dustbowl at Dong Tam where the Seawolves were kept.

We were all billeted in little fifteen-foot-square rooms, four men to a room. The rooms were screened to let the breeze through and keep the mosquitoes out. There was one bathroom and a shower. Mostly, we wore regular civilian clothes or issue jungle greens, noncamouflage. Going around the hotel and the town, we would just look like anyone else. We would only change into our field uniforms, the cammies and web gear, down at the PBR base, where our gear was stored. That way, no one knew we were Joe Commando, nighttime killers of the wetlands. At least that was the theory.

Uniforms on operations was what you liked. Some guys wore blue jeans. I liked tiger stripes the best, but initially I just wore what I had been issued. Sometimes I would change and wear regular camo pants with a tiger stripe top. Nobody really gave a shit how you looked.

The camouflage face paint we would carefully apply before a mission gave us our nickname, "the men with green faces." But those patterns never stayed long. After you had been wandering around in the bush for a while, sweating and rubbing your face, half of it was gone by the next morning. You would have to cammie up more than once if it was a long op. But for the most part, by the next morning you were either compromised or had gotten your job done. Either way, you were hauling ass for home.

When we first arrived at My Tho, we had no real idea how to operate in Vietnam. We had practiced and trained back home, but now something was added to help give us a little more edge. Guys from the platoon that was being relieved, in our case Fourth Platoon, would break in the arriving platoon by taking them out on their first few ops. It wasn't the whole old platoon that would remain behind. Only two SEALs on the average would stay back to show the new platoon the ropes. Beginning ops would be planned as easy ones, just something to cut your teeth on, nothing hairy.

Moose Boitnott was the officer who stayed back from Fourth Platoon, along with an enlisted man. Our first op was going to be at night, and Moose coordinated the whole thing. Out of the two squads in Seventh Platoon, one squad went with Moose and the other with the other man. It was basically a hunting expedition. We knew that there were VC in this one hamlet and we were going to try and capture them. It wasn't even fully a snatch operation. Just an easy go-out-and-look-see.

This was my first op, and I was going as Joe Stoner. I

was going to carry a Stoner M63 light machine gun and be a major part of the squad's firepower. Meticulously, I went over every inch of that weapon, cleaning it fully three times before the op. No one knew I was doing that, but it probably wouldn't have come as a surprise to anyone. We were all fairly nervous, except Bob Gallagher.

There were 150 rounds in the drum of my Stoner, and I carried an additional 500 rounds Pancho Villa–style, in crisscrossed belts around my body. Along with that I had a standard ration of M26 frag grenades, a Ka-bar knife, Mark 13 flare, and an assortment of other gear. All of that weight and I still would have liked to carry more ammo.

We were inserting from a PBR. The boat crew slipped the bow of the PBR onto the bank and we quietly got off. I slithered over the side of the boat's bow and immediately sank into the dark water. We hadn't hit the shore— the boat was nosed into a mangrove tree. As the water closed over my head I thought, Oh God, I'm going to drown on my first op.

Coming back up to the surface, I tried to be real quiet while spitting and sputtering, still trying to play it cool. Not that it mattered much—everybody was making noise that time.

And it was dark. I had no idea where we were. If we had been told to break up and meet back here, I couldn't do it. I didn't know where in the hell "here" was. It was three in the morning in the middle of the jungle. I wasn't quite the kid I could have been. I had seen some action a few years before in the Dominican Republic operations. But that didn't make this spooky situation much easier.

Going in towards shore, we finally made it to the ground. Quickly, we set up a perimeter. Following SOP, we each covered our areas. Watching the area that Moose had pointed out to me, I gave no thought to the other guys. Training had drilled in us the importance of doing your own job and trusting your Teammates to do theirs. If I had seen anything, I would have either told someone or blasted it.

Finally, the move-out order was given. Going through the boonies, we couldn't see anything. All I could see was the man in front of me trying to move quietly, just like I was. The time for playing "I got you, you got me" was over. These weren't blanks we had in our weapons. This was the real shit and we were playing for keeps.

Walking in about eighty or ninety meters, Moose said, "Okay, we're going to stay here." Settling down, we silently waited for it to get light enough for us to walk and not run into booby traps. We had stopped about ten or fifteen meters from the targeted group of hooches. Daylight was coming soon and the Vietnamese were just getting up. Using candles for light, they were moving around and doing their morning routine.

Moving out, we surrounded the hooches. There was a lot of bush and scrub around and I was stuck right in the middle of an area where you couldn't see three feet in front of you. But I was acting the part of rear security, so whatever they had told me to watch, I was watching.

Noises started building up as more and more Vietnamese were starting their day. Deciding it was time to move, Moose made the motion for us to go in. Saying to myself, "Here we go," I got up. We all moved in just like we were supposed to, watching our own fields of fire.

Walking across this one area, I decided to go through this one spot that looked closer to the target. I moved about two or three meters closer to the target and stopped when I felt a straining across my chest. Thinking I had struck a vine, I was pushing and tugging, trying to break through. Suddenly, it flashed through my mind, Holy shit! What am I thinking about?

Looking down, I could see it was a piece of monofilament fishing line I was pushing against. Holy shit, I thought again, I'm in a booby-trapped area. Looking around, I could see this big round thing on a tree, about where the line would be going. It sure looked as if there was a land mine staked up on that tree.

It was just getting light and I might have been mistaken at what I saw. Backing off, I gasped quietly for a moment. Waving my hand slowly in front of my body, like that was really going to do a lot right then, I moved back to the way I had been going earlier. Lesson learned—don't ever take the path of least resistance, it isn't. And don't go in the shortest line, because things don't work that way.

Finally I got to where I was supposed to be. Nobody had seen my little show; they were all busy doing their own part of the op. I had been told where to go, not how to get there. Watching my field of fire, I thought that if that mine hadn't gone off by now, it wasn't going to.

While I was sitting there, Moose slid over to me. "We've got to get back into the water," he whispered. "We think there's some gooks coming down the trail."

Moving back to the water, we all got in, and Moose told us to go all the way down. I crouched down until only my nose and eyes were showing. But my Stoner was underwater. Son of a bitch, I thought, if I have to get up and use this thing, it's gonna be full of water.

If we were going to initiate something, I would have to get the water out of the Stoner's action quickly. As it turned out, nothing happened. After twenty minutes had gone by, Moose signaled us to get up and move out. Working the charging handle, I made sure the weapon was free of water before we moved. After getting out of the water, I had my first of many experiences with leeches. Those suckers get attached to you—*muy pronto*!

There were some Vietnamese we caught and questioned. Moose pushed them around a bit, but they were just fishermen who couldn't tell us anything. I didn't venture an opinion of what was going on. This was my first op in Vietnam, and there was a lot of learning yet to do. After we'd farted around the area for about twenty minutes, one of the Vietnamese interpreters with us, I think it was an LDNN, told us that none of the locals knew anything worthwhile. Apparently the VC we were after had been there and weren't coming back. So the op turned into just a dry run.

Calling our boat in, we extracted and started home. Once aboard the boat and moving down the river, the guys started to relax and kid around with each other. The posturing blew off steam a little, but that was all. I realized that we hadn't done shit this op. But everybody thought it was neat since we all came back alive. There was a lot of joking and "Hey, what did you think of that?" going around. But inside, we knew what could have happened. As far as my little encounter with the mine went, I never did tell anybody. It may not have been a mine and trip wire, it could have been my imagining a mine and some lost fishing line. But it scared the shit out of me, that's for sure.

After getting back to My Tho, we went out on the town to celebrate getting our feet wet. A little later, we went out on another op with Moose leading, but it turned out to be another dry hole. Moose went back to the Creek after our second op and we started out on our own.

Things soon settled into pretty much a pattern. We went out about every other night, sometimes more often than that. You'd prep for an op, attend a briefing, and get your gear ready. If it was a late-night op, say it started about two in the morning, you'd grab a bite to eat before leaving. After that, you'd get your gear on and join the others. Once the insertion ride showed up, usually a boat, we'd climb aboard and move out.

The ride would take a while, enough time to grab a nap if you could. Arriving at the insertion point, you wouldn't land right at the site. You'd go past the spot and land somewhere else first. Conducting several fake insertions before the real one was one way to deceive the VC a little bit.

We started getting some good hits once we learned our own way of operating. A VC tax collector and district-level people were among our haul. In those days, 1967–1968, we went after the guys with the guns. What we wanted was a body count, information, documents, weapons, and kills. That was a major part of what we were trained to do. Later on, we picked up on the smarter way of operating, targeting the brains of the VC. But that really came on strong during my second tour when I was a PRU advisor.

During the first tour, we did pick up on the idea of cutting off the VC's head. With the troops the VC had to work with, if you took out the leaders, the shooters didn't know shit. In the VC structure, it was very hard to replace the higher-ups. Especially those province-and-district-level people who had been on the job for years and years. Later on, that became the guiding premise behind the Phoenix program.

Though we were out for a body count early on, nobody did any of the things you hear about. Nobody took any ears. If they had, the rest of us probably wouldn't have stood still for it. And when we interrogated a suspect, we didn't torture him. SEALs are just men, regular guys who do more than the average man. Most of the stories came about because of the veil of secrecy that covered all of our operations. And we didn't talk to outsiders. Surprise was a major weapon of ours, and a large part of our protection. Talking to others can cut back on that surprise. When there's an information vacuum, it's human nature to fill it up with whatever stories are available, real or not.

The guys I was with did nothing out of the ordinary. Some of the guys would talk differently than others. One man might say, "I've got more kills than you." Privately, I would think to myself, Well, who really gives a shit? I certainly didn't. But if that was the way that person thought, that was fine.

On patrols, we switched positions around a lot. I did rear security, and I did point. As far as equipment went, I carried everything but the radio. The squad had one man who always carried the radio, and that helped keep me from packing that heavy mother around.

My personal web gear was about the only piece of equipment that I modified a lot. Since I carried just about every weapon that our platoon had available at one time or another, I set up my web gear so I could carry ammo and supplies in a way I found most handy. The platoon T&E'd [tested and evaluated] a lot of gear during our tour. We had the Stoner, the duckbill shotgun attachment, the Remington 7188, and other items.

The shotgun with the duckbill was an Ithaca Model 37, and the duckbill was a muzzle attachment that changed the spread of shot from a circle to an oval four times as wide as it was tall. After we started to get some good hits,

I picked up the shotgun as a preferred weapon for close-in, especially around hooches. With the duckbill, you didn't have to lead a moving target as you did with a regular shotgun. The spread of the shot made up for any target movement at the short ranges we fought at. The No. 4 hardened buckshot was my preferred load. Double-ought buck was good, but you could hit more with the greater number of pellets in a No. 4 load. Flechette was also good, at least I thought so. You could hit a man at longer range with it than with a regular shot load. But when a man was hit with flechettes, he would keep on running as if he hadn't been shot at all. The targets would bleed to death with a flechette hit rather than get knocked down as with a buckshot load.

I liked the Remington full automatic shotgun, the Model 7188, a lot, as well as the Ithaca. It didn't have a duckbill, and the recoil of that sucker would really put a hum on you, but who cared? During a firefight, your adrenaline was pumping so hard you didn't even feel the buck and recoil of the weapon much. The only trouble was, boom, boom, boom, boom . . . eight times and whoops, you had to reload. I used the weapon on full auto a lot. It really got everyone's attention, especially the people you were shooting at.

The Stoner was a particular piece that we suggested a lot of modifications for. After our return to the States, a lot of our suggestions were adopted into a new version of the Stoner. I really loved the weapon. Not much heavier than a large rifle, say a fully loaded M14, but the Stoner carried lots of bullets. But the weapon was sensitive, it needed a lot of care and maintenance, and there were some bugs still to be worked out.

On one op, I had caught this guy just dead to rights, we're talking black pajamas and all, a bad gook without question. I was carrying the Stoner with a 150-round belt drum attached. With the VC in my sights, I pulled the trigger and click!

The plastic foregrip, up underneath the barrel where it attached to the metal, had cracked from all the usage we had given the weapon. With the plastic cracked the way it was, the bolt couldn't go all the way forward and the weapon wouldn't fire. My target got away that day. But things were all right. We wrote a nice letter to Cadillac Gage saying, "Hey, you've got to fix this because this sucks. There's no lead coming out of the son of a bitch."

But in spite of that, I loved the Stoner. But I also carried other weapons. For hooch searches I would carry the CAR-15 and a Chicom pistol. Both weapons were light and handy, and the pistol was especially nice for those closed-in spaces like bunkers. I also carried an M60 machine gun, several different kinds of shotguns, and an M16.

It didn't really matter what an individual carried. As long as the squad's firepower didn't suffer, nobody really gave a shit what you had. At the beginning of our tour, things had been different. Layout of the squad had gone right by the book. Before an op we would have a meeting and get briefed on the mission.

During the briefing, we would be told where we were going to go and what our objective was. No LDNNs or other outsiders would be invited along. Who knows which side some of those guys are on? But the early briefings were more detailed. It would be explained that we were going to go here and then here, with the locations being indicated on a map or photograph. Even the coordinates wouldn't be said out loud—occasionally the walls did have ears in Vietnam.

The briefing would continue, "We're going to go here, here, and here. And this is what we're going to do. And the intelligence is such and such. We're going to extract here by this means. And our support is such-and-such with these call signs."

At the beginning, even more information was put out. The operations went almost straight by the book, with instructions going out to each man, such as "You're going to carry two hundred rounds of 7.62mm. You're going to carry four smoke grenades and you're going to carry two CS grenades." And on and on until each man had been accounted for. Emergency actions were stated as well: "If this happens, that is where we're going to be.

And if this happens, we're going to meet here." And on and on the briefing would go.

After two months of operating in the bush, everybody in the platoon knew what everybody else had and where they carried it. You knew what the other guy carried, and we were proficient in each other's weapons. When I carried a Stoner, I would pack along five or six hundred rounds in belts over my shoulders, Pancho Villa–style. With other weapons, I carried ammo loads that I developed a taste for over time. After operating awhile, our briefings became much simpler affairs: "We're going to go over here and this is what we're going to do. See you down at the boat." That was all it took.

We had quickly gotten to the point where a simple briefing was all that was needed. Telling each man what he would carry and do was unnecessary. Everyone knew what he and everyone else would do. We had become, and operated as, a well-oiled machine. That's what was nice about operating the way we did. It didn't take long to get that way, either. Nobody wanted to come home in a bag.

We respected each other for what the man could do. And we respected each other's privacy, what little we had. When a guy would get a bad letter from home, or something like that, we would tend to leave the guy alone. On the other hand, if a man wanted to talk about it, he could approach you. And that happened from time to time and was one of the sad things about being over there. Things would happen back home and you were too far away to help.

All the good things about working together outweighed the bad tenfold and more. Sometimes on ops, the situations did get a little dicey, but that was what the SEALs were trained for. We had a lot of dry runs, but had a lot of good hits as well. Camaraderie was strong in the platoon and squads and we depended on each other a lot. That made us tight together.

As far as the other services went, I didn't have much involvement with them on my first tour. We didn't work with other units much, even other Navy units, except for two. The PBR sailors who would take us in and pick us up were good. I respected those sailors, who would drive us up on the banks in their boats, not much more than plastic coffins with guns. Mind you, I felt safe enough on the PBRs when they were running on the rivers. But coming up with a big thing like that and nosing into the shore was tough. I don't care how much you silence those engines, they're going to make some noise. It took brass nuts to crew those things like that. Especially if you were the gunner in the bow gun tub.

It didn't matter if you had 7.62s or twin .50s to hide behind, a B-40 rocket or RPG-7 [rocket-propelled grenade] would take you out. And those gooks knew how we patrolled and they could hear us coming, especially the boats. We might have owned the river, but Charley held the land. At least he did when we first got to Vietnam. But I have to give credit to the PBR sailors. Those guys knew their jobs, and I felt good, and safe, when I traveled with them. And I felt better, when extracting, when the PBRs came into sight. Of course, all the weapons they had on board including those twin .50 calibers in the bow may have colored my vision a little bit.

A lot of other SEALs as well as myself really have a special admiration for the Seawolf pilots. Those Navy pilots in their Army-supplied Huey helicopter gunships saved my ass more than once. They were really good in getting everything out of their choppers that they could. There were certain ops where nobody else would come out to us, but the Seawolves would always be there.

The whole package of units, the SEALs, Seawolves, and PBR sailors, came together as part of the Game Warden forces, Task Force 116. We all worked together and had mutual respect for each other. But there was nobody a SEAL was closer to than his Teammates.

There was one SEAL—well, he was sort of a SEAL—that I liked but never thought much of over in Vietnam. Rinnie was a pain in the ass over in Nam. Starting with our having to carry nine hundred pounds of dog food with us for him and ending with our having to carry him. But there was one thing Rinnie was great at, and that was interrogations. I'm not sure who taught him the trick. He was Fraley's assigned dog, but all of us took care of Rinnie at one time or another. I even had him over at my house more than once. He liked us and didn't like the bad guys. Maybe he just came at it naturally, but when we brought in a captured gook for interrogation, Rinnie wanted after him in the worst way.

Imagine the situation from the point of view of the prisoner. Here he was, captured by some guys who didn't act like any soldiers he had ever seen. And now he was facing a large German shepherd, as big as or bigger than the average Vietnamese, and the dog was just slavering and snarling trying to get at the man. And when we released Rinnie, he'd be all over that prisoner, snarling and tearing his clothes off.

The prisoner never seemed to notice that Rinnie just tore the clothes—the dog just didn't seem interested in biting the man wearing them. Those prisoners would shit in their Fruit-of-the-Looms big-time. Black pajamas, soiled immediately. Braaaap, thank you very little.

We never let Rinnie rip all the prisoner's clothes off, just have a little fun and then pull the dog back. Often the guy would talk after just seeing Rinnie and his enthusiasm. Rinnie just scared the shit right out of them. Some gooks would see him and just pee their pants. What could you expect, anyway? Those people kept dogs as alarms and the Sunday roast, or at least the Vietnamese equivalent. Dogs as big as Rinnie just weren't seen in Asia.

Sometimes we would get the information we wanted, sometimes it was something else. And the trouble with a forced interrogation is that you can't be sure that the information isn't bogus. The guy could just be saying what you wanted to hear to make you stop, or in our case take Rinnie out of the room.

One thing about interrogations was for sure—you couldn't make the senior VC cadre tell you anything. Those hard-core card carriers had lived under Ho Chi Minh for years; some of them had a history going back to World War Two. They wouldn't tell you shit. But a young VC or lower cadreman, he just had a gun for the cause, and to impress the girls, those you could make talk. But in their case, they usually didn't know anything of real value. All he would be able to tell you is about the other two or three guys in his cell. The VC used compartmentalization for just that reason. One guy couldn't blow a whole area, just the few people he worked with.

Though he was great at camp, Rinnie was lousy on ops. We took him with us on one operation early in the tour and quickly learned our lesson. The dog just couldn't move quietly in the mud and brush. The patrol sounded like a herd of elephants. I thought for sure that we were going to be compromised and get blown away because of the damned dog. And he couldn't walk in the deep mud or get up and down the canals—we had to carry him or lift him over the banks. At the compound, Rinnie was great at watching our stuff. And occasionally we used the interrogation trick. We didn't employ him all the time, just now and then as a scare tactic.

We mostly operated at night and early in the morning. As our intel net built up, we could specifically target things more and more easily. We never went into an area and just wandered around. On an op, we would always be going in for a particular hit. But sometimes the party didn't show up to our dance. Perhaps our intel was bad, or the target had showed a day early. Whatever the case was, we didn't dally around in Charley's backyard. We got the hell out of there.

There were some SEALs who operated differently. Even after an op was compromised, they continued operating in the area. And the compromise didn't have to necessarily be shooting. Perhaps they hadn't gotten everybody during a shooting or they had questioned a local and let him go. Either way, news was going to get to the bad guys that the men with green faces were in town. And Charley knew all of the short cuts in his own neighborhood as well as where all of the booby traps were. He could move much faster than we could on the ground. Often enough, a platoon or squad of SEALs could find themselves on the wrong side of an ambush. I know of several times that SEALs were wounded when they had overstayed their time in an area.

Overstaying was a cardinal sin in our platoon's book, and we didn't do that, at least not often. If we were compromised, or had made contact with the enemy, or somebody had slipped away, personally, I wanted to get the hell out of there. We didn't do that all of the time— sometimes we continued patrolling, meandering around enemy territory. That was not something I liked to do at all. But I did it, because if you wore the name, you had to play the game. It wasn't my place to say anything. But I didn't like the situation at all.

Things came out all right for the most part. But I always had the thought in the back of my head that if you were compromised you got the hell out of there. I did tell myself that if I was ever in command and calling the shots and a compromise happens, we were going to leave. Because if you stay in a hot area after there is a good chance the enemy knows you're there, you lose too much. Once the element of surprise is gone, the mission is down the toilet. If the enemy knows you're around somewhere, it's just a matter of time before they find you.

There weren't that many times when situations came around against us. When they did, we were lucky. We never walked into an ambush or counterambush. And nobody got seriously hurt. I do know of JOs [junior officers] who did that, overstayed their time, just to help make a name for themselves. But that was their own personal thing. I didn't have to operate with them.

For the most part, there were two kinds of SEALs in Vietnam, operators and hunters. In my mind, an operator who was doing his job didn't just take chances. If the particular target of an op wasn't there, he got out to fight another day. That's my perception. You didn't go into an area and just hang around looking for a slope to walk down the trail with a gun in his hand. Blasting him wasn't getting a hard target. That situation would just be a target of opportunity. There were a million VC kids walking around that you could hit on. They're just gun fodder. It took discipline to pack up and get out, without anything to show for it. I don't see anything rational about just going out and stalking around.

The hunters were people who did their jobs and more. They could turn away when it was necessary. Bob Gallagher was one of those. But hunters were also men who would go after Charley, work through the really hard areas and take him with the maximum surprise. Going in on light intel and working on a target, making the situation work for you. But because of the way I feel about staying in an area just to hunt the enemy, like you would wander a field looking for a rabbit, I don't use the expression "hunter" to describe these men.

Strong operators developed constructive tactics. The "stay behind" ambush, where a false extraction is made and an ambush team lays in wait for anyone who was following the patrol, is an example of this. As is the parakeet op, where a single helicopter would carry a crew in to the target covered by helicopter gunships that wouldn't expose themselves until the last minute. Those are tactics, and the men who developed them are called hunters by some SEALs.

Going in on a target, not finding it, and then just walking down the trails looking for the enemy is not the way to operate in Vietnam. At least it's not the way I operated. Some guys did do just that, walk down the trails. But usually, they stopped as soon as they realized what they were doing. Sometimes a leader would do this sort of thing. Mostly just putting everyone at risk for self-glorification.

Later on, when I was in charge, I didn't change. As the head banana, I always had in the back of my mind the thought that I was responsible for the lives of the men who followed me. We were all in it together, and we made decisions together. But if something happened and things went wrong, it was the man in charge who had to stand on the carpet.

But we also had a job to do, and we did it. I didn't slack off on my part no matter what was going on. And I made my share of mistakes as well. But the luck hasn't run out when you can still live through your mistakes.

But always remember, sometimes the luck runs out and you go home in a bag.

Young officers had the edge in getting through an op with minimum mistakes when they listened to their senior enlisted men. We had good young officers and some great senior enlisted men. Bob Gallagher was in my platoon and had one of the best heads in combat of any man I know. Today, the Eagle, as we called him, is still something of a legend in the Teams. But even Bob didn't always have the luck he needed.

It was a good op we went on with Bob one day. We had gone all the way down to the end of the Ca Mau Peninsula right on the South China Sea to sweep some villages with the platoon. The whole platoon had traveled in the Mike boat, a heavily armored LCM modified with overhead cover, armor, a 106mm recoilless cannon on the overhead, lots of gun mounts on the gunwales for .50 calibers, M-60s, and Honeywell 40mm grenade launchers, and an 81mm mortar in the bow. Along with all of this was the minigun we had brought from the Creek. Not a bad chunk of firepower. But it was all in a boat that could barely make five knots and was a hot, smelly, crowded pig yard when filled with the boat crew and a platoon of SEALs.

The squads split up, each going to its assigned targets so our people were spread out over an area. My squad didn't have any contact, but a member of the other squad nailed a VC armed with a BAR. There wasn't any question that the area and village were VC-controlled, not if you counted all the booby traps that were around. Trip wires were everywhere, all of them connected to little silver fragmentation grenades. Apparently the gooks cast the grenades themselves in jungle workshops and filled them with explosives they either made themselves or steamed out of unexploded U.S. ordnance.

Roy Matthews and I had completed our sweep and were just standing there looking at the japs. I heard a noise some distance away, but nothing looked out of place, so I didn't pay it any mind. I think Roy went over to check it out, and when he came back, he was chewing on a piece of sugarcane. Walking up to me, Roy said, "Hey, Bob [Gallagher] just blew his hand off."

"What?" I exclaimed.

"Yeah," Roy continued. "He's over there."

Heading over to where Roy had indicated, I saw what was going on. Apparently, Gallagher had been examining one of the grenade booby traps and it had gone off in his hand. Bob was EOD-qualified, so something must have gone wrong. The grenade hadn't detonated high-order or there would have been a lot less of Bob for the corpsman to work on. As it was, by the time I got on the scene, Rio [Riojas], our corpsman, was finishing up his bandaging of Bob's hand.

With this big old bandage on his hand, the only thing that the Eagle said to Rio was, "Is this thing going to survey me out?" It was obvious that Bob was in pain— you could see the tears in his eyes. But I don't know if Rio gave him a Syrette of morphine or not. What was important was to get in a dust-off chopper and get the Eagle to a field hospital.

With the 106mm on top of the Mike boat, there wasn't room for the bird to put down. To get the cannon down would take our disassembling it into pieces small enough to move. The bird had already been called in, so there wasn't any time to lose. We hadn't had any trouble with the village where we were, so we secured the perimeter and the dust-off set down on the beach.

It was with a heavy heart that I watched the medevac helicopter take off with Gallagher aboard. In one instant, a majority of the platoon's experience was gone. Many of us felt the loss of a vital link, but we pressed on and completed the mission. I had known Bob a long time and probably felt his loss the hardest.

The squad and platoon pressed on with operations. We made some hits, but mostly we had a ration of dry runs. It wasn't that we weren't trying, our intel quality had taken a nosedive. What little information we did get turned out to be wrong or late. One thing that stood out was that we were taking some Vietnamese LDNNs with us as scouts. It may just be my own feelings, but maybe those LDNNs were leading us in the wrong direction. Many of them were notorious for not wanting to make contact with the enemy. Whatever the reason, the squad had a long run of just nickel-and-dime skirmishes, none of the big hits that really made operating worthwhile.

Another problem was that we weren't using our heads and targeting the people of importance, the VC leaders and infrastructure. What we were going after was the shooters, and those guys are a dime a dozen. Not only that, but the VC shooters could see us coming from miles away, and they would just haul ass out of an area. Sophistication in operations was still something we had to learn more of.

Our primary source of intelligence was the NILO [Naval Intelligence liaison officer] up in My Tho. As far as I could tell, the guy was just sitting in the officers' club up in My Tho getting his information from who knows where. And I really didn't care anyway; he was a nobody to me. I answered to one guy, Lieutenant Pete Peterson, who had gone through training with me.

But the lack of good ops was taking its toll. Mistakes could be made when you had a long time between contacts, as I learned. Some nights we didn't operate at all and spent our time taking it easy. It was on one of these off nights I was relaxing at the Red Dog Inn after watching a movie. The Red Dog was a place for the enlisted swine the Navy ran. It was conveniently placed in the hotel across the street from our quarters. It wasn't as classy as the Officers' Club, and that was just fine for me.

While I was sitting down and having a couple of beers, these two PBR sailors, kids really, came over to me. I knew the PBR sailors, because we worked with them all of the time. I never got real chummy with them, they weren't Teammates, but we'd certainly share a drink or two. But what these guys wanted to do was share a story with me.

After exchanging pleasantries, these two guys sat down and started telling me their story. "Hey, Mike," one said, "you know when we leave and go up the river and take a right? Well, at that point there's these two huge bunkers on the shore. We're getting sniped at all the time there. And these goddam B-40 rockets are coming out of that position too."

I knew what area these guys were talking about. And the VC had built two huge, thick-walled bunkers there. But the bunkers weren't occupied regularly enough for us to schedule a raid. This was the first time I had heard about any real trouble with them. "Yeah, I know the spot," I answered. "What about them?"

"Goddam, no one's doing anything about it," the sailor said. "We're going by that spot all the time and taking fire. It's just a matter of time before somebody gets hit bad."

It had been a slow night, and I had several beers in me. Actually, I was about half in the bag. "Fuck 'em," I said. "Let's go and blow them up."

"Come on," they said. "We can't do that."

"The hell with that," I said. "Who's going to know?"

And they agreed to an impromptu mission. After making sure that the guys knew they couldn't tell anyone about what we were going to do, we decided to get the bunkers that very night. After making our plans, I went back to the hotel to get a little sleep.

About three o'clock that night, I got up and went down to the compound. Opening up the magazines, I made up two twenty-pound C4 charges in haversacks primed with nonelectric firing systems, time fuses, and pull-igniters. The PBR sailors were in their boat and ready to go, so we just quietly pulled away from the dock and moved upriver.

Along with my two charges, I had an M16, a flashlight, and my Ka-bar knife. Not exactly heavily armed for a night trip into Indian country. "Look," I said to the sailors. "This won't take long. I'm just going to this bunker and throw the charge in and then slide over to the other bunker and do the same thing." The two bunkers were only about ten meters apart, so I didn't see any real problem in my "plan."

The kids agreed to what I was going to do. It was pretty obvious that they were starting to get a little scared.

Maybe they were smarter than I was. But I couldn't let them know that. "Look," I said. "When you go in, I'll be up on the bow. You just snug it up there and I'll get off. Then you guys back away from the shore and I'll call you in with a red light when I'm finished."

"Okay," they whispered, too afraid to make much of a noise. But I hadn't quite finished. "Now you," I said, pointing to one of the men, "you stay in the bow on those twin .50s. If I get into trouble and I need you, you just start strafing the place."

"But what about you?" he protested.

"Don't worry about me," I said. "I'll be sucking mud. I just want you to shoot."

"After he agreed and got into the bow gun tub, we nosed into shore and I got out of the boat. By this time I had learned how to get out of the boat quietly without making an ass of myself. Lying down in the grass, I waited to hear if there was anything there. Well, shit, I thought to myself, if there's anyone here I'm dead meat anyhow. So taking my two explosive packs, I moved out to the bunkers dimly visible in the darkness. Going up to the first bunker, I put my back against the wall near the door opening.

What I was trying to do was hear if there was anyone inside the bunker. But I couldn't hear anything, my heart was beating so loud. Looking up at the sky, I asked myself, Just what in the fuck am I doing here? Then I ducked into the bunker.

No one was home, so I packed the charge up tight against the wall and pulled the fuse. Moving out, I slithered over to the other bunker on my belly like a snake. By this time I was more than sober and realizing just what the situation was that I had talked myself into. But it was far too late to turn back now. Doing the same thing at the other bunker with my charge, I pulled the fuse and headed to the shore. I signaled with my flashlight with a red lens over the bulb, and the PBR came in and picked me up.

Now we could relax for a moment. Slipping quietly away from the shore, we boogied up the river a little way to wait out the charges. I had built the firing assemblies with thirty-minute delays, so we didn't have long to wait.

While we were waiting, a little old guy in a sampan came paddling along the river. As he passed the bunkers, the first charge went off. The explosion scared the hell out of that fisherman or whatever he was. But when the second bunker went up, the guy was so scared that he fell out of his boat. Shit was flying everywhere as the bunkers came apart. There wasn't going to be any more sniping from that position for a long time. As the fisherman swam back to his sampan, we put the PBR into gear and moved back to the base.

Getting back, I put my gear up, took a shower, and went to breakfast. By this time, it was getting to be dawn, and activity at the base was picking up. Pretty soon the only thing to be heard was the question "Who blew the bunkers?" Most of the people were glad of the situation, but neither the PBR sailors nor I were taking any credit. There was a lieutenant commander going around saying that no one had been authorized for a mission and wondering what in the hell had happened.

Nobody knew who did it or exactly what had happened. I was playing dumb and doing a good job of it. Then some officer piped up, "I don't know who did it but I'd give them a medal for it."

Things were going okay until Peterson came up to me a little later. "Hey," he said, "We're missing some demo [demolitions]. You're in charge of all that stuff, Mike. Where is it?"

Looking at me square in the eye, Peterson said, "You dumb fuck. You did it, didn't you?" Then he proceeded to give me a royal dressing-down. After voicing his displeasure at my actions and listing the amount of paperwork he would have had to fill out if I got myself killed, Peterson ran out of steam and had to stop and catch his breath.

"But what about my medal?" I asked plaintively.

"Fuck you and your medal," was his answer. Then he was off again chewing me out.

"Okay, okay," I said. "Enough already. Get off my ass. I won't do it again." But it didn't take me long to realize just how stupid a thing I had done. Boy, what a dumb shit I had been. Here I was married with three kids and I'm running around the countryside like an idiot blowing things up. Not the brightest action I took while in Vietnam. And I had been scared, but not so much I couldn't operate, and it had been a neat explosion.

Bob finally returned to the platoon, and we continued operating, a few ops here and a few ops there. Things started getting better; the ops were getting more productive. Some guys did get wounded, myself included. None of the wounds were major. For myself, I caught a few fragments in the chin. We had been blowing up materials during a sweep, denying them to the enemy. VC were in the area, but we didn't receive fire from them. The Vietnamese had these huge earthenware pots they would store just about anything in. The VC would put weapons in these pots and bury them. While we were blowing up some of these pots, a fragment from one struck me under the chin. No big deal.

The closest I got to action on that op was when one of the village dogs kept barking at me. Didn't have a hush puppy, but a normal weapon works just as well. Besides, the noisy little barker was getting on my nerves.

For the most part our operations stayed light. We didn't come across any heavy competition on the part of the VC. The enemy was there and fired at us, but we had Stoners, M60s, M16s, shotguns, everything we could want. The firepower was definitely on our side. For the most part, the VC had Chicom carbines [Model 1944 five-shot bolt-action rifles] and some SKSs [a ten-shot semiautomatic carbine]. Once, we crossed paths with a VC patrol of eight guys and two of them had AK-47s. That was the meanest group we ran into.

Most of the encounters we had were just nickel-and-dime Chicom stuff. One morning, 16 January 1968, we went out looking for some VC tax collectors. Gallagher was back leading the squad, and it felt good to be following him. Ming, our platoon's interpreter, was with us, as the other squad was away pulling their own op.

Having inserted in the dark, we set up a hasty ambush

by a trail and settled in to wait for light. The ambush was just to cover our asses in case Charley came wandering down the road. Our target was a group of VC tax collectors, a premium target at the time. We had intel that the tax collectors would be performing their job in our area, and we knew about when and where they would be. The plan was to hit the collectors while they were taxing the locals. If we captured, or even wasted, the collectors in front of the locals, that would show them best what we could do to protect them from the VC.

At the time, as Joe Young Guy, I thought that tax collectors were pretty big targets, prime meat for our grinder. Later on, after I had spent time as a PRU advisor and learned more on targeting the VC infrastructure, I would have a better idea of what was a good target and a great target. But back during my first tour, a tax collector was something to get warmed up over.

Now the sky was getting lighter and we could move out from our hide. Patrolling along, we traveled through a banana grove, skirting this huge rice paddy. Along the way, we snatched up Joe Farmer, just a Vietnamese going about his morning business. Rather than let the guy go and alert the countryside, the squad put out a secure perimeter while Bob Gallagher and the interpreter, Ming, talked to the farmer.

Bob told Ming, "Ask him where the japs are."

With their rapid Vietnamese, the exchange between the farmer and Ming just sounded like a lot of jabber to me. The rice farmer ended up saying, "There's about three hundred of them [VC] in the tree line right over there." And he indicated the tree line on the far side of the rice paddy.

That answer kind of set Bob off. "There isn't three hundred VC in this whole damn IV Corps. Who the hell does he think he's kidding? Ask him again where the VC are."

The farmer's answer came back, "There's three hundred that came in last night. They're over there in the tree line."

So much for that. Bob still thought the farmer was full

of it. But we couldn't let him just trot off. It was too early to let people go. We weren't compromised, we had just run into this one dude and still had a chance at our tax collectors.

After asking where his home was, we went over to the farmer's hut. The farmer's domain was this huge rice paddy, so we skirted the area, just chugging along to the farmer's hooch. We passed along a tree line, opposite the supposed VC tree line, and walked along a rice dike till we came to a hooch. The place wasn't anything special, just a thatch/frame building with a little outhouse to the side and a small bamboo/wire fence beyond it, running along the top of the wide dike, to protect what was probably his garden. Off to the side was a small bunker which wasn't anything special. Almost every hooch in the country had a bunker for protection. Just a normal Vietnamese pastoral scene.

Getting to the farmer's place, we held a short war council. The farmer was still insisting that the bad guys were in the tree line. Our intel had said that the tax collectors were coming today. We expected them to hit everyone in the area during the early part of the morning. If there were VC in the tree line, we could wait in the hooch and see if any stepped out of the trees. But by playing wait and see, we could still nail our original targets. What we didn't know was that the tax collectors had hit the area the night before. The farmer didn't tell us that. The locals had to deal with the VC and us, depending on who was there. Volunteering information was not usual for them. They just tried to survive from day to day.

The rest of the squad took up positions in the hooch and the bunker nearby. Gallagher and I went down to the tree line to kind of scoot along and see what could be seen. I was armed with an M16 and about four hundred rounds in magazines along with a couple of frags and a couple of smoke grenades. As we traveled along the rice dike, we had the small fence on our right side. In front of us, extending to the left, was the rice paddy and then the tree line on the far dike. As we approached the tree line, we learned that the farmer hadn't been telling stories.

As Bob and I got near the trees, some overexcited VC sprang the ambush too early. When about half a dozen shots rang out, we knew we were in trouble.

The time couldn't have been more than a couple of seconds at most, probably microseconds. The fence line was too high for us to jump and the bunker too far back to reach. There was no way we could get to the tree line in time, so Bob and I came to the same conclusion at the same moment—we both died.

Falling over like we had been shot, Bob and I landed in the rice paddy. The rice was high enough to hide us, and that was all that was keeping us alive. Because of the fence, we had to roll into the paddy water on the same side of the dike as the enemy. We didn't have any real cover between us and the VC, just a bunch of tall rice stalks. And the bullets were flying by, close by.

As we lay there, a bullet went through the sling of my rifle and another zipped close by my boot. Pretty close, in fact just a little too close. And then the fire let up as the VC stopped shooting. "Don't get up," Bob said. "Don't get up and run."

"No shit!" was my answer. I was sucking mud now.

Now Ming, our LDNN interpreter, was shouting at the VC from where he was near the hooch. He was bellowing Vietnamese, something along the lines of "You stupid bastards," or words to that effect. Was there three hundred VC in the trees? You bet your ass there was, and some of them opened fire.

Maybe there wasn't actually three hundred VC, but there was sure thirty or forty of them. Apparently they had stayed quietly in the tree line, waiting to see what we would do. They had seen us without question and knew how many we were. All the time we were dicking around in the hooch, the VC were getting ready.

While the main body of VC remained in position, a small group had moved along the tree line closer to where Bob and I were. They figured that we were dead and wanted to get our weapons. The first seconds of the firefight were now stretching into minutes.

But this didn't make things any easier for Bob and me.

We were still lying in the mud and water trying to figure out how to get out of our situation. Bob's CAR-15 and my M16 weren't going to do us much good right now. It was time to use grenades.

We could see the VC moving closer. They thought we were dead and were concerned with staying under cover from the hooch, not us. Moving carefully, I pulled an M26 grenade from my harness as Bob did the same. As soon as our little friends got close enough, we would pull the pins and nail them. After the blasts, we would try to haul ass. The chances weren't in our favor, but they were better than just lying there.

A lull came into the paddy as the firing died away. Our VC friends weren't getting any closer, so I chanced lifting my head higher to see what was going on and couldn't see anyone. Crawling along slowly, Bob and I came to a spot where the dike wall was lower. Putting out a base of fire, we quickly rolled over the dike. Some VC had been in front of us, and I think we hit several of them. But with the dike between them and us, I began to breathe a little easier.

The squad had called in a FAC [Forward Air Controller] plane, and he circled the area. Seeing what was going on, the FAC called in an air strike on the tree line. Now that I was on the far side of the dike, I had time to get scared. Before, while hiding in the rice, I was too busy doing stuff to try and stay alive to give any thought to fear. Now I had time and I was giving it a lot of thought.

With the strike coming in, we extracted. Bob and I got back with the squad, and we all pulled out. Later on, another team went in and counted ten or so VC bodies. We had gotten some of them, but they had nearly gotten a few of us in the bargain. I was later put in for the Bronze Star for that operation, but it was downgraded to a Navy Commendation Medal. At the time, I didn't care. I just drank many, many beers that night.

But for all the hairiness of the operation, I was glad that Bob was leading us. Bob and I had wasted at least a few of them, and he had been wounded not long before. SEALs just heal faster, probably since we're in such good shape. I still heal fast today, which isn't something I'm likely to complain about. But the op had been a good one and one I strongly remember. Of course, the ops you live through are the best. I couldn't be telling this story if I was dead.

But some SEALs didn't make it through the war. And not all of the SEAL losses were due to combat. There were men lost through helicopter accidents, parachute accidents, even simple automobile mishaps. Seventh Platoon lost one of our own in Vietnam, but not directly due to a combat action.

Gene Fraley had been with Team TWO for a number of years. Before Gene had come into the Teams he had served in the fleet, where he survived a number of aircraft crashes. In at least one of the helo crashes Gene was in, he was the only one to survive the situation. Gene claimed to be lucky but appeared to be the most unlucky man in the Teams. Actually, he just seemed to be accident-prone. And the weirder the accident, the more likely it was that it happened to Gene.

Before the platoon had left the Creek for Vietnam, we had a party at Hook's place. Gene was late, and when he finally showed up, he was covered with stitches and bandages. As it turned out, Rinnie had attacked Gene.

Rinnie was at Gene's house and Gene was taking care of him and training with him. Before the party, Gene had been doing something in his garage up on a ladder. The ladder slipped and fell on Rinnie, probably while he was asleep. The dog was disoriented and hurt, so he lashed out at the nearest person who seemed to be the aggressor. And that person was Fraley.

I had Rinnie over at my house a number of times, and he was a good dog. Though trained as a scout dog, Rinnie was far from being uncontrollable. Fraley just dropped a ladder on him and pissed Rinnie off. Not the kind of accident that happens to every dog owner.

Fraley and I weren't big buddies, but we would go around the bars together sometimes, especially in Vietnam. Gene was big on amateur magic, and he would do tricks in the bars to impress the bar girls. One time Gene did this sleight-of-hand trick where he suddenly seemed to be holding this one girl's white bra in his hand. It was a laugh when her eyes got big and she quickly checked her blouse to see if anything was missing.

Over in Vietnam, Gene and I were in charge of the ordnance at My Tho. Fraley just loved to make up booby traps and other weird shit to use against the enemy, and I would help him. We made all kinds of stuff to mess with the enemy. Such as taking the bullets out of 7.62 intermediate rounds [7.62x39mm] and replacing the powder with C4. After packing the casing full, we would replace the bullet. Leaving rounds like this in enemy ammunition caches could cause Charley to distrust all of his ammo.

While Gallagher and I were up in Saigon, working at the EOD facility there, Fraley's luck finally ran out. Gene had been making a booby-trapped flashlight with one of the special fuses China Lake had produced for the SEALs. Something screwed up. When Gene took the flashlight out of the sandbagged enclosure where he had assembled it, the charge went off.

The blast killed Gene immediately. As Bob and I came back from Saigon, a PBR sailor on the dock told us that Gene had just been killed. Bob and I ran over to the compound and found out that the sailor had been telling the truth. I ended up cleaning out Fraley's locker back in the hotel, and Gallagher took care of the stuff Gene had assembled in his locker down in the compound. Apparently, Gene had a number of booby traps and other stuff in the compound that didn't exactly let Bob relax when he cleaned the place out. I ended up escorting Gene's body back to the States. By the time I got back in early February, most of the Tet offensive was over, with just little pockets of in-city fighting still going on. Getting back to the platoon, I went back to operating.

It was on March 13 that I had my biggest op with Seventh in Vietnam. We were supposedly looking for someone specific, but I believe we were looking for a VC POW camp. It took nearly an act of God to get clearance to go in after a POW camp early in the war. Later on, the powers that be set up special procedures for POW rescues under the code name BRIGHT LIGHT. But for us, it was a lot harder to get the absolutely airtight intel needed for an authorized POW op.

The insertion was made about thirteen miles east of My Tho off the Cua Tien River, traveling there in the armored Mike boat, our "Mighty Mo." The platoon was split into two squads for the op. Bob Gallagher was with my squad, along with Ron Yeaw, an ensign who came in to replace Charles Watson. Watson had come down with some kind of jungle rot and they sent him back to the States.

Yeaw and I knew each other pretty well. I had put him through training back at Little Creek. Here Mr. Yeaw was, on his first op in Vietnam, and one of his squad mates was his instructor from UDTR. I was reasonably hard on him during training, but not much more so than I would have been on any other commissioned puke who wanted to be a SEAL. Yeaw showed up at My Tho and was just in time for this deep penetration op of ours.

The site we were heading for was four klicks in from the river. A hell of a long way for folks who always liked the water at their backs. And we went in heavily armed. For myself, I was carrying a CAR-15, a 40mm M79 grenade launcher, and a 7.62mm Chicom pistol, along with two knives. For the 40mm, I had both canister and high-explosive rounds.

In an earlier op, I had used a canister round on a gook not more than three yards away from me. That was what the canister rounds were intended for, and they sure worked. The twenty or so No. 4 buckshot in the 40mm canister tore this one VC's shoulder and arm clean off. The flechette rounds for the 40mm or the shotgun were like shooting needles at the guy, no stopping power, although they were lethal. On the March 13 op, I was packing about twenty-four rounds of HE and a dozen or so canister rounds for the M79 along with four hundred rounds of ammo for the CAR and a good handful of M26 fragmentation grenades. No water, salt tablets, or Syrettes. Just the tools for killing, and a lot of them.

It was a long trek in, especially with all that gear. We

inserted and started to move in with the other squad operating about a klick away from us. Before the operation, Army slicks had been laid on to extract us, and Seawolves were on call for air support in case we fell into some real hot shit.

We inserted and settled in for a wait. We waited and waited and finally I asked, "What the hell are we waiting for?"

"Gallagher's not here," someone said. "I think he's back on the boat."

"Well, leave him there and let's go," was all I could think to say. What had happened was that Bob had fallen asleep on the long trip aboard the Mike boat. No one woke his ass up when we inserted. Everyone thought that he was behind us, but when we settled in, no Bob.

I didn't think it was all that big a deal. So Bob got to sit one out—this was just another op. But Bob had gotten on the radio and told us to wait for him, so we did. The Mike boat came back and Bob was right there alongside of us, madder than hell. "You guys didn't wake me up," he said along with other colorful expressions. Didn't make no never mind with me. My ass wasn't in hot water for Bob not showing up.

We moved out and began the op in earnest. There were a lot of bad guys in the area, and we didn't want to be compromised. So we moved slowly, skirting hooches and avoiding contact. The next thing I knew, we were three klicks in. It was a long trek and a hot one even at night, especially with all the stuff we were carrying. Suddenly, we could hear a lot of noise coming from the direction of the other squad. They had made contact and were compromised. Later, I learned they had run into a VC doctor and corpsman, who tried to run away. They couldn't let the VC get away and warn anyone, so the squad hosed them.

Calling us up on the radio, they told us what had happened, that the squad was compromised, and to head for the extraction point. There wasn't any argument. Charley knew we were in town, so we headed for where the slicks would pick us up.

Moving along, we passed a number of dry rice paddies. The bush was getting pretty thick and making the going hard. Just as we had crossed a canal and were going up the other bank, we spotted a huge hooch. This was unlike anything I had seen before. The hooch was almost the size of a U.S. barracks, ten by fifteen meters, a huge sucker by Vietnamese standards. Off to the side was another, smaller hooch, and trails ran all through the area around the buildings. Well, boys and girls, what have we here? Shall we take a peek?

Quickly, we set up a skirmish line and assigned fields of fire. Bob, Ron Yeaw, Ming, and another guy decided to go into the building itself. As Bob and the others moved in to the building, I kept a watch over my part of the area. Suddenly, everything seemed to happen. There was automatic weapons fire and a loud explosion. Curtis and I were hit in the first few seconds of fire.

Someone yelled, "Get the son of a bitch, get her!" and I could see this woman running like hell for the bush. Pointing my CAR, I stitched her up the back.

What had happened was that the guys had gone into the hooch and discovered that it was a barracks. All these bunks were in the building covered in mosquito netting. Racked up close to the bunks were VC weapons. And the owners of the weapons were asleep in the bunks. Maybe thirty VC total. So Bob and the others started hosing down the room. The woman had been staying in the other hooch. As soon as she heard the firing, she ran out of her hooch to the large one with a couple of M26 grenades in her hands.

Showing real concern for the other VC in the barracks, the woman threw the grenades into the building. The blast blew Gallagher and Ming under the beds and threw Ron into the canal. Gallagher ended up fighting one VC hand-to-hand. The blast fragmentation hit Curtis and me just outside of the building. So in one action, five guys were hit, three real bad.

Ron was in the canal screaming in pain from his wounds. I was hit and still on an adrenaline rush, so I shouted down to Ron, "If you don't shut up, I'll kill you.

Quit screaming.'' Bullets were flying by, but then suddenly it became real quiet.

Ron called up to me about how his foot was hurt bad. "Okay," I said. "I'll pull you out of the canal, but you have got to shut up. Be quiet."

Be quiet—that was a laugh. We had just made enough noise to wake up the dead. But the instinct is to be silent and not draw attention. Pulling Ron out of the canal, I noticed he was trying to keep quiet. I think he really did believe that I would kill him—his training days weren't that far back for him to ignore his old instructor. Pulling Ron from the canal, I told him to lay still. I still had to check out what else had happened and what the situation was.

I could hear Bob call my name. Moving around, I could see bodies all over the place. I didn't know how many of the VC were wounded or just lying stunned. I do know that after I passed them with my CAR, they weren't anything to be concerned with anymore. Getting to Bob, he said, "Grab Ming."

Moving a bed out of the way, I picked Ming up from where he was on the floor. I could see that he was in a lot of pain and not in good shape. For that matter, neither was I. My wounds were just nickel-and-dime frag cuts compared to what the other guys had gotten. But picking Ming up was adding another 130 pounds or so in addition to all the gear I had on. I wanted to put Ming over my shoulder, but there wasn't any way for me to do that with the wounds he had. I ended up cradling Ming in my arms like a baby.

I didn't know how bad Ron was hurt, but it didn't look very good. His legs were all peppered with fragmentation wounds, and one piece had sliced in enough to have severed one of the muscles to his foot. Gallagher, after he came out of the building, was also torn up pretty bad in the legs. Ming was hurt the worst and couldn't walk at all. Ron could kind of stagger along.

Ron, he's an ensign and in charge. Only Ron wasn't in charge, Gallagher was in charge; Ron was down for the count. And when you get right down to it, Ron was having just about the worst day. Here he was, his first op, and already mostly wasted. Along with the wounds, he had his old UDTR instructor threatening to kill him if he wasn't quiet. What would you think?

But Gallagher was calling the shots, and none of us were arguing. "We've got to get out of here and hit the extraction point," Bob said. I had a lot of respect for Bob and knew how he cared for all of the guys. And now we had to get out of here before more VC showed up. This was being compromised big-time.

Calling over to the other squad on the radio, we told them about having made a major contact and having three serious WIAs [wounded in action]. At that time Bob didn't know about Curtis Ashton and myself being hit. Along with scrambling the Seawolves for air support, the slicks were being scrambled to pick us up.

We moved away from the building, leaving fifteen or more bodies behind us. I still held Ming in my arms—it was the only way to carry him without making him scream. Trying to move as fast as we could, we started walking down a trail in the direction of the extraction point. Probably some VC had gotten away from the building, but the amount of noise we had made would have had everyone's attention for some distance around anyway. Before the VC could get their act together, we had to get out of there.

Moving as quietly as possible, we traveled south for about one thousand meters. Carrying Ming the way I was, I couldn't use my weapons. But most of the other guys had a hand full of gun with their other hand helping to hold up the wounded. VC were moving all around, but it was so dark no one spotted us. Enemy fire was continuing sporadically, but none of it seemed to be aimed directly at us. Finally we came up to a rice paddy with a hooch in the middle of the paddy. Going into the hooch, we took it over.

We tried to keep control of the Vietnamese family that was living in the hooch, but two of the kids got away. We weren't going to waste the kids, and if we did shoot, the VC would know where we were anyway. In the meantime, I was getting Ming and Ron taken care of with first aid. Bob was in a lot of pain from his wounds but was still talking. To add to our troubles, the radio quit working.

With all the fire we had been taking along the way, I figured the radio had stopped a bullet. With some swearing, praying, and dirty looks, along with changing the battery, the radio went back on line. The choppers were on their way, only it looked like they might not get here soon enough. The whole operation had been taking place at night, and now, with the full moon shining down, we could see what was coming.

We were laying low and looking around. With the big rice stacks around there was plenty of cover. But there was so much movement around, cover didn't matter. It was plain to see that the VC were arriving. "Goddam," I said. "Look at them all—it looks like hundreds of them."

It wasn't really hundreds, but there were a lot of VC out there. All the moving around they were doing made it hard to get a count, but I could see dozens of them milling around. The VC didn't seem to know exactly where we were. It did look as if they were trying to encircle the area we were in. By closing the circle, they would have us no matter where we hid.

By now we had the choppers on the radio and they were closing in. The plan was that we wouldn't let the chopper know where we were until it was within range. We weren't going to lay down smoke or flares or anything that would draw fire. While Gallagher continued talking to the bird, I was paying attention to what was going on around us. And what I could see, I didn't like.

The VC were getting closer, much closer. They were in the tree line, some not more than twenty meters away from the hooch. Things were starting to get a little dicey, and we still hadn't fired a shot.

One slick was going to pick up the other squad, the other bird was going to come down to get us, with two Seawolves putting down covering fire. The Seawolves would come in at treetop level, not twenty feet above the ground, and hose down everything but the hooch. The slicks were up at around one or two grand [thousand feet], and they came back over the radio: "Hey, we're not coming down. We're getting fired at."

This was stunning. "What?" we asked.

"We have standing orders from our commanding officer," the choppers answered. "We cannot come into a hot LZ when taking fire."

Just what the hell was their job, anyway? These were Army slicks, and right now we didn't think too much of that branch of the service. Lieutenant Commander Savage, up in the Seawolf, gave voice to our feelings and saved our bacon. "Fuck them," he said. "I'll put out as much ordnance as I can and come in to pick up your seriously wounded. The rest of you are going to have to hightail it to the river."

Great plan—we're going to run for the river, three klicks away, with nine zillion Indians on our ass. "Okay, sounds good."

"Hmmm," Gallagher said. "It looks like the fucking Indians are going to start coming over the gunwalls, doesn't it, Mikey?"

"Yeah, it does," I answered. By this time I was checking over all my weapons, laying out magazines and 40mm rounds for quick reloading. I was as ready as I could be. "Yeah, well, okay," Bob said. "Let's see what happens here."

We were cool—none of us had fired a shot since the initial exchange one thousand meters ago. The VC probably knew exactly where we were by this time. They just didn't know how to come in and get us.

The choppers had been on the radio all this time, talking to us and among themselves. Radio telephone procedure had taken a backseat to expediency. There wasn't any of the official "Silver Fox this is Stingray 35 over" kind of talk. Conversations were more along the line of "Hey, goddammit, come in and get us. Our asses are hanging in the wind down here."

Finally, the choppers agreed to come in and get us. The Seawolves would pull in at low level and cover the pickup slick. "Now look," I said back to the birds. "This is going to start awfully fucking quick. I'm going to put out a flare. At the count of fifteen, you start your run in to the hooch. At the end of the count, I'll throw the flare. You open up with everything you've got right above this hooch."

That was the plan, and the two Seawolves came in. At the end of my count, I threw the flare, a Mark 13, out into the paddy. The wolves opened up and their muzzle blasts and rocket exhausts were ripping the roof right off the hooch. The tree line was being cut back big-time, and the VC along with it. The noise was unbelievable, and it looked like something not of this world. The slick came in behind the wolves and landed. It was obvious that the Army pilot was scared spitless.

The first thing I did was grab Ming, run over in the mud, and get him into the helicopter. Heading back to the hooch, I was now covered by all the SEAL weapons. Fire was being put out by everything from Stoners to 2.75-inch rockets. VC bodies were flying everywhere.

Grabbing Ron, I helped him over to the helicopter. Bob Gallagher was limping along with his weapon in his hand, and I half dragged him to the bird. Getting to the door of the helicopter, I literally picked Bob up and threw him into the bird. I weighed maybe 205 pounds without all of my gear, and Bob had to spot out above 190 with all his stuff. But the excitement was so much that I could throw the man into the slick. Into the slick and right out the other side.

Running around the chopper, I said, "Sorry about that," and tossed Bob back into the bird. As I climbed aboard, the helicopter started to take off. Pounding on the pilot's helmet, I yelled, "Hey, we've still got men on the ground." The pilot put back down and the rest of the squad climbed aboard. Now we could lift off.

I don't know how old the bird's engine was, but we put some strain on it. With the crew of the chopper as well as a squad of SEALs and their gear, we had some weight in the air. The shooting suddenly stopped and things got real quiet. The chopper fought its way into the air, and we made for home. But as soon as the bird reached about one hundred feet, every VC opened up on the slicks. It looked like the Fourth of July with all the tracers going by. But we got out of there and headed for Dong Tam.

Pete and his group had already been pulled out and were waiting for us on the pad. They took the five of us over to the hospital right away. I was still decked out in my combat gear and looking a real mess. Covered in blood and camouflage, my face a green smear. But the first thing I did when we landed was kiss that Army pilot. "This," I said after I kissed him on the cheek, "would have been better than this," and I pulled up my pistol. He knew what I meant. If he had left our guys down there and pulled out, it wasn't VC fire he would have had to worry about.

But things weren't over yet. At the hospital they were working on Gallagher big-time. He was so cold and slipping into shock, they couldn't get any blood out of him to cross-match. They finally took it from Bob's neck, a dicey procedure, I've been told. But the doctors hadn't dealt with me yet.

Bursting open the doors to the hospital, I shouted, "Where's the Eagle?" I was still armed and looked like some kind of war creature. Pointing at the door to the OR, the stunned hospital people indicated where Bob had been taken. Slamming open the OR doors, I again bellowed, "Where's the Eagle?"

One of the people there was so shocked he dropped the IV bottle he was holding. Seeing Bob on the table, I walked over to him and planted a big kiss right on his bald head. Looking around at the doctors and then back to Bob, I said, "I'll see you later." And I walked out the door.

That was an excellent op. Bob got the Navy Cross, I was awarded a Silver Star, and the rest of the guys all got Bronze Stars for their parts in the op. We learned later that what we thought was a VC company was a little bigger than that. During the time that we were walking in those four klicks, intel had come in that two VC battalions had moved into the area. Eighteen hundred VC were hidden in a two-mile stretch of tree line. We had just caught a corner of that line when we headed for our extraction point.

Did I get ripped after that or what? The beers were popping that morning. We took a PBR back up to My Tho from Dong Tam. When we pulled up to the pier, every American at the base was down there to see us, the SEALs who had taken on two battalions of the enemy and lived to talk about it. Personally, I would rather have taken a couple sacks of demo and blown another bunker by myself than have gone through that little adventure. Especially after we learned just what we had faced. But we had kept our heads and played it cool. If it had been necessary for us to get out overland, we would have E&E'd [escape and evasion] and done it. Luck was on our side, and Savage had convinced the slicks to come in and get us.

Bob was later flown to the hospital in Vung Tau. Ron Yeaw was sent to Japan. Ming ended up in Vung Tau with Bob, and I went up there a few weeks later to see them.

Bob's mail had been building up back at the hotel, and I suggested I could jump a chopper and take it up to him. Grabbing up Bob's mail and a couple of paychecks, I flew up to Vung Tau. After we landed, I told the pilot that I would be a couple of hours. As I walked away from the chopper, I was taking off my second class insignia and putting on a set of captain's bars.

Going in to the hospital, I asked, "Hey, where's the Eagle?" But now being an officer, I couldn't do it with the same panache as I had as an enlisted man.

"Oh God," one of the nurses said. "We were just talking about that Frog and what we were going to do with him."

"Well, don't worry about it," I said. "I'm here to bounce his ass out of this place."

"You can't do that," the nurse protested. "He's still got stitches in."

"Let me be the judge of that," I shot back. "Where is he?"

"Over in the beer tent."

Good place for Bob to be. When I got to the tent, Bob was sitting there talking to a couple of Aussies. He was glad to see me. After a little talk, Bob indicated that he really wanted out of the hospital. "I'll see if I can't do that," I said as I went out the door.

Finding the nurse again, I asked him if I could take Bob back with me. "Well, you can't do that. He's still got stitches in."

"I don't care about that. I want him to go back with me. Come on and help me spring him." Well, the nurse wouldn't help and directed me to the doctor. Finding the doc, I continued my act with him. "Doc," I said, "I want to take the Eagle back with me."

"Eagle? Who's the Eagle?"

"Senior Chief Gallagher. I want to take him back with me. Do you mind?"

"He hasn't fully recovered yet, and . . ."

"Come on, I promise that I won't let him go on any operations and that he'll behave himself."

The doctor finally agreed, reluctantly. I didn't give anyone a chance to think much. I grabbed up Bob's records, and we both hightailed it out to the chopper. Two nights later, Bob was back out on an op, stitches and all. Who cares, we live for the moment.

Finally, it was getting time for the platoon to rotate back to the Creek. I stayed back with Peterson to help break in the incoming platoon. The reason I was staying back was that I had gotten some time in the States when I escorted Fraley back. Soon enough, I was also back at the Creek, my first tour in Vietnam over and memorable.

At Little Creek, Ted Lyon was now the Team's CO. While on a deployment to Europe with Ted I told him that I would like to go back to Vietnam as a PRU advisor. Later, after he had checked my records, Ted agreed and said that I would be sent to PRU school on the West Coast.

In 1969, I went out to San Diego for PRU school up

in the Cuyamaca Mountains above the city. As students, we did whatever we had to. Some of the training was a farce and other parts were good to learn. The admin stuff was especially good. The structure of the Phoenix program, how the PRUs were used, and the job description were all useful. Except for the part about signing your life away if you talked about the program. We had homework from the classrooms as well. Going back to your room at night, you would have to plan out an op in writing and the next day present it orally as well. Good training, even for the guys who don't like paperwork.

But running around in the mountains, knee-deep in snow, is not the way to prepare for Vietnam. Some of the field training was useful, giving briefings and laying out missions for the guys. That sort of thing was good. But the environment wasn't conducive for the best training. But I passed the course well enough. For my second tour I went to Vietnam strictly as a PRU advisor.

On my second trip to Vietnam in late July 1969, I flew over with two other SEALs who were also pulling special duty. We weren't with a platoon or anything, which was a little different way to travel. I was assigned as the senior advisor to the PRU in Ba Xuyen Province, the largest province in IV Corps. Under my direction were 125 PRU troops and two PRU chiefs. It was unusual to have two PRU chiefs, but I had one for admin and the other for operations. The group was so large because of the amount of area we had to cover.

A big plus for operations was the great intel net I inherited from the previous advisor, Bob Gallagher. Bob had been hit during a body snatch and left to go back to the States. That situation left me with some pretty big shoes to fill. But the setup was real good and working smoothly.

One of the PRU Chiefs, Bai was his name, was like the XO of the PRU and had been a VC company commander before he changed sides. The man was good, real good. He had six guys covering my ass every time I went into town and I never knew it. Going into town on business sometimes, I'd be taking some of the local bigwigs to lunch, and these six bodyguards would always have me in sight.

Along with the setup of the PRU, I had a pleasant little safe house in town and a jeep to get around in. In my large room was a big wall map where I could plan out ops. All in all, a nice arrangement, especially for a guy who was still just a Navy first class [E-6]. The position had a lot of power that came with it, but I never flaunted it in anyone's face. Doing that is a good way to lose your men's respect, and those PRUs gave their respect grudgingly.

But it was a good job and it kept me busy. My first boss was great, a retired Army NCO who knew how to play the game and get results. Later during the tour, his replacement was a paper pusher who didn't know how to operate. But you get all kinds, especially in Intelligence work. I never gave my superiors anything to complain about, and the second boss wasn't the kind of guy who liked to mingle with the field hands.

The whole time I was with my second boss, we only had one argument. The argument took place when some bigwig came down from Saigon just as I was getting ready to go out on an op. I was called into the safe house and told that all advisors were under orders not to go out on ops with their PRUs. The most I was able to do was go forward to my last CP [command post]. The My Lai incident had hit the streets back home, and the politicians in charge didn't want to take the chance on any more embarrassments.

That caused me to pull back and regroup for a moment. This was serious. If I couldn't go out, what was I going to do for fun? Another big heavy came down from Saigon and interviewed me. This guy was some kind of retired four-star—I didn't know exactly who he was and didn't care. I'm just a shooter and never was much for the politics of these situations. "I've got to ask you this question," he said. "Do you go out on ops?"

"Yes," I answered.

"How far do you go?"

"Only as far as my last CP. Just as I was instructed to do."

That was all he wanted to hear, and he left happy. Of course, my CP was way up front, right in the middle of things, but who was going to know? These guys going to go out there and watch me? So I always conducted the ops from my last CP. And the CP wasn't always right behind the point man. It could be a little farther away, depending on the op.

The intel net I had was excellent, and that complemented my men. The fighters I had were very good, and most of them really had some balls. That situation is illustrated by the fact that out of over four hundred operations conducted during the six months I was there, I only had two wounded and two killed. Out of the two KIAs I think one of them was targeted by the other side and the other PRU just stopped a piece of fragmentation.

The majority of the ops we ran were K-BAR ops. In a K-BAR op, I would take about sixty guys out, broken down into ten guys per chopper [slick]. Either a heavy or light fire team would be supporting the op. For my time, a light fire team was two slicks with door gunners. A heavy fire team was a pair of Cobra gunships. Above the whole thing would be a C&C [Command and Control] bird containing a South Vietnamese officer, usually a major or lieutenant colonel, along with a MAC-V [Military Assistance Command–Vietnam] Army officer of equal rank.

I would go in with one of the slicks. The only way to put on a K-BAR op was if there was an American on the ground calling the shots. That made me the token white on these things. But a K-BAR was worth the trouble because of the size of the enemy force we could take on. When I had the intel for a K-BAR, I could have the request in fast and the op going out quickly. With my people and the proper support, we could take on three or four hundred VC at a time.

There were only sixty guys with me on the K-BAR, but we had air cover right on hand. Medevacs were at my disposal for wounded, and I could call in air strikes from the carrier offshore. Ba Xuyen Province borders the South China Sea, so reaction time could be short for an air strike.

It wasn't just the people I worked for that got me this kind of cooperation. Personalities counted for a lot as well. Talking to the chopper and fixed-wing aircraft people directly had a lot more to do with the actions I got rather than the Company being at the head of my little road show. Of course, when we captured stuff that made good souvenirs, I saw to it that the air jocks got what they wanted. I didn't want that stuff. If I did I could have had drawers full of it. What I wanted was to target the VCI [Viet Cong infrastructure] and tear it down in my province. That was my mission and something I excelled at.

About my second month in-country as an advisor, I went over to the Army base to meet the air people. I was authorized to use the facilities available to a commissioned officer, including the Officers' Club. It wasn't that I particularly liked the O-club, and I certainly didn't want to flaunt any position I may have had. But I did want to meet the local pilots, and the O-club was where they hung out.

Meeting the guys, I could tell them who I was and what I did over a couple of drinks. A good way of unofficially breaking the ice without stepping on any toes. I could tell them what I would like from them, and they could talk to me as well. Good things came out of these meetings. One pilot gave me the frequency needed to call in a fixed-wing air strike from off the coast.

That information saved my butt when I found myself pinned down big-time by about three hundred VC. We were on an op against a VC stronghold, and I had intel that there were several VC bigwigs around. The area was built up better than I thought, with a number of heavy weapons dug in. The frequency I had been given got me a flight of F-4 Phantoms coming back from somewhere still loaded up. They had to drop their ordnance before they could land. When I asked them to make a run, they just said, "Sure, mark it for me," and came on in. Napalm and whatever else they had blew up big-time and sent the VC packing.

The pilots at the base knew I was an advisor, but they also knew me as an average Joe. I never threw my weight around. These young JOs had a job to do and they did it well, but they had an asshole lieutenant colonel for a CO.

It was the day before payday and I was at the base in the O-club watching a movie. A MAC-V major was with me, and we were just enjoying the evening. A bell was hanging over the bar, and if you rang it, you had to buy drinks for the house. They were changing reels for the movie, and I knew most of these guys were short of cash just before payday, so I rang the bell. With a happy yell, the young officers headed for the bar, all except the CO.

Looking down his nose at me, the CO said, "Who are you?"

"I'm Mike Boynton," I answered. "Who're you?"

"I'm Colonel"—whatever-the-hell-his-name-was—"and I'm the Commanding Officer of this airfield. Why did you ring that bell?"

"There's a sign here . . ." I started to answer. And the MAC-V major groaned and just shook his head.

"Major, you stay out of this," the colonel said. And he started dressing me down for ringing his damned bell.

All I had wanted to do was buy the flyboys a drink. And now this short colonel was starting to piss me off. When he asked me for ID, I dug out my card, the one that says I could go anywhere, commandeer anything, and to generally stay off my ass. What was known as the "Get out of jail free" card. Dropping my card on the floor, the colonel went away.

The young officers there said not to be concerned about the CO, that he was just a dick. And these were his own men talking that way. But I knew I had to prevent any trouble before it started and to let this jerk know just who the big dogs were. Petty tyrants like that can get you killed in the bush.

Getting back to my safe house, I made a couple of calls to Saigon. I told my people at the other end of the line what the situation was, that I had a little problem, and asked them to take care of it. The man in Saigon said okay, that he would take care of the situation. He went on to say that the next time I heard from that colonel it would probably be for a visit to his office and that he wanted to buy me a cup of coffee.

Just as I was told, within a few days, a driver from the colonel came over to pick me up. My Cambodian guards wouldn't let anyone into the safe house, especially not some driver. Later, one of the colonel's flunky captains showed up at my door. Again the guards weren't about to let the guy in, but they did bring me a note. I spoke to the captain and let him know that I was busy now but could make some time to see the colonel later. This was a game I could play at.

Later on, I went over to the colonel's and was ushered right into his office. The man was all smiles and told me that if I had any trouble with anything, to just let him know. I played the dumb role and didn't force him to lose any more face than he already had. No need in rubbing it in. He knew now where the big dogs were.

That was the way I handled the situation, reasonably subtly. Other guys in the program would lord it over the local officers. That made for bad relations and just helped the rumors that circulated about Phoenix and the PRUs being out of control. In fact, we operated very well and with good, sometimes great, results.

Much of the time I could run multiple ops. My K-BARs were limited, because I couldn't be two places at once. And I could send the PRUs out after only a certain number of targets, since I only had so many guys. Even so, my PRU conducted over four hundred ops during my tour with them. Transportation was "What's available?" Truck, boat, or whatever, we used them all. The only limitation was that I couldn't get helicopter transport unless I was going along. The system worked for us, and we stuck it to the VC.

A number of ops stood out in their own way. We did a sweep and hit a VC hospital. On another op, we came across a VC POW camp as a target of opportunity. We didn't get any Americans at the camp but did liberate thirty or forty Vietnamese and Cambodians.

The intel net was my most important tool in preparing for any ops. The quality of our intel showed up in the quality of our ops. In total we neutralized—isn't that a neat word?—over 105 VC and VCI personnel. These successes had a drawback as well: I was targeted by the VC and they put a price on my head.

My intel net told me that the word was out to get the province PRU advisor. They even showed me a wanted poster listing me, the Co Vahn of BA Xuyen province, as being worth a 35,000-piaster reward. That was worth what—about twelve dollars and a nickel.

Later on, the reward got quite high, like so many thousand dollars American. Bob Gallagher had much the same situation before I got there, so mine wasn't any kind of special case. Most of the PRU advisors who were worth their salt were in the same boat. Those advisors who were mostly armchair quarterbacks and led from their desks didn't have a price on their head. Charley knew that if the guy never left his office you couldn't get a shot at him anyway.

There was an attempt on my life in town one afternoon. I was taking a couple of secretaries out to lunch, a reasonably official situation. I tried not to frequent the same place too much, but I did like this one restaurant. We took our meal on the second floor, decorated in Vietnamese style with wire mesh on the windows to deflect grenades. While we were enjoying our meal, the sound of gunfire erupted downstairs.

I always traveled armed and pulled my weapon out. Shoving the secretaries into the kitchen, I crouched down next to a table and waited for whoever was coming to move up the stairs. The shots died away downstairs and the screams of the wounded faded. Time went by as I waited and waited. Finally, I could hear someone coming up the stairs. It was Bai, my ex-VC company commander.

"What the fuck are you doing here?" I asked. He just smiled at me. Going downstairs, I could see the two or three guys lying in the restaurant with an additional couple of gunmen in the street outside. Standing around were my six PRU bodyguards. I recognized them from the out-fit, but up to this moment, I didn't know they were fol-lowing me around. "Hey, all right," I said. "You guys want a beer?"

After all, what could I do? Those guys saved my bacon that day. One thing was for sure—I wasn't hungry enough to finish lunch. And all the time Bai was just standing there smiling quietly.

When I asked him what he had done, he explained to me about the bodyguards. He went on to say how I had been good to them and was worth the trouble. I had been paying the PRUs the regular pay and whatever bounties they could earn. I had a slush fund authorized and would pay out amounts against what they would bring in. A crew-served weapon would be worth so much money, and so on. Some advisors screwed with the system for their own gain, and then we had to account for all the money issued. But I never crossed the line on that score. I have no trouble sleeping at night, and anyone can come knock-ing on my door, I'm straight and have nothing to hide.

When we pulled an op where a tax collector was hit, I would give the money to the PRUs who were on the op. The guys knew I stood up straight with them and appar-ently respected me enough for it to assign bodyguards. Lucky for me.

Sometimes we had intel captured on ops that was very time-sensitive. We had to react on it in a matter of hours. The setup we had allowed us to do that. Intel could come in about a VCI meeting in a village that would take place in two days. Great stuff—you can plan a lot given two days lead time. Other times, the people would be showing up in three hours—then you had to hustle.

One afternoon I was sitting in my safe house office doing paperwork. There was a weekly report about what had been accomplished by the PRU that had to be sent up to Can Tho and from there to Saigon. In came my intel chief with some news about some hot information. Putting my stuff aside, I asked him what he had. The intel was COSVN-level, really hot stuff.

COSVN was the highest level of the VC infrastructure

there was in South Vietnam. The levels of VCI importance went from the hamlet level, through village, district, province, and COSVN, the Central Office of South Vietnam. The people who were at the COSVN level were hard-core card carriers who probably knew Ho Chi Minh personally. The major COSVN headquarters were in Cambodia and Laos, beyond our official reach at the time. Hitting a COSVN-level official was about like nailing a U.S. senator in our country. Not the kind of target that came along every day.

The intel came in from an informer who said that I had two COSVN-, one province-, and two district-level VCI coming my way. The group was working its way along the commo/liaison route, hamlet to hamlet. By moving that way, the VC could keep their security as tight as possible, only moving it from point to point. The cell structure used by the VC compartmentalized their people tightly. One guy in a hamlet might know another guy in his cell who lived in a hamlet down the road. That way intel and messages could be passed along, but any one guy being captured would only cost the men of that one cell.

The VC security had slipped up, and we learned about them. I understood that the group had been on the road for a number of weeks and were heading back to their base across the border. They had been canvassing their people up in the Can Tho area and would be passing within my reach in about nine hours. The informer pinpointed the place on the map where we could expect the VC to be at about two o'clock the next morning. It was about five in the afternoon, and I had plenty of time to get a good op together.

Of course, there were a few questions in my mind. Is this a setup? Could this be bad information? I knew I was being targeted, and intel like this would be sure to draw me out. I asked how good the intel was and was told that it had come from my Chiefs' number one man. It was left up to me to decide how far I was willing to stick my neck out. "Let's do it," I said.

I decided to take twenty of my best PRU guys and go out after the VCI. Going over to the PRU camp, I was going to pick the men myself. With my Chiefs' help I picked out the twenty guys I wanted. The problem was that many of the PRU people were mercenaries—they were out for the highest dollar. The op was going to be a hairy one, and I didn't know which ones I could trust completely. Putting the team together, I had the PRUs get a truck ready for the op. Then I gave my interpreter a list of the gear I wanted brought along.

While the PRU was getting ready, I went back to the safe house. Going in to the MAC-V officer, I explained where I would be going and why. There were South Vietnamese people in the outside office, and talking in specifics there was a good way to get sent home in a box. I made sure the correct people knew the right story, but I sure didn't broadcast my intentions. That was one less source of leaks I had to worry about.

Getting back to the PRU, we piled onto the trucks to head out. I asked my man if he had picked up all of the stuff I wanted, and he said he had it in the truck. A lot of ordnance, thirteen claymore mines, stuff like that. I wanted this ambush to go off with a bang and not miss anyone. For myself, I just had a CAR. Going out with all the PRUs with me, I could travel light.

In fact, my PRUs often wouldn't let me into the fight. There was one time during a firefight that I stood up, shooting at the enemy. All of a sudden my PRU people were diving on me, tackling me into the ground. "What the fuck is going on?" I asked my interpreter.

"Hey," he answered. "Something happens to you and we don't get paid."

That was a hard point to argue with. So when I went out on an op I would usually carry just a pistol and a CAR-15. The pistol would be either an issue S&W .38 or a Chicom 7.62mm [a PRC Type 51 Tokarev]. The CAR had a little Colt three-power telescopic sight on the handle. Not that I used the weapons much—my PRU didn't really give me the chance. But I had to be armed in case someone suddenly popped up close.

Driving out, we soon parked the truck at an outpost. Telling the driver when we would be back, we picked up the gear and started humping it by foot to the ambush site. We walked about a klick to where I had planned to set up the ambush.

Putting out the claymores, I planned out the killing zone to be sure everything was covered as much as possible. With the men in place and the ambush set, we settled in to wait for our target. And the wait wasn't anything at all.

Within about fifteen minutes of our settling in, here came our targets, right on schedule. The only trouble was that it wasn't the six or seven bodyguards the intel had reported, it looked more like sixty of them. There was a forward platoon of VC out in front of the main body, flank guards on either side, and a trailing platoon covering the rear.

My interpreter had all the claymore clackers [firing devices] in his hands, and I could just see his thoughts: "I hope this guy doesn't expect me to fire these things." We were outnumbered at least three to one. Reaching over to the interpreter, I whispered to him, "Give me the clackers." He was a little reluctant to let them go, so I repeated my whisper a few times—"Give me the goddam clackers!"

Finally he let them go, and I quickly divided the firing devices between myself and Bai. "When I count three," I said, "we fire." Bai nodded and we waited. Just as the main body entered the center of the killing zone, we fired the claymores.

The mines going off sounded like an ARC LIGHT strike [B-52s]. Then my PRUs opened up, covering the entire area with a swath of fire. As the firing stopped, there was only dust and a ringing kind of silence.

Running over, we started to check the bodies as fast as we could. There was one guy laying there who had an AK-47 literally blown into his chest. When I grabbed hold of the AK I couldn't pull the weapon free, it was embedded so deeply. Calling one of the PRUs over, I told him to get the weapon out of the man's chest. The VC was obviously dead and he wasn't going to need an AK anytime soon.

Moving through the bodies, I had my PRUs grab anything that looked of intelligence value. The escorted group of VC had been carrying a bunch of ammo cans with them that were probably full of documents and money. Whatever was in those cans, I wanted it. I made sure the PRUs took those and then told them to check and see if any of the specific VC we had been looking for were still alive.

Going back to the man with the AK, I asked him if he had gotten the weapon out yet. Finally, the guy had to cut the weapon free with his knife. On the end of the AK was a homemade rifle grenade launcher that had gone through the VC's chest. It was crudely machined and must have been turned out in one of the many VC jungle workshops that were around.

By this time, the bad guys were starting to recover. We must have killed a third of the VC forces, twenty guys or so. But that still left enough around to make our lives interesting. The informer who had supplied the intel was with us, and he identified the bodies of the VCI we had been looking for. Until we found those VCI members alive or identified their bodies, the guide wasn't going to get paid. Once he pointed out who we wanted—they were all dead—I pulled out the wad of cash I was carrying and gave it to him. He had done his job, and no problem, I could account for this money easily.

By now a hornet's nest of VC was waking up. It was time for us to haul ass, and we did, running for the outpost shooting over our shoulders. Grabbing the radioman, I said, "Get on the phone and tell those people at the outpost to give us some HE over our shoulders out here." Jabbering away at the ARVNs in their outpost, the radioman got my call for fire support through.

As the mortars in the outpost fired, the illumination rounds they put up lit up the area nicely. Illumination, just what I wanted, thank you very little. It's the dead of night and I'm in the middle of a rice paddy running towards an outpost. A couple of VC platoons are chasing my ass and my support puts up illumination.

It wasn't as bad as it could have been. One of my men caught a round in the calf. We made it to the outpost with only that one wounded. Not stopping to catch our breath, we piled in the truck and headed back to base. Getting back to the safe house, we opened up the cans.

As I had thought, some of the cans held money, lots of it. Handing the piasters to Bai, I told him to give it to the men who were on the op. He knew what I wanted, and I trusted him to do it. In the meantime, the intel people were going through the documents we had collected. "Hey, we've got some hot shit here."

Going over to his room, I got the chief of station up—it was around six in the morning—and told him what we had. He got the secretaries in early and started translating the papers.

By eight o'clock, enough material had been translated to tell us that we had some very hot stuff here. "Do you know what you've got here?" the Chief asked me. "All I know is that it's hot," was my answer. I knew the op was going to be good—I felt it in my bones before we even started.

What we had was documentation outlining the new Tet offensive in IV Corps for 1970. This was the biggest hit I had ever made. All the documents were bundled up and a special Air America flight came down to pick them up. The documents went from my place to Can Tho, to Saigon, to Washington, D.C., and finally ended up at the Paris peace talks within thirty-two hours of the hit. I don't know if the papers influenced the Paris peace talks, but I received a telegram from D.C. thanking me for the results. Another attaboy came to me from the State Department by way of my boss in Saigon. Those kinds of things aren't given out easily, so the documents may have had some kind of effect at the talks. That was a big hit.

As my time in Vietnam drew to a close, I started cutting

back on my ops. I didn't want to press my luck, so I would stay at the CP, the real one, or on the boat, whatever, and direct by radio. There had been a lieutenant at another PRU who came down from Can Tho and had been forbidden to go out on ops. He went out on one and got his ass killed. That was just two weeks before he was to go home, this West Coast SEAL goes out and gets his ass killed. He had a wife and two kids back home. That wasn't going to happen to me. The last week of my tour, I didn't go out at all.

And my turnover advisor wasn't even a SEAL, he was some Army puke. He relieved me and I went home from my last tour in Vietnam.

When I had been running my PRUs, there hadn't been any problems out in the field. There were no excesses done by my men which made such great copy back in the States. I just wouldn't allow it. I kept control of my PRUs whenever I was in the field with them. And I never got any feedback that things happened when I wasn't there. The men knew that they would get paid and there wasn't any reason for any kind of excess. I told them what the rules were and they knew them. If I had people who were going overboard, killing, torturing, or collecting ears because they liked it, I would have gotten rid of them. The work was hard enough without that kind of shit.

Other PRUs I didn't know about. But I'm certain that the stories being circulated about the Phoenix program are more than a little exaggerated. There was little I could do if the PRUs stole anything on the ops where I wasn't with them. And that did happen on occasion. One time coming off a K-BAR op, I had my men lined up and was putting them out, ten at a time, to board the choppers. The guys were happy and milling around, so that was the way I had to handle getting them on board.

Over in the back of the crowd, I could see a commotion going on. At any time an LZ could turn hot, so I wanted to know what was happening. The PRUs had a three-hundred-pound pig they were trying to get on board the bird. The situation was actually kind of funny—the pig was kicking and squealing and not about to get on the helicopter. And if they did get the pig aboard, the chopper wasn't going to get off the ground, not with the crew, ten PRUs, and a three-hundred-pound porker. Finally, I told the guys that I would buy them a smaller pig when we got back. I didn't condone that kind of thing. The natives were having a hard enough time just getting by.

Nothing I did over there bothers me at night, or any other time. I have dreams, but not nightmares. We had a job to do, and I'm not ashamed of the way I did it. My PRUs were successful, and there is no way of arguing against that. While I was in Vietnam for that last seven months, I felt that my part of the Phoenix program was working. I never saw the whole picture, but the results from what my PRU was doing were positive.

For twenty-eight years, until my retirement as Command Master Chief of SEAL Team TWO, I had the pleasure of being a part of the best the Navy has, SEAL Team TWO and Naval Special Warfare. When you spend most of your adult life in an organization like SpecWar, you wonder where all the time has gone. I know that the last ten years blurred, they passed so quickly. The beauty of the Teams is growing old without growing up. There is always something new going on. The good times outweigh the bad tenfold.

To the men of the Teams today, I say this. The price of patriotism is high—you only buy the farm once. Keep the body bags where they belong—on the shelf. The stakes are high in real missions; it's not a crapshoot. You must know and evaluate the mission in your own mind. The ultimate objective cannot override the risk factor. It cannot be suicidal and it must not be morally repugnant.

If you are ever called upon to fight another "Vietnam" or "JUST CAUSE," I know that all of you will excel. Remember this: There are mistakes to be made by every man. No one is perfect. In war, do what you have to do, help your Teammates, and never leave anyone behind. That is all anyone can ask of you.

SEAL Team TWO, I applaud you, I will miss you.

Before the Teams sent direct action platoons to Vietnam, a great deal of preparation had to be completed. Not only new training but new weapons and equipment were examined and tried. Existing materials were modified and adapted to the SEALs' expected methods of operating. But far more important than the exotic materials available to the Teams were the men who would use them.

Enlisted men in the Teams could spend their entire careers in the same Team. This allowed men to establish families and as stable a home life as possible for a SEAL who could be deployed at a moment's notice. Officers had a different situation.

If an enlisted man was awarded a commission as an officer, established procedures would send him to the opposite coast from the one where he had served as an EM. But qualified officers were in very short supply in the Teams. Often, men could receive a commission while in the UDT and volunteer for the nearby SEAL Team. Very quickly, a new officer could find himself leading the very men he had been following just a short time before. The overall quality of the men serving in the UDT and SEALs prevented this situation from being much of a problem.

One reason that officers were in such short supply in the Teams was the special attention they received from the instructors in UDTR. During training, instructors would take extra pains to be sure that any officers who would enter the Teams would measure up. "I may have to put my life in that man's hands when I follow him someday, and when I do, I'll be sure that he can lead" was a thought enthusiastically shared by several generations of UDT instructors.

An officer's tour of duty was often short in the Teams. With so few men in all of Special Warfare, there were accordingly few slots for an officer's advancement. To continue his career in the Navy during the 1960s, an officer would often have to return to the fleet to gain experience and rank. With the later growth of the Teams and the addition of an officer career development track in Naval Special Warfare, many of the earlier officers could return to the Teams and continue their professional growth. The shortage of experienced men also made it possible for officers who had left the Navy to later rejoin the service and the Teams.

CAPTAIN

LARRY BAILEY

USN (RET.)

Captain Bailey joined SEAL Team TWO prior to the Vietnam War commitment. As an officer with strong interest in engineering, he assisted in helping to create the first specialized SEAL combat boat, the STAB (SEAL Team Assault Boat). After deploying to Vietnam with the first Team TWO platoons to go into combat, Captain Bailey left the Teams to enter civilian life. In the early 1970s, Captain Bailey returned to Naval Special Warfare, and he later became the Commanding Officer at the Basic Underwater Demolition/SEAL school (BUD/S) at Coronado, California.

I was raised on a little farm in East Texas between Marshall and Longview. I was born in 1939 and went to school in Marshall through high school. My dad was a farmer. My mother was sort of a schoolteacher—she had a two-year degree. My family wasn't dirt-poor, but we weren't rich, either.

The family had only one vacation in its entire history. We rigged a pickup truck with wagon slats and put a tarp over the back and a mattress in the bed, and we went to Tennessee to visit my aunt and uncle—and had a great time. We never had vacations 'cause you have to milk cows twice a day.

So I had a real neat upbringing for a kid. I learned how to work, learned how to tell the truth, and I probably learned a little more patriotism than is healthy these days. Then I went to Stephen F. Austin College, a small school in Texas, graduated with a major in history, and joined the Navy in 1962.

I wanted to do something as far from milking cows as I could get, as milking cows is not my idea of a vocation, so I went to OCS and was on a destroyer for seven or eight months. Anything was better than being seasick on the bridge of a destroyer, so I volunteered for Underwater Demolition Team training in 1963. I graduated in January 1964 and went to Underwater Demolition Team 22, and that was the beginning of my SEAL career.

The most memorable incident at UDT training camp occurred at Camp Pickett, Virginia. Now it's Fort Pickett, but then it was Camp Pickett. There was a traditional problem that we conducted there, a field exercise called the Kennedy Bridge Problem. It would have been about October of 1963.

The Kennedy Bridge Problem had every class doing the same thing, just different circumstances depending on whether it was a winter or a summer class. Mine was a summer class, happily. The class would carry forty-pound packs of simulated demolitions to the Kennedy Bridge, which was many miles through the woods along the Nottoway River. We had to navigate through the river bottom and over farms and hills and dales and what-have-you. We had to get within range of the bridge, set up camp, then do a quick reconnaissance and plan how we would assault the bridge to take out the enemy, who were the instructors. Then we took our demolition packs, placed them in strategic points along the bridge, and simulated blowing it up. It was a major U.S. highway bridge, so it was a pretty big structure.

Well, as bad luck would have it, we got so hung up in that river bottom that we got to the bridge literally at the crack of dawn when we were supposed to be assaulting it. So we did a hurried reconnaissance and conducted a hasty assault on the bridge. That turned out to be absolutely beautiful, precisely because we did not have the opportunity to cross over the river and assault the bridge from the other side, as we had briefed we would. Of course, the instructors had heard all our briefings and had set up their defenses on the north side, and we hit them from the south. Well, we never owned up to the fact that we'd screwed up. They credited us with doing some great planning. Anyway, we took the bridge, laid our charges, and blew it up.

They did a quick debrief and told us we'd done a fantastic job slipping in from the south when we'd originally planned to come in from the north. And our demolition charges were properly placed. They left us on our own to get back to camp, and they said that we could hike the roads getting back to camp, since we'd done such a good job.

Well, one of our guys saw some Army two-and-a-half-ton trucks in a little campsite up a hill to the south of the bridge. He went up there and convinced one of the drivers to let us jump in the back of his truck, pull the blinds shut, so to speak, and take us ten miles or so to this little bridge close to our camp, where we knew we were going to get ambushed by the instructors. That was always done, class after class.

So we jumped in the six-by and were carried about ten miles down the road and were put out alongside this bridge. Whereupon we went into the woods about a hundred yards and set up camp for the next ten or eleven hours and got a good night's sleep. Then we were up and ready for the instructors when they came to set their ambush for us. And we waxed them—just really blew them away.

The instructors really thought that was wonderful too. And they told us how great we were and gave us the rest of the day off. Then that evening the senior officer instructor went over to the Officers' Club at Camp Pickett and met this Army warrant officer who said, "Hey, we gave some of your SEAL guys a lift this morning."

And he said, "Oh, tell me more."

Well, the lieutenant came back to camp about ten P.M. and told the two chief petty officers, two bad boys, what we had done. So Chiefs Blais and Waddell, they came

down to the student bivouac. I was the class leader and
Petty Officer Ed Jones was the senior enlisted guy. Tom
Blais and Bernie Waddell called Jones and me forward.
"Oh, you sorry so-and-sos, you lied," blah blah blah.
"You tricked us. Now you're going to pay us back."
They were drunk. I mean, they were *mean* drunk, too.

So they had Jones and me in the leaning-rest position
for about forty-five minutes. Sweat was rolling down our
hands and forming puddles of mud under our hands. We
were about to collapse. Finally they said, "Okay, that's
enough; form the class up."

So we formed the class up and they said, "Okay, boys,
get in the six-by. We're going to give you a little ride."

They took us back. We were loaded up with our weapons and packs again and taken back to Kennedy Bridge.
I forget the exact distance, but it was about fifteen miles
or so. They said, "Okay, you boys like to hump the road
so well that we're going to let you do it on your own.
What would be a good time for you to make it back
here?"

The previous class record was two hours and thirty
minutes. "You've got two hours and twenty-two minutes
to make it back here. And we're going to do it all night
until you make it back under that time."

It was impossible to complete the march in that time,
it just couldn't be done. But we did it.

That's pretty much the story. Every time Class 30 (that
was our class number) gets together we talk about the
Kennedy Bridge Problem. And although at the time we
were absolutely mortified that we had to do all this mess,
it was a great memory, knowing that, when we had to,
we could do that march in two hours and nineteen
minutes.

I don't remember a whole lot about Hell Week except
about guys who quit. I think one was named Jadrnicek,
one was named Farmer, and one was named Stants. These
guys were all physical studs. And the thing I remember
most about Hell Week was that all three of these guys
quit on the afternoon of the first day. There was just no

way to predict that these guys wouldn't make it, but they sure didn't.

I wasn't a particularly graceful or athletic person, or particularly strong. I had a lot of endurance. I guess my biggest asset was that I was hardheaded, I never even thought about quitting.

And here these three superstars, great swimmers, great runners, great PT-ers, and they quit. I remember one of them was absolutely crying like a baby. He said, "I just don't know how you do it." So that's my big memory of Hell Week.

After the first couple of days, we didn't get any sleep at all. It all just kind of fades into oblivion.

I was supposed to get out of the Navy in October of 1966. I had planned to get out. I didn't intend to make a career out of the Navy. We found out that SEAL Team TWO had a Vietnam commitment coming up early the next year and I wanted to go to Vietnam. So I extended for a year so I could go to Vietnam.

I was excited. Every young man has to have his war.

It was kind of like the old Marine gunnery sergeant told us it would be. He was the lead instructor of the Vietnamese village course in Camp Lejeune in North Carolina. And he said, "Boys, when you get over there you might as well take everything out of your rucksack and throw it out on the ground in the rain, get it soaking wet, and say 'Screw it,' because that's the way it's always going to be for the rest of your time there."

And that's the way it was when it started raining. Happily we got a bit of respite during the dry season.

Upon arriving in-country we went to the Rung Sat Special Zone for four or five days to get oriented by the West Coast SEALs who were there. SEAL Team ONE had the Rung Sat responsibility, while SEAL Team TWO was the first American combat unit of any kind actually in the Delta. Rung Sat was not in the Delta proper. It was a special zone, a so-called secret zone.

So we went down to Can Tho in IV Corps and there were no U.S. Army people or Air Force people. In fact, we were the first American ground troops in the entire

Delta, so they didn't know what to do with us for about three weeks after we got in-country. We just cruised up and down the rivers trying to do things without a great deal of success.

Finally the bosses in Saigon said, "Hey, let the SEALs start doing some of their stuff." That's when our combat started.

The thing I'm proudest of is that we did the first-ever night land navigation using Firefly helicopters. These were helicopters with huge umpteen-million-candlepower lights that they would shine along the river to uncover Viet Cong river traffic. We were going in to try to rescue a couple of Americans who had been located in a Viet Cong prison camp alongside a certain canal, but there was no way we could navigate. We had to go in at night when everything was pitch-black.

So I came up with what I thought was just a brilliant idea for a country boy, that of letting the helicopters set us out anywhere within a reasonable walking distance of this camp. And then at given times we'd have these Firefly helicopters go over known locations, known landmarks, and, when we told them to, shine their beams on these confluences of rivers or canals or pagodas or villages or whatever. We'd just take a compass and cut a bearing to the beam. By using three compass readings we were able to triangulate almost precisely where we were. And then we'd do checks every now and then. We knew what the tree lines should look like in silhouette. And we came out exactly where we had intended to. I was kind of proud of that.

We didn't rescue any prisoners, as the VC had moved them the day before. But what we did do was kill a couple of Viet Cong and have a good time.

There's one incident that stands out in my memory. It's not a happy memory. Since we weren't working with the LDNN, we worked with local militiamen. I killed one of these militiamen who accompanied us on an ambush one night. This happened through a series of errors of various types. One time I counted seven different mistakes that resulted in the kid dying. But the last mistake was that I was the guy who pulled the trigger, so that's a very traumatic memory for me.

There were a lot of things that happened that night that shouldn't have happened. All I can say is that it helps to be a little fatalistic about things like this, because if any one of those things hadn't happened the kid would still be alive. But war is full of tragedy.

During one particular operation over there, a Vietnamese sampan came out into the river. We were on boats in the river supporting a land operation. Before we were allowed to go ashore this sampan came out. Obviously the occupants were in a great deal of distress. We pulled alongside the sampan and there was this woman in there with half her face blown away. I mean, literally half her face was gone. We found out that some Vietnamese soldiers had thrown a grenade in the tunnel where they were hiding.

This woman was lying there in the sampan. One eye was gone, her nose was gone, her jaw was gone. She was not in shock, she was looking around and was able to talk. She was absolutely under control. She didn't show any indication that she was in pain or in shock. And I found out later that the next week she was back home.

The Vietnamese are an absolutely incredible group of people as far as stoicism is concerned.

The Viet Cong were very competent at night, when they were on the offensive. But if we could get them on the defensive at night they were absolutely hopeless. They did not plan to be hit at night. If we hit them in the daytime they would just disappear. But if we hit them at night they were just totally helpless.

It's kind of ironic. The Vietnamese Army was probably best on the defense during the hours of darkness, and they were best on the offense during the hours of daylight. They just flip-flopped the Viet Cong. So we were a kind of happy medium as far as our side was concerned. SEALs, and some of the other elite units, so called, would go after the Viet Cong at night and they didn't know how to defend themselves. They just weren't ready for you to hit them.

They were effective and they were so well propagandized that they were a motivated enemy. And when someone knows there are some hard-core cadres behind him that will shoot him if he retreats, that motivates him too. There was a lot of that.

We had great relations with other services. We didn't try to bully people around but rather tried to cooperate with them. The Air Force and the Army supported us. In fact, the Army helicopter pilots preferred to fly in support of us more than their own people.

The only "vacation" most of us took was one R&R out of country. For example, I went with Pierre Birtz, one of the guys in our platoon, to Kuala Lumpur, Malaysia, and had a great time. It's really kind of strange, and I'm not sure R&R was the way to go. We went out of country for five days. We got bathed, shaved, had our hair cut and poo-poo juice put on us. We slept in nice clean sheets, and we ate great food and played tourist—just did all kinds of relaxing things.

And then we had to go right back and were expected to get the same warrior mind-set all over again. I didn't think that was good. I enjoyed my R&R and I'm glad I did it, but it kind of ruined my focus.

The best combatant, bar none, was Bob Gallagher. He wasn't in my platoon, but he made, I think, three tours in Vietnam and had a Navy Cross and two Silver Stars, all of them well earned, unlike a lot of the decorations awarded in Vietnam. There were some pretty significant awards that weren't really earned. Everybody knows that, so it's no big deal.

We were pretty pleased with our weapons. Apart from a few Marines, we were the first Americans who went over there with the original AR-15s. Shortly after we arrived in Vietnam we were issued M16s, which were an improved version of the AR-15. There were a lot of Marines who were killed because their AR-15s jammed as they didn't have the chromium-lined chamber that helped keep the corrosion and mud from jamming the weapon.

We had some really fantastic weaponry, including the hand-cranked 40mm grenade launchers that were really great to mount on the boats. And we had the XM-148, the experimental 40mm grenade launcher, which attached to the bottom of the M16; this led to the M203 40mm that is standard issue today. We also had the Stoner weapon, which was .223 caliber and had a much higher rate of fire than the M60 and was a much lighter weapon. The ammunition load was much lighter because the bullets were small, but they had the same effect. The advantage of the M60, of course, was that it did have a longer barrel and a heavier slug and was more effective at long range. But we weren't concerned with long range anyway. The Stoner was just great for our close-in type of operations.

We improved things and adapted; even while I was over there we were starting to change certain things about our web gear. It started out as personal customizing, and then toward the end of the war guys were developing all sorts of flotation vests that carried ammunition and what-have-you. We did this because, if we were going across canals carrying a big ammo load, we were going to be walking on the bottom of the river, whether the water was over our heads or not. So if we had an inflatable vest that also carried our bullets, grenades, and what-have-you that we could blow up slightly as we went into the water to allow us to stay on the surface, that was much better than walking on the bottom.

I only had one full tour there, and then I got out of the Navy because I had planned to. One of the things I did when I was out was to work with the treasure-hunting company that found all those wrecks off the Florida coast. I worked with Mel Fisher, the guy who found the ATOCHA. In fact, until Fisher found the ATOCHA off the Keys, we were the most successful treasure-hunting operation in history. What we found on today's market would have been worth, oh, 120 or 130 million dollars. I got none of it, since I was just a hired hand. They gave me a few silver coins.

I got to travel and made three or four trips to South America as their representative, as I speak Spanish and Portuguese. Later on I was executive director of the Re-

publican Party down in Fort Worth, Texas, where my secretary asked me one day, "Can I ask you a personal
question, Larry?"

And I said, "Sure."

And she said, "After doing all that exciting stuff that
you've done, being a SEAL and all, are you really going
to be happy doing this for the rest of your life?"

I said, "Sure, why not?"

And she said, "Well, I'm just thinking that it might get
kind of boring."

That started me thinking, and within thirty days I had
started the paperwork to get me back in the Navy. I went
right back to SEAL Team TWO.

Right now I'm working with a group called Ecogas
Incorporated. We've got a contract with the State of Lou-
isiana to convert several hundred state-owned vehicles to
natural gas, and then we will sell the fuel to power the
vehicles.

*The major entry qualification for any man who wanted to serve
in the UDT or SEALs was to complete UDTR. Later renamed
UDTB and still later BUD/S, the course of training was, and
still is, considered one of the hardest in the world. The only way
to make the course any more difficult would be to start shooting
at the trainees, and that's a little extreme even for the SEALs.*

*Completing the course, and especially Hell Week, is the single
most uniting factor in the Teams. Each man remembers what it
took for him to complete the training and knows that the man
he serves with also made it through the same course. Teamwork
above all else is stressed in the Teams. From their time in UDTR
until they leave the quarterdeck, each man knows the importance
of teamwork in completing the mission.*

*This emphasis on working together also develops some fierce
loyalties among the men. Attack one and you attack all, and a
Teammate, living or dead, was never left behind.*

*These feelings and attitudes are even more strongly forged in
the fierce heat of combat. A good leader who had proved himself
in front of his men could ask for almost superhuman effort on
the part of his people. In many cases, the men would have al-*

ready anticipated an upcoming need and taken care of the problem long before even being asked.

If a native unit they fought alongside of proved itself in combat, the SEALs would extend their loyalties to include it. Individual natives and units could find themselves being awarded the trust and loyalties the SEALs normally reserved for themselves.

HENRY S. "BUD" THRIFT, JR.

Bud Thrift was a mustang officer in the Teams—that is, an officer who was an enlisted man before receiving his commission. After joining SEAL Team TWO, Warrant Officer Thrift was the assistant officer in charge of what may have been the most successful individual SEAL platoon of the war. Sixth Platoon of SEAL Team TWO received a Navy Unit Commendation for its actions during its tour of duty in Vietnam in 1970. Bud Thrift was in command of Bravo squad of the Sixth Platoon during that tour.

My name is Henry S. Thrift, but I'm usually called Bud. I was born in Richmond, Virginia. My father was in the Army, and we traveled all over the world. His last duty station was in Florida, and that's where I joined the Naval Reserve in 1960, when I was seventeen. Since I felt that I'd already been in the Army for almost eighteen years, I wanted a transfer out of that outfit, so I decided to try the Navy.

My first two years in the Navy I served at the Naval Weapons Annex at Charleston, South Carolina, where they built the Polaris missile. I made E-3, Boatswain's mate seaman, by the end of that time. About thirty days before I was due to get out, I heard about the Frogmen, who I thought had been disbanded. There was a guy coming around and testing people for entry into UDT training, and since I had no other plans, I went down and took the test. Nobody had told me it would include a physical test. I ended up doing my running in my dress blues and the swimming in nothing at all because I didn't have a suit with me. It was an interesting way to start off my new career, but I passed the physical test and entered into the program.

I did my training for UDTR at Little Creek, Virginia, in June 1963. One of my classmates was Ensign Lockerman, who had already been through two previous classes but had been hurt each time and still hadn't passed the course. There were so few officers in the UDT at this time that Ensign Lockerman, even though he hadn't officially passed the training, had checked into the Teams while waiting for a new class to start. He had even become the acting commanding officer of one of the Teams! Lockerman was hurt again in our class when they dropped a boat on him and injured his back or his leg, or something. So we had a big joke going on. Whenever we went out to this little Reserve unit bar down the road during training, we'd set this helmet on top of two shoes, call it Mr. Lockerman, and pour beer on it.

We started off with a really large class, about 130 or 140 people. There were guys in there who looked like body builders, were great swimmers, and could run like gazelles. And these guys were quitting right and left. I weighed about 165 pounds at the time and couldn't understand why I was there, and they were quitting. That was nothing unusual; I suppose that's true of everybody who made it through training. But it seemed strange to me that some of those guys dropped out.

There was one time when I would have quit training, but I couldn't find anyone to quit to. I had poison ivy from about the third week of training until the eleventh or twelfth week. I get poison ivy really bad, and it was all over my wrist and growing all up and down my legs. We were up at what they call Camp Pickett, out at an ambush site, and all the instructors were supposed to drive trucks down through there so we could ambush them. So we were sitting up there in the bush. The mosquitoes were eating me, and this poison ivy had been on me for about nine weeks. Finally I just said, "Bullshit! I've had it up to here!" I sat up. "I'm tired of this bullshit!" And everybody said, "Get down! Get down!" Taking out my Ka-bar knife, I scraped all the poison ivy off. It scabbed over the next day and got better. That's one day when they would have got me if there'd been anybody there. But there was nobody there harassing me, I was just sitting there on my own. More than any of the physical stuff, the poison ivy really bothered me, but once it stopped itching I didn't have any more trouble.

We made swims down in Puerto Rico. One time we were supposed to swim from Vieques Island all the way back to Puerto Rico, but they had a hurricane at the time, so instead they made us swim five miles around this pier. But there were sea wasps [jellyfish] in the water—not the big ones you get in the Indian Ocean, but smaller ones. All you could see was the four little black threads that were the tentacles. Every time we made a circle, we swam back through the sea wasps, and everybody was getting stung. I had a sore on my neck already, and one of these sea wasps hit me there. I started cramping up and foaming at the mouth from the neurotoxin, and had to swim in a bent position. But I did finish the swim, although I slowed the class average down. The sea wasp had left a mark like a Z on my neck, so afterwards I used to say that Zorro had got me.

This was back at the time when you did all the training together, and didn't go to the Teams until after parachute school, so we did our initial training at Little Creek, the heavy demolition work in Puerto Rico, and then went on to the Army jump school at Fort Benning. We were one of the classes they thought of not sending to Benning, and a lot of the guys were kind of excited that they weren't going to go ... until they found out that when we went to jump school we got to use parachutes. After jump school, we were flown down to Key West for underwater diving school. It was six months of training straight through without having to report in to a Team. You knew you were a trainee for six entire months. Instead of saying "Okay, I made it here" and joining a Team, you just went on to another school after finishing the one before.

We finally graduated the program at the beginning of January 1964, and the class was split up and sent to the Teams. I went to Underwater Demolition Team 21, stationed back at Little Creek. My first trip I was sent down to the Panama Canal Zone. The Communists were trying to take over there. The Navy put a ship into the area, and we went to jungle warfare school while we were there. They sent us out on a three-day escape and evasion problem, but on the first day we ran all the way back in three and a half hours—it was twelve miles through the jungle. We beat all of the roadblocks and were in the bar having a steak that night while the rest of the class was still out in the jungle for three more days.

Our officer in charge on that particular deployment was Lieutenant Gibby. We weren't authorized liberty downtown, but we were sneaking down there anyway. One night Gibby decided to go along with a group and they ended up in a big fight. I don't know how Gibby got hold of the Commodore's jeep, but he lost it. We got back to the States in the first week of April, but Gibby had to stay aboard ship for another week to finish his time in hack. I thought that was kind of funny.

The next cruise was to Vieques, and then I made a cruise as a first class Boatswain's mate to the Mediterranean with Pete Dirkx and Pappy Munson. Pete Dirkx was an enlisted man who had made ensign. Because we were still so short of officers they sent him out with Pappy Munson, who was probably the oldest E-9 in the Navy at the time, as his AOIC [assistant officer in charge]. I remember an interesting thing while we were parachuting in Naples, Italy. Pappy Munson wanted to bring one of the other chiefs on board the plane to watch the parachute jump. So Pappy's got on his camel's-hair overcoat—he's in civvies—and is hanging out the door watching the jump, and I'm trying to keep him back so he won't fall out of the airplane. He was about fifty-five years old then.

We also spent some time with the CDs, the British Clearance Divers, in Malta. That was at the time when they [the British] were being thrown out of Malta, and we had to watch our p's and q's there. We found a German torpedo underneath one of the ships in Valletta Harbor while we were doing a practice bottom-search swim, and the British CDs wanted the torpedo. So we hooked on to it and towed it. The officer in charge had to go by the ship to drop off some messages, so I dropped him off while underway and kept making circles while we were towing the torpedo. If I had stopped the boat, the fish would have nosed into the bottom, making a need for another dive or maybe a large explosion.

I circled around and picked the officer up again. We then went over to the harbor where the CDs were located. They dragged the torpedo up on the bank and got their torches out and were going to cut it open to get all the brass and copper out of it to sell. Well, that's where I got everybody and told them to leave. It didn't blow up. Later we took the 750-pound warhead out to sea and detonated it.

After that, I made warrant officer in 1969. I had a good skipper at the time, Fred Kochey. When I put on warrant officer, I asked him, "Don't I need to go to the other coast?" And he says, "No, you don't want to do that. You'll probably end up getting yourself killed. Even though it's going to be harder for you to go from the enlisted to the officer ranks staying here. There's a shortage of transfer funds right now, and I can make you stay here." So I said, "Well, I'll take your advice," so they shipped me right from UDT 21 over to SEAL Team TWO when I made warrant.

When I arrived at the Team, I became the Ordnance Officer, a job that I really enjoyed. At that time we had about 180 people, and we had about twelve hundred weapons to keep track of. Every time that they would find any kind of weapon in downtown Norfolk, the FBI or somebody would show up at my door wanting to inventory our weapons. They were getting so concerned about it that we finally had to put out the word to the platoons that anybody who had brought back weapons from Vietnam, if they'd just bring them in to Ordnance, they could turn them in with no questions asked. I'd just pick up the extra weapons on inventory as part of our weapons cache. So every day I'd come in and slide my feet, slide up to my desk, and crunch! What the hell was that? And I'd look down and see an AK-47, small mortars, you name it. Everybody was bringing guns in to get them picked up on the inventory. We had over sixty AKs that nobody could trace, which is nothing compared to what they've got today.

Once you were in a SEAL Team, you knew you were going to Vietnam. We only had so many people available, and each platoon had a rotation schedule. When you joined a Team, you started training with a platoon, as a group, to go to Vietnam.

Throughout the war we had SEAL Team ONE on the West Coast and SEAL Team TWO in the east. At their highest manning, Team ONE had maybe 290 men, and we were up around 190 or 200. Our Team had Det Alfa, two platoons, in-country in Nam, while Team ONE had Det Golf, four platoons. When we deployed, we went as a group for a six-month tour. It wasn't like a Marine group where one guy replaced a guy that got hurt or whatever. Maybe people would be replaced, but at the end of the six months we came out as a group.

You took all of your own weapons and equipment in-country with the platoon. Other services would send men to Vietnam and, once they arrived in-country, they would draw their weapons and fight the war. When the men came back out, they'd leave their weapon and come home. But SEAL platoons each had their own weapons assigned.

When we got our orders for Nam, our only reaction was that we'd been training all our lives, it seemed like, and now we were going to get to go and use it. Everybody wanted to go and try themselves. I'm not saying it was a good war, but it was the only one we had. And it was our job.

I arrived in Vietnam in April 1969, and we left in October that same year. I was the assistant platoon commander of Sixth Platoon, which meant I had one of the squads. The platoon commander, Louis Boink, had already had a tour in Vietnam. He knew what he wanted to accomplish, and he was into the hierarchy side of things and knew how to get support for what we needed to do. Boink ran what was probably one of the best operations over there, the POW op where they went in and freed eighteen POWs, using Canberra bombers and naval gunfire to support them. That was a good op.

We landed in Tan Son Nhut and stayed the first night with the platoon that was in Nha Be. They had a nice concrete barracks with tin roofs and all. My first reaction was, "This is how we fight a war?"

We shipped out and went on to Song Ong Doc, where we were living on a barge. At night, you'd see groups of rats swimming out from shore in a column maybe twenty feet long, trying to reach the barge and climb up to get into the potatoes that were stacked amidships. When we didn't have operations, the guys would get M16s with silencers on them and sit out on deck shooting the rats. As long as they used the silencers the officers didn't know what they were doing.

Louis Boink wanted to get us ashore up in Ca Mau where we could operate with more Vietnamese troops and get more operations. We were having trouble getting things to do while we were stuck down there on the point. So he finally got us moved to Ca Mau. Soon after we moved, someone called in for gunfire support from the USCG USS HAMILTON, which was offshore to provide us with fire support. The HAMILTON had the barge locked in on their fire control computer. They fired off eight rounds real quick, right into the barge. It killed one and wounded six men. The rounds hit right at the end of the barge where our quarters had been, but luckily we'd left the day before.

Once we got up to Ca Mau, Lou Boink kept one squad, and I took a squad seventeen klicks south to a little town called Hai Yen. Now the story goes that Father Hoa [pronounced "Wa"], who was a Chinese Catholic priest, had left China with Chiang Kai-shek. Father Hoa went to

South Vietnam when Chiang went to Taiwan and had built up this town of Hai Yen and put a minefield around it.

After he had finished building the town, Hoa knew that all the people who had helped him build it and put the mines in were Viet Cong. So he waited outside of town when they were coming out to be paid. According to the story, Father Hoa then lifted up his black robes, where he had hidden an M3 submachine gun, and killed all the VC. A good priest. And Father Hoa effectively ran the town of Hai Yen.

Anyway, that's how the story went, but we didn't know anything about it when we first arrived. The problem was that for the first four months we were in Hai Yen we operated without an interpreter. It got exciting. One night, we had a mortar attack, and the Vietnamese perimeter guard ran the attackers off. The next day they went searching and found some of the mortars. These were like sewer pipe tubes, corrugated metal tubes with a wooden block on the bottom and a nail stuck into it for a firing pin, a one-time-use mortar. The VC left them laying about with the mortar shells in them. The Vietnamese weren't sure if they were booby-trapped or not, so they didn't want to move them.

The Vietnamese came to us, since the guy that normally blew up things like that for them wasn't there. Without an interpreter, they got the message across that they wanted us to go blow these abandoned weapons up for them. So myself and Duke Leonard made up some explosive charges and some short fuses, shorter than I should have made. A Vietnamese paddled us out to this rice dike where there were some trees and these three mortars, one on the ground and two hanging from the trees. We decided we didn't need to move them, we'd just blow them in place, right in the trees. After we placed the charges, I told this guy with the sampan to get the hell out of there, we'd just run out. But the Vietnamese wouldn't leave. We shoved the sampan off and told him to go, and he paddled back, he just wouldn't leave.

Finally I screamed at him and he got the idea and left.

We lit the fuses, which were short, and took off running through the shallow water of the paddy. Running along, I said, "We better not run any further. Let's dive behind this little dike and wait for this thing to go."

So we dived down behind the dike. Have you ever been looking past something, like a bush, and then you pull your focus back and concentrate on the bush? Well, this bush had three little things sticking out of it, the firing mechanisms for mines. We'd been running through the minefield and didn't know it. That was why the guy in the sampan didn't want to leave us out there. But we didn't have an interpreter, so the message never got across.

"Duke," I said, "look at this!" As we started looking around, we noticed that every bush around us had these things sticking out of them. That's when I realized that we were in the minefield. We called the guy in the sampan back over, and he paddled across and picked us up. The charges we had planted failed to fire. But that was just as well—the fuses had been too short and we were still too close. Finally we patted the guy on the back and said, "Now we know what you were trying to tell us." Going back and getting some longer fuses, we waited a full thirty minutes to make sure the charges were safe. Then we went back and blew up the mortars. That was an interesting minefield.

Hai Yen was so far south that we only had one bar in our town. There was no electricity, and they brought ice up the river wrapped in rice husks. The shower we had was four fifty-five gallon drums on top of a building that you had to go up and fill with water if it hadn't rained. When the Army couldn't get us food, we'd take our outboard motor and go out to an LST that was off the coast. We'd trade sea stories with them, grab a hot shower, and get some food to take back ashore.

Once I was going to take some time for R&R and go to Bangkok and visit my wife's brother. But when I got up to Nha Be, I found out that I couldn't get on the airplane, I didn't have enough time in-country. So I stayed with the other platoon in those nice concrete barracks where we had spent our first night in Vietnam.

One time, when some of the troops didn't have anything to do, Eddie Leasure went out one day with what
we called the Ruff Puffs, the regular Vietnamese troops,
to provide them with air support if they needed it. They
were riding down the river in a Mike boat that had a
helicopter deck on top of it with all the troops underneath.
While Eddie was standing on the helo deck, somebody
fired a B-40 rocket into the boat. The round went in between the side of the boat and the helo deck before it
detonated, so that all the shrapnel hit the troops inside.
But Eddie, standing out in the open on the overhead,
wasn't touched. There were enough uninjured troops left
to continue the operation, so they completed the op.

When the op was over, Eddie said he wasn't going to
ride the boat back, he'd fly back instead. So he got into
the helicopter. As the bird was taking off, the door gunner
accidentally discharged his weapon. The pilot got excited
and thought it was incoming fire. Dipping the bird down
low, the pilot tried to fly out fast. A skid caught on a
barbed-wire fence and flipped the helicopter into an old
French minefield. Nobody was hurt, so they all got out of
the minefield and got on another helicopter.

When Eddie finally got back to Ca Mau, he walked
into the little bar that was set up there and said, "This is
the end. I'm not going out with those guys anymore." He
sat down, and the chair collapsed, dumping Eddie on his
ass.

Another time, we were trying to take a province tax
collector. We went out about midnight, paddled about fifteen klicks to get to this area, and set up an ambush where
we thought he would come through. The target didn't
show up the next morning, so we got into a relaxed mode.
It was cold. You can't believe this, but as hot as it was
over there, if you were wet all night, then you were cold
when morning hit.

So we set three guys up on the trail and the rest of us
went into this one little hooch to take a nap. We were
going to relieve each other so everyone could get some
rest. Just then the VC we had been waiting for came walk-

ing down the trail. Duke Leonard jumped out in front of them with his Stoner. The VC wouldn't stop, so Duke opened fire. He killed the tax collector and we captured the man's assistant.

When we were getting ready to extract—this is again before we had an interpreter—we headed back to the boats. The boats that we had paddled fifteen klicks through the darkness with now had motors on the back of them! In the dark we had never noticed the motors. Looked like a yacht club, with these Vietnamese we had left with the sampans just sitting there. We were all wondering what the hell was going on.

Just as we got into the boats to leave, an ambush opened up. The VC had been expecting us to go the other way, and they were all behind us. It sounded like a 20mm being fired at us, but after we got back and listened to other weapons again, I think it was a BAR the VC had captured.

I was the last one getting into a sampan—everybody else was in front of me. "That's the PBRs coming to save us!" I said "There's nobody shooting at us." And then the water started splashing into my face and I did a real quick flip out of that narrow sampan and into the water. Everybody thought I was shot. I wasn't, and I stood up in the water and started returning fire.

Then one of the Vietnamese was hit. Now whenever I called for a medevac extraction of a wounded man, I'd never tell the helicopters whether it was a Vietnamese or an American who was hit. Sometimes the pilots wouldn't come in to pick up a wounded native. The Vietnamese liked this, saw that we cared about them and would get them taken care of. We carried serum albumin with us as part of our first-aid gear. It's a blood expander, to help fill up your system and prevent shock again when you've lost blood. Duke Leonard and John Porter administered serum albumin to the wounded Vietnamese while we were waiting for the medevac.

A Seawolf came in and hovered right in the middle of this firefight and took our Vietnamese. Duke and John stood up in the boat and handed him up to the helicopter.

He'd had one bullet go all the way through his chest, but they got him back and saved his life. Later he recovered and came back to work for us after about six weeks had passed.

But for those of us still in the sampans, the situation was tight. We still had ten klicks to get home. Everyone was shooting, until I said, "Everybody cease fire! Cease fire! How many bullets have we got left?" With ten klicks to go we had only seventy-five rounds left between us. We were real careful going back.

We did do one thing that almost got us in trouble. We went on an op, and the guy we were after turned out not to be around. His wife and kid were there, so we took them. I left a note telling him that we were the men with the green faces, and where he could find us and his family. We took the gal back, but nobody showed up. I couldn't just keep this woman at the hooch where we were, so when we found out that this VC we were after had a brother who was a major in the Vietnamese Army, we turned her over to him. That way her brother-in-law could hang on to her until the husband surrendered.

Later on, we found out that the woman's VC husband had a girlfriend and that he'd been wanting to get rid of his wife anyway. Of course, he never came to get his wife and kid. Then the higher-ups got on me for capturing and holding a woman hostage.

The last two months we were there we finally got an interpreter. I can't remember his name now, but he had a big scar on his face that he was very sensitive about. He always tried to talk to you with the scar turned away. I finally asked him how he got it. He said he went to the dentist to have his wisdom tooth pulled, and the guy decided it was easier to cut his jaw open and pull it out than to go in like a normal dentist.

On one operation we went on, we were supposed to go after this VC "rest area." That was what we called hospitals, because you couldn't attack a hospital. We had three Americans and eight Vietnamese on the op traveling in three sampans. As we went into this canal, we were stopped by an armed Viet Cong. The VC wanted to know who we were, and I just stayed quiet and kept my head down. I had my interpreter then, so there I sat, right next to the interpreter, as he explained that we were Viet Cong troops who were going north to be resupplied. The VC accepted our story and we traveled on.

So we continued paddling upstream, and turned up this one canal. I was in the middle sampan with one boat in front of me and the other trailing. It was so dark that when we made the turn to go down the canal, the last sampan missed the turn and continued traveling straight on. We were almost to the objective before we realized the sampan behind us wasn't behind us anymore. Now we were missing one American with a Stoner along with two Vietnamese, who were ex–Viet Cong. I quickly told the others that we were canceling the op.

We went back out the way we had come and found the VC who had stopped us still waiting at his post, so we captured him. As we were starting out again, my interpreter somehow let our prisoner get away. The bad guys had set up an ambush for us, but we avoided it by cutting across a big dike carrying the sampans instead of paddling out the way we'd come in. We waited outside the VC area, and I called back on the radio and gave them code to tell them we had some trouble. But I couldn't tell them what the trouble was because I didn't want anybody who understood English to know that we'd lost a guy. We waited in the sampans until about ten o'clock the next morning. Here came this civilian water taxi moving downstream, and there was old John Porter, my missing SEAL, along with the other two men who had been with him. That was the most relieved I think I've ever been.

Lou Boink and I went to the provincial police chief's house in Ca Mau one night for dinner. We only carried one pistol between us for protection. We both got so drunk that night that on the walk back to our quarters, we tripped and the weapon fell into the mud. So we both crouched down in the mud feeling about and trying to find this pistol. If anybody had wanted to shoot us, they would have had us.

We worked with the Army a great deal. They had control, furnished all the provincial governors, so to speak, the district and province chiefs. The Army was also providing us direct support, as in places to live, food, that sort of thing. They were glad to have us operating in their area. The Army had more constraints on them in how they could operate and engage the enemy. The constraints were supposed to be on us as well, but we were a loose-knit organization and could get away with ignoring the details a lot more than a more regular unit. Towards the end of the war, the rules of engagement said that you couldn't fire on anybody unless they were firing on you. So there was a lot of gunfire going on by the radio. "They're firing at me, and we're shooting back!" That sort of thing.

An Army group with some Kit Carson scouts came into our operational area one time and said, "We have our own op here, and you can't operate." So we just shut down and let everybody go on liberty for a week, picking up later on where we had left off. That's the way it worked.

One problem was that the Army helo people would not support us at night. They wouldn't fly at night to come and help us. The Seawolf units, which were Navy helos, would come in and get us or provide air support whenever we asked. They did a hell of a job for us; those Seawolves were just top-notch. They had all the old, used helicopters, whatever the Army threw away. Last year's model, that's what the Navy had. So the Army got the new, powerful engines, and we got what was left over. On one occasion—I wasn't on this particular op but Jim Watson was leading it—they had to strip the guns off a Seawolf in order to make the ship light enough to pull everybody out of a bad situation. I've been in some of the helos where the pilot said, "All right, everybody hold on. I may not be able to control the torque with all this weight in it. So if it starts spinning I want you to all fall out together."

It was really enjoyable when you'd be out on an operation and the Black Pony Broncos would come over, the OV-10s. They were fixed-wing aircraft run by the Navy to supplement the Seawolves. Heavily armed with 2.75- and 5-inch rockets along with machine guns and a minigun pod, the Black Ponies were nice to have around. "Good morning, sir," the pilots would say over the radio. "Is there anything we can do for you today, sir?" Real gentlemen, you know?

"Well, if you could go and kill those guys over there, that would certainly help."

"Where was that, sir? How can we identify them?"

"Well, you can identify me by this." And one of us would pop a colored smoke grenade. "Tell me what color you see. Yeah, that's me. All right, anybody else you see, you pop 'em."

The differences between the services worked this way. The Air Force, before they could do anything, they had to have a regulation saying they could do it. The Navy would write a regulation telling us what we couldn't do, so we could do everything else. It made you think on your feet, a lot more so than some of the people in the other services ever had a chance to.

For the most part in Vietnam we had no one looking over our shoulders. Oh, in some cases if you were up around Nha Be where the staff was and they could get hold of you, maybe you'd get some specific operations. But the tour that I made in 1970 in the Ca Mau area, nobody gave us any direction at all. We'd gather our own intelligence and do the job. And when the op was over we came out.

Back in California, China Lake had a special section where they would build different weapons for us. One of the things they made for the SEALs was a pump-action 40mm grenade launcher. The weapon was a repeater that would fire four grenades. A good operator could get all four grenades in the air before the first one hit. The pump-action was made of aluminum, so it was very light to carry for its size. Every unit of SEALs would carry some M79s. The M79 40mm grenade launcher was a good weapon, much like a big single-shot shotgun.

Later during the war, we were issued an experimental weapon, the XM-148 40mm grenade launcher, which you could mount under the barrel of a CAR-15 or M16. The XM-148 fired the same ammunition as the M79, but you had the firepower of the M16 right there in your hand after you used the 40mm. A later weapon, the XM-203, was an improved version of the XM-148 and was adopted as the M203 for standard issue to all the services.

But the four-shot grenade launcher was a good squad weapon, and only the SEALs had it. You have to appreciate how the M79 operates in order to understand what a great weapon it was. The 40mm grenades were large, fat cartridges, about the size of an orange juice can. Each round would lob a high-explosive grenade out to about four hundred meters, without kicking the operator on his can with the recoil. There were all sorts of ammunition for the 40mm, high-explosive fragmentation rounds, canister rounds like large shotgun shells, and some other rounds even more exotic.

Have you ever seen how you make Jiffy-pop popcorn? You start out with the flat pan and it just expands—the gas never escapes. They made us an M79 round like that, the XM-463 flashless/smokeless round. When the powder went off, the gas remained in the aluminum shell and just popped out the little green-and-black egg [grenade] downrange. It had no noise except for the thump, and usually no flash coming out of the barrel. So you could have bad guys down in an area, and you could be hidden where they couldn't see you. With the pump-action and the flashless/smokeless round you could fire four rounds on the other side of them, and they'll run towards you because they don't know where the fire came from.

I think the average SEAL kills people from about four feet away, so we didn't really have to do a lot of marksmanship training.

I wouldn't single out anyone I knew as an "operator" or a "hunter"—they all were. We didn't have anybody who would sneak out nights when we weren't operating to cut people's ears off or anything like that. We had enough excitement without that sort of thing.

We captured a doctor there who had been to medical school for three weeks. He wanted to quit because he didn't like the sight of blood. He was going to turn Hoi Chanh, tell us where the medical school was and so on.

So we went in and got him out, and then we told him we'd go back and get his family. But he said no, somebody had to stay and tend the rice field.

I hated to think that I was going to be shot by some guy who hadn't had any training. I mean, if the VC would use a doctor who had only been to school for three weeks, how much training would they give a soldier?

There were VC over there who were shooting carbine-type bolt-action weapons, but when they couldn't get the right Chicom ammunition, they were using M60 machine gun rounds. The cartridges the carbines used had large rims. The M60 ammunition had the same size bullet, but the casings didn't have the large rim. The VC made do. They would use the American ammunition and carry a long rod, like a musket ramrod. Using the rod, they would knock out the fired shell and put another one in by hand so they could shoot again.

We also found a jungle factory over there where they were taking minigun barrels and machining them to accept bolts so they could use them as weapons. They were ingenious, but still, here I'd been trained to do all this fancy killing, and somebody who doesn't know what the heck he's doing is going to shoot me.

After the war there weren't any slots for warrant officers in the SEALs. I'd been to EOD school already, so I became an EOD warrant and left the Teams. I retired in 1982 with the rank of lieutenant. I still do some bomb disposal work today, but don't tell my insurance company. Last year I was in Laos working for an oil company, making sure it was safe. After the Gulf War was finished, I was over in Kuwait and Saudi Arabia for a while. I also teach an OSHA class for people who handle hazardous chemicals.

We're always seeing pictures, "Send money for these poor kids that are running around with no diapers on and are living in houses with no floors." Well, it's cooler to live in a house with a dirt floor, and if you've got diapers, that's something you've got to wash, and you don't have washing machines, and you don't have electricity, so what do you need diapers for? All they [the Vietnamese] really wanted was to be left alone, to tend their rice fields or whatever.

It was a terrible war. Our Team lost nineteen men in Nam, I think, and the West Coast Team lost about twenty-eight. We lost a few of our guys to some dumb things, like our own ambushes. One guy got the wrong blood type in a transfusion. But I think man for man we did a good job.

Even completing UDTR was not a free pass into the SEAL Teams. First an "apprenticeship" had to be served by would-be SEALs in the UDTs. Normally, only after a man had served well in the UDTs with at least one deployment in his record would his request for the SEALs even be considered.

And time in the UDTs was not an easy ride. Deployments went on constantly. Frogmen could find themselves on their way to the Mediterranean, the Philippines, Europe, South America, the Arctic, and even the Antarctic. Several UDT platoons were deployed to Vietnam as well. The primary mission of the UDTs was to scout beaches, charting them and declaring them clear for amphibious forces to use. In Vietnam, the clearing of muddy rivers and canals was added to the UDTs' assignments as well as the recovery of lost equipment or enemy materials in the water.

Important missions were also performed by the UDT in the humanitarian support of locals. Among all of the tasks performed by the UDT and the SEALs, probably the most publicly spectacular was the recovery of all the returning manned space capsules. Anytime a capsule splashed down, be it Mercury, Gemini, or Apollo, the first people to greet it after its return to Earth were the men of the UDT and SEALs. Jumping into the water from hovering aircraft, Navy Frogmen would quickly attach flotation equipment to the capsule proper and assist the astronauts for recovery. Other duties included assisting in the training of astronauts, as a weightless environment could be simulated underwater.

The long tour of duty for the UDT, from the beaches of World War Two to the splashdowns of the lunar missions, finally came to an end in 1983—though it wasn't really an ending, more of a final evolution. On May 1, 1983, UDTs 11 and 21 were decommissioned and became, respectively, SEAL Teams FIVE and FOUR. UDTs 12 and 22 were also decommissioned and became SEAL Delivery Vehicle Teams (SDVT) ONE and TWO.

★ ★ ★

THIRD CLASS ELECTRICIAN'S MATE

DICK POULIOT

USN (RET.)

Not all members of the Teams made their reputations in the rice paddies and canals of Vietnam. Many other duties had to be performed by the SEALs and UDT besides combat. With his contribution to NASA and the space program, Dick Pouliot stands out as an example of the Special Warfare operator excelling at those other duties.

I grew up in the small town of Franklin, New Hampshire, in a Catholic neighborhood. I grew up in the sixties, and as far as I was concerned it was America's playground. I had a lot of athletic success. I made All-State in football in my sophomore year in high school.

Then I had a compound fracture in my femur from a ski accident. Actually, I went off a ski jump in a toboggan. They nearly amputated my leg. I was told I wouldn't walk normally again. Then I started walking and they said, "Well, you'll never run." When I started running they said, "Well, you'll never play ball."

Thinking back, that gave me the mind-set I needed to get through SEAL training. The easiest way to get me to do something, and a lot of people haven't figured it out, is to tell me I can't do it.

When I broke my leg I had to focus all my ambitions in a different way. I would have gone to Holy Cross and played football. That's where my life was focused. Then when I broke my leg I had to show people, at least in my mind, that I could do it.

I had a ski instructor who had been a Frogman. His name is gone; it was just a casual meeting. He told me stories that captured my imagination, I had to find out for myself what it was really like. I wish I could find this guy. He changed my life. When I couldn't play football in college, that was the only thing I wanted to be, a Navy Frogman.

I went into the Navy specifically to go into the Teams. No ifs, ands, or buts. I enlisted after the holidays in 1965. I was on a plane for the first time on January 5th, flying to Chicago for boot camp. After boot camp I went to an A school and was taught to be an Electrician's Mate. After A school I took the exam for UDT training. I was the highest scorer, and when I graduated from A school they gave me orders to training.

I got off the plane on August 3rd here in Norfolk and thought I was going to have to swim through the air. I'd never, never experienced such heat and humidity. That was Sunday evening. When I got off the plane, I had never been anyplace by myself. This was my first time in my life. I called my mother. I said, "Mom, I'm in Norfolk. I have no idea where to go."

"What did you call me for?" she said. "Get in a cab."

So I did. I got in a cab and said, "I need to go to UDT." I didn't say training. He took me to the Team area. Well, I have never been so embarrassed in all my life.

There I was, a young nineteen-year-old carrying his seabag up to the Team area and here are these guys who have already been through all this training. That's when it started.

Luckily the cabbie waited for me and took my wounded tail from the Teams to training. I didn't tell anybody that I had done that for ten, twenty years. I got there at ten minutes to midnight. I would have been AWOL at midnight.

I didn't start training on the best foot. I was two weeks late. I didn't know I was two weeks late. There was a preconditioning period and a trainee would just get in and go.

My prime motivation, then as it is now, all hinges on that compound fracture. Now my primary motivation is my wife, but I didn't know her then. I met her here.

I was a country bumpkin. I thought that with the success that I'd had, I could do anything.

After I broke my leg I made it back to varsity basketball. The doctors would not allow me to play football my senior year, although I broke my leg in the winter of my sophomore year after basketball. I had a steel pin inserted through the hip into the bone marrow. They pulled that pin out because they were afraid if I bent it, then I'd be in serious trouble. But I played basketball my senior year in high school, and went on to play baseball and track that summer.

And then I worked in a woolen mill in New England, which gave me additional motivation. I didn't have a scholarship; there was no way in hell I was going to go to school and my family didn't have the economic background. I was a success because I had graduated from high school. Neither of my parents did. They were Canadian immigrants who came down in the thirties to get jobs in the woolen mills.

All those things combined was the motivation that got me into the situation to begin with. I think what my father taught me was to put myself into a situation where I would have to perform. That's why I played sports. And that's why I joined the Navy and that's why I wanted to be a Frogman. It would put me in a situation where I would be forced to perform.

When I got to training there were fifty, sixty people just like me. I didn't know these people existed. But we all had very similar stories.

Most of us in the training class were in the eighteen-to-twenty-five-year age group. I was at the bottom, being nineteen. Here on the East Coast the trainees were mostly from the Northeast.

So I had a lot in common with these people. I had scored touchdowns, I had scored a whole bunch of points in basketball. I was talking to these guys and they all had done that, too. Right away I had friends that it seemed like I had known my whole life. I felt comfortable.

It was easy to compete with these people, because if I lost or if I won it wasn't the end of the world. Being an athlete I think prepares one for life, 'cause you don't win all the time. Going through life, if you don't know how to lose, it could affect your psyche.

In training, we were molded. The one big saying in training was "It pays to be a winner." We had a mind-set and here I am in this exceptional group of people. We had maybe two dozen officers who had already been to college. I had an All-American swimmer in my class. Four or five of the officers had been on their swim teams in college.

I grew up in New Hampshire. There were about three or four months in the year when I could swim. I had never swum in a pool until I got here. There weren't any indoor pools in New Hampshire then.

I had swum in races with the recreation league and I did well, but that was just sheer energy. It wasn't that I was coached or had techniques. I couldn't turn in the pool. I'd just touch it and kick off and go the other way. When we had races we'd swim in the lake. So we just swam to the end and whoever got there first won.

When I got to the Teams, well, not to the Teams but in training, it didn't take me long to figure out there were six or seven people in this class of 150-something that there was no way in hell I was going to beat them to the end of the pool. The first swims we had in the pool—150 men dive in and the first one out at the other end is finished. He can go sit in the sun or shade, wherever. Everybody else has to swim and win to get out.

Not only did a guy have to get across the water fast, he had to make sure that nobody knocked him in the head or kicked him in the face. It's like piranha on top of the water.

So, my plan was, the first ten races or so I kind of sat back, kind of stayed behind. The second week in training one of the instructors was watching me and caught me sandbagging. My overall plan, and I talked to my bunk-mates in the barracks about this, was if they didn't know our names then they couldn't pick on us. Be low-key, be in the middle. Never be first, never be last, be in the middle group. Well, that was blown two weeks into training because the instructor caught me sandbagging.

I think the first day we had maybe 150, 160 people. I don't know the exact number. And we lost, oh, it was tremendous, two in the morning, two in the afternoon. So by the end of the first week we were down to maybe 140. And the second week we were maybe down to 120.

And here this instructor was watching me and I'd be the tenth man to win in a swim and he'd never seen me up front in the other nine races. He caught me. He was a French Canadian from upstate New York by the name of Blais, Tom Blais. I knew I was in trouble when he grabbed me and he looked me in the eyes and he pronounced my name right.

"Well, Mr. Pouliot."

Oh, no! And he had me duckwalk from the swimming pool back to the barracks, which was about maybe half a mile. I was his project. He was going to drum me out.

I lost my friends. My buddies didn't want to be seen hanging around with me because I was singled out. But the longer I stayed, I think I gained Blais's respect. He was after me, but there was nothing he could do that was going to change me. I knew he really couldn't hurt me. He wasn't going to kill me. As long as I had food to eat and I could sleep every once in a while I was going to do it. This is what I wanted to do. I told him later that what he did that early in training really was best for me because it made me operate on a higher level.

I told him and he growled, "I already know all about that bullshit." It wasn't unique to me. I thought it was.

Training, for me, was like trying out for the football team. I knew there were so many spaces and I knew that I was good enough and all I had to do was show them that I could perform. With me, just getting on a football team wasn't good enough. I had to play. One of the biggest challenges in my life was not only making the football team as a freshman, but starting the first game of the year. And I did it. I just took that experience and played it into the early part of training.

In that business a person becomes a veteran quickly. It's so hard and so all-consuming that if he doesn't absorb everything he's just going by the wayside. It's funny, I haven't thought about training in a long long time. The more that we absorbed, the easier it was. It wasn't that hard physically, because we were all at the same level. There were dozens of guys who could swim faster and there were dozens of guys who could run faster; maybe there were dozens of guys who could do more PT. But put them all together, and it's all pretty even. It's a mind-set. I was an average size and I'm six feet and two hundred pounds, I was maybe fifteen pounds lighter then, 185. But there were guys smaller and guys a lot bigger. I always thought, and I still think, that smaller people have an advantage.

I know what motivated me, and I know how I used that. During Hell Week we wore a red helmet liner, and to stop it all, all a guy had to do was take the helmet liner off. Nobody would have thought any different of him. But that became the hardest thing to even think about.

And I could never understand why anybody would quit. It never crossed my mind. I would have to be seriously hurt to quit.

The first beach run I ever went on, they got us all down to the beach and we had boondockers on, which were Navy-issue boots. We were in fatigues, long pants, long-sleeved shirts. They put us in the back of stake trucks, which are big cattlelike trucks. There were four trucks with forty or fifty of us in each truck. If one guy fell down they'd all fall down. They drove us down to the beach and we all piled out and the instructor said, "Okay, line up here." And we all lined up. "Take off your jacket, fold it up, and put it down. And form up on the beach."

Our first beach run, this was maybe ten o'clock in the morning, was three minutes in soft sand and then two minutes in hard sand and then back. It was maybe a twenty-minute evolution, so it was five times switching.

I'd never seen a beach before. I grew up in New Hampshire where the beach was maybe eight feet across and then it was all grass. So we ran in the soft sand and then we got out on the hard sand, and one guy dove in the water. Splash!

The instructors yelled, "Grrrr, don't do it again."

He got back in formation. That gave us a longer break too, because they yelled at this guy. So we got a three-minute break. We got back into the soft sand and then as soon as we came out into the hard sand, this guy ran into the water again. He did it three times. And then he disappeared.

I didn't see him again until that night about seven o'clock. We saw him walking down the road with his seabag on his shoulder. He was gone. That was the first guy I ever saw quit.

Twenty-three finished in my class. And I've got five guys that are friends for life. I communicate with them often.

I feel like when I go back to the reunion that I have hundreds of friends that I haven't met yet. It's that close.

Hell Week is a blur. We had five hours' sleep in five and a half days. It started at midnight on Sunday and ended at five o'clock on Friday. The instructors came into the barracks and woke us all up at midnight. Well, there was nobody asleep. Who in the hell can sleep when we've got Hell Week hanging over our heads? We had no idea what it was.

What I remember about Hell Week was constantly moving. I remember a lot of pain, confusion, and lack of sleep. We did the Around the World and I saw parts of Virginia Beach I haven't seen since. We paddled an IBL [Inflatable Boat, Large], I swear it was eighteen hours. We urinated on our hands to get warm. This was the latter part of October.

I've done some crazy, crazy things. We thought we were hiding from the instructors and we tried to build fires. It was windy—there was a northeaster blowing. We started on Laskin Road, which is thirteen miles from Little

Creek, and it took me five or six years to find that spot again because it was such a secluded area.

We had four or five boat crews, and a boat crew was basically seven people. So we had thirty-five people who started.

I did things in Hell Week I didn't know I was capable of doing. We ran a marathon. The body still functions. And if a guy had to move his bowels in a marathon, the poor guy would have to drop his pants and everybody else would jog around him till he was finished. You dropped your inhibitions or you dropped out of training.

And we were acting as a group. By this time we realized that we were going to be going on missions and we were going to be doing things where we absolutely had to trust who's on either side of us. We were starting to gain that trust.

After I graduated from training I went to UDT 22. I still had no idea what to expect, but the first thing I did was report in. That was the quarterdeck where I had gone on my first day of training, so I walked across the quarterdeck. It was one of the high points of my life because I belonged. It was so satisfying to be there.

After training we still had to go to underwater swim school and jump school before getting assigned to a platoon. I was at the top of the world. I got to a platoon and I'm a new guy.

Right down to the bottom again. It was like going from grammar school to high school when I was a freshman. And I thought I had all these major abilities to contribute and here I was back on the bottom. Lower than whale shit again.

My first deployment took us to the Caribbean for three months. It was fantastic. I was in a platoon and I'd proved myself and I'd carried the bag, done all the freshman initiation again. I was almost on a level with everybody else, but I wasn't really there until there were other new guys. It's a step up the ladder.

But being in the teams was a dream come true. It was everything I thought it would be. We went to Cuba, we went to Guantanamo Bay, and we did a lot of reconnaissance of the beaches.

That was the first time I was shot at. Cuban sentries were shooting at us as we were out on the water. Having somebody shoot at me—I think I lived more during those few minutes, the intensity of it, than any other time in my life.

There was a hurricane. We were down there, I think it was August through December, and we were caught in a hurricane. We were on an APD [high-speed transport], which is a ship smaller than a destroyer. I think they're old destroyer escorts.

The ship went to sea. We tried to get around the outside of the hurricane. Fortunately I never got seasick. But we couldn't walk around on this ship without our hands on the bulkheads. The captain was very gracious and he allowed everybody a few minutes on the bridge to look outside, because all the hatches were closed. The bow of the ship would disappear under the waves.

We ran around for two or three days and the hurricane went by. The captain got a radio message that a village on Hispaniola was flattened. They hadn't had any medical aid and nobody'd been able to get to them. They'd lost their dock and a helicopter wasn't available. They asked if we could swim supplies ashore.

Well, I thought this was great. They lowered our boat loaded up with everything the ship could do without. We didn't have a doctor, we carried a corpsman with us all the time, and we took one of the ship's corpsmen and put him in our boat and we carried all the gear ashore.

I saw things I never dreamed could happen to people. Third World poverty, and the hurricane had flattened their homes and they didn't have anything to eat and no medicine. There were no public facilities. It was terrible.

One old lady, her whole head was bandaged. They had taken horse manure, put it on her face, and put on palm leaves and then wrapped her up. We had to soak the bandages off. Her face was gone from her upper lip to her eyes. A piece of metal had caught her and ripped her apart.

We carried a couple of pregnant women into the aid station, and we stayed there nearly two full days. From there, we went back to Cuba and did the very same thing we did the first time. We were looking for explosive devices that had been placed there.

We came back to the States for the holidays. I had met my future wife and she was going to college in Georgia. I drove her down to Georgia for spring semester and I took the month of January off. I hadn't had any leave up until that time, though I had been in the Navy for two years.

It was decided while I was gone that I was going to be the parachute rigger for the platoon. So when I came back they sent me to Army parachute rigger school. As it turned out, that changed my whole career.

I loved it. My mother was really happy. When I told her that I was going to be a parachute rigger she said, "Oh, my God, that's so great, now you won't be swimming anymore."

And I said, "Well, Mom, actually we're going to be parachuting into the water. We jump out with our tanks and the parachute . . ."

And she said, "You're going to be doing this for other people?"

And I said, "Yes, yes, that's what it's all about now."

So I spent the three months in Fort Lee, Virginia, which is just south of Richmond. My wife was going to school in Georgia, so every weekend I would go down and spend some time with her. My weekend trips eventually got her kicked out of school. She wasn't supposed to be away from campus, and I would stop and get a case of Michelob and a big bucket of Colonel Sanders and we'd hole up in a motel all weekend. We have been married for twenty-seven years and she says it has been a purely physical relationship. We have yet to have a meaningful relationship.

The next deployment was the first time I went off for sub training. I lost hearing in an ear in that, and that was the beginning of the end of my career in the Teams. We were in four-man SDVs [Swimmer Delivery Vehicles] coming back to the sub. I had the position where I was the aft lookout, so I couldn't see the sub.

Seeing a submarine underwater is a thrilling sight. They have the flag aft of the sail, and I'd always try to take a look at it because I wanted to see it. I wanted to remember this because I didn't know when I was going to have the opportunity to see it again.

My swim buddy was one of the platoon officers, and he kept talking—"Go down, do what you're supposed to do." Well, I was doing what I was supposed to do when the minisub hit the sail of the submarine and sank. Both my ears burst, cold water rushed in my head, and I went unconscious. The next thing I knew, I was on the surface waiting for the safety boat to come and pick me up. As a result of that I lost hearing in my right ear.

We had a physical every six months. All the hearing tests that I took, I didn't tell anybody that I couldn't hear. Being in the Teams was what I wanted to do. During hearing tests, they would always start with the left ear. When they went to the right ear I would just turn the headset around. They never caught on.

When it was time for me to reenlist I was married and we wanted to set up a household. I was debating then whether I wanted to get out because I always knew I wanted to go to college. Another reason I joined the military was for the GI Bill. We decided to wait for a year and for me to do another tour. This was what I really wanted to do—I'd have more time to mature and maybe get back into the tour as an officer.

After I lost hearing it was hard for me to dive, so I focused on my parachuting. My mother taught me how to sew, so when I went through rigger school it was very easy for me. What a rigger does is patch the chutes. I was the fastest, the biggest, the best. At this time we started experimenting with parachutes, and I would cut panels out. It wasn't against the law, but the military didn't advise us to do this. We were doing this on our own.

In the summer of '68 I was assigned to the headquarters platoon and I ran the paraloft. I was third class and here I was running the multimillion-dollar facility. It was beyond my dreams. We started up the Leap Frogs, the East Coast parachute demonstration team. I was one of the first in the East to jump a parawing. Things just snowballed with the parachuting.

Then my son was born, and that started to change my life. I was beginning to realize that my life wasn't just me, it's a wife, it's a family. Now I had these responsibilities, and I started to think, maybe I am being selfish. I was having trouble with my ears.

My time at the paraloft was up. I'd transferred to SEAL Team and I was in predeployment training to go to Vietnam. This was accelerated training, and I was as excited as I was when I went through UDT training. My wife was a basket case.

During this time there was a rumor going around that the Navy was going to supply NASA with ten divers. If someone wanted to go he put in a chit. What did I know? I put in a chit and forgot about it. Time went by.

Two weeks before my platoon was scheduled to go to Vietnam, the XO called me in his office and said, "You've been selected to go to NASA."

I said, "I don't understand."

He said, "Well, you've got a choice. You could go here or you could go to Vietnam."

This was in 1971. I'm not a political person, but at that point my ideas of why we were in Vietnam had started to change. And my wife was going to be a fruitcake if I went. I said, "Well, tell me about NASA."

He said, "You've been selected, along with nine others, and you've got to be there in three weeks. What do you want to do?"

I said, "Well, how long do I have to make up my mind?"

"Before you get out of that chair," he said.

I think that was the first time in my life I thought of other people. And I went to NASA.

That was a thrill. We trained the *Skylab* astronauts for their EVAs. We had a tank that was seventy-five feet across, forty deep, a million and a half gallons of water. It had a one-to-one mock-up of the EVA area and the telescope mount. The astronauts would come up, get in their space suits, and get in the water. We'd put lead weights all over them to be neutrally buoyant at twenty feet, and they'd go rehearse the task they were going to do in space.

And I was there. We were the divers that did this. One of the responsibilities we had was to make all the equipment neutrally buoyant at twenty feet. We had an unlimited budget to neutralize all this equipment. We were just limited to our imaginations.

I was the second-youngest one there, one of the junior people, but I had a talent they could use. I could sew. I worked in a suit lab. I worked with astronauts Pete Conran, Joe Kerwin, and all the *Skylab* crew.

When *Skylab* went up it broke. They had to send a patch up to fix it, because one of the solar arms was damaged and the heat in the capsule went up tremendously. They had to send up something to fix it.

Houston was going to manufacture a great parasol. They were going to stick it up through a hole and open it up. Our crew at the Marshall Spaceflight Center in Huntsville, Alabama, came up with what they called the "sail." They were going to pack it in a little container, with telescopic pulls, and it would just be like running a flag up a flagpole.

I was in the water. Somebody said, "Dick Pouliot, report to the so-and-so." And so, dripping wet, I went down to the main office.

They said, "We just got a call. They need you up at the headquarters."

I said, "Who needs me?"

They said, "Rocco Petrone's office." Well, Rocco Petrone was the director of the base. "His office called down and they want you up there now."

I said, "Can I change?"

And they said, "No. Now."

So I went up and they said, "We ran records through the computer and you're the only person on this installation that has a master FAA parachute rigger's license. Is that correct?"

I said, "I don't know if I'm the only one, but yes, I do have an FAA parachute rigger's license."

They said, "Well, we have this material, and we want to fold it up so it'll come out the same way every time. Can you do that?"

What they had was ripstop nylon and it was silver on one side to reflect the sunlight, and it was white absorbent material on the other side. They wanted it to come out with the silver side every time. They asked, "Can you fold it so that it'll come out the same every time?"

I played with a little sample and said, "Yeah, I don't think that'll be a problem."

They manufactured a mock-up. I was part of the group. We would go to a clean room and pack this. I directed how it should go. And then we would go to another building, put it in an altitude chamber, and run a vacuum on it. Then we would go into another building and open it up. And everything would be filmed.

They'd say, "Okay, worked that time. Do it again."

We had three days to get ready, to get it manufactured, to get the procedures. So the astronauts would come up, get in the tank, do it, and fly.

This was April '73. I would have gone down to Cape Kennedy and placed this sail in the capsule, but my daughter Robin was ready to be born and I didn't get to go. The sail worked. *Skylab* was repaired and I received the Skylab Achievement Award for my efforts. What a thrill!

I did a lot of different things because of the Teams. I don't know if I would have been involved with the sail if I hadn't gone out and gotten my FAA parachute rigger's license. I was always, and I hope still am, the kind of person who, if opportunity knocks, will go through the door.

I got out of the Navy in Huntsville. By then my ear was starting to bother me more. My knees were getting bad. Eight years was long enough for me. It was time to do something else. And I had always wanted to go to college.

I went through the business school at Old Dominion

and received an undergraduate degree in business administration. In seventeen years I was vice president of a manufacturing firm. This was '89, '90. I went back to school to get my master's degree in history. And the end result was the publication of *Shipwrecks on the Coast of Virginia and the Men of the Lifesaving Service*, with more books to come based on Team experiences.

Among the new equipment developed by the SEALs and UDTs during the 1960s were the Swimmer [now SEAL] Delivery Vehicles or SDVs. These small submarines were the "wet" type—that is, the occupants had to wear breathing rigs, as the inside of the submarine was flooded with water. These relatively simple wet subs could transport two or four swimmers, depending on model, along with a pilot and navigator, much farther and faster than men could swim. Along with traveling over long distances, an SDV could carry much more in the way of demolitions or other materials than a group of swimmers could tow with them.

Piloting and navigating SDVs became more difficult as the vehicles became more sophisticated. Specialized training had to be given to the pilots and navigators. Maintenance of the SDVs was also specific to the vehicles and took extra training. In spite of these difficulties, the SDVs proved a positive addition to the missions of SEALs and UDTs. Eventually, specialized SDV Teams were commissioned. These SDVTs support all of the SEAL Teams within their groups. SDVT ONE is on the West Coast with Special Warfare Group ONE and SDVT TWO is on the East Coast with SpecWarGrp TWO.

Not all of the SEALs' unique equipment worked out as well as the SDVs. Even some weapons that were favorites of the SEALs had their share of problems. The Stoner light machine gun required a lot of care and close attention to its maintenance, something the SEALs could do very well. But as a new weapon system, the Stoner still had some bugs in the design that required modifications for improvement. One problem of the Stoner for the SEALs was that of ammunition. Though the Stoner fired the same caliber as the M16, and that was plentiful in Vietnam, the weapon used its own unique metallic link to form ammunition belts. Though cartridges could be found, links were often in such short supply that gunners were told to pick up (police) expended links whenever possible. Evenings would be spent cleaning links and relinking fresh ammunition belts for the Stoners.

The SEALs suffered through a constant problem during the Vietnam War that was seen in varying degrees of intensity. Because of their constant security-consciousness, the men in the Teams rarely spoke to outsiders about their mission. Ignorance about what the SEALs were and especially how to employ them was common throughout the fleet Navy. This problem became even worse when the SEALs worked with other services than the Navy.

COMMANDER

TOM HAWKINS

USN (Ret.)

Tom Hawkins was Special Warfare officer involved in the development and fielding of the Swimmer Delivery Vehicles back when they were a new concept. His work helped lead to the commissioning of the new SDV Teams that operate today. As a combat officer leading SEALs in Vietnam, Tom Hawkins had the unenviable task of operating with the "support" of commanders whose knowledge of the SEALs came from rumors and stories rather than fact.

I grew up in a small town in West Virginia called Philippi. I'm one of three children and I'm an identical twin. I went to a small college in West Virginia where I graduated in 1966 and went on to the officer aviation program in Pensacola. I left the naval aviation program and went straight to UDT training in Little Creek.

I actually got my commission through the aviation officer candidate program. For a lot of reasons I was not happy with the naval aviation community. I had not known before I joined the Navy about the UDT community. In fact, while I was in OCS and just prior to getting my commission, I saw this somewhat sophomoric recruiting poster on the wall at the Navy Exchange at Pensacola. It had Frogmen in the water and guys parachuting out of an airplane, and I knew that that's what I really wanted to do.

After I got my commission I went in and resigned from the aviation program. I got a lot of flak for doing that and I had to go before a review board. They told me I was making a great mistake, that I didn't understand what UDT training was, that I would fail and be sent to sea and have a horrible Navy career and that I should stay in aviation.

So I said, "Thank you very much," and took thirty days' leave and went to Little Creek for training. And they were right. I had absolutely no idea of what I was getting into.

On the physical side of it, nobody is ever prepared entirely for what they put us through. The mental side of it is that we didn't realize what they were doing to us until after we had left training.

I had two motivating forces when I went through training, and I would never have quit no matter what they did to me. The fact this aviation captain had said "You'll never make it through training" was something that continually drove me so that I would never quit. The second thing was that all the UDT guys had this little sticker of Freddy Frog in their back window. I really wanted Freddy Frog in the back window of my car. Other than the fact that I wanted to dive and parachute, I guess that those were two things that I had in my mind all the way through training.

I was small in my training class and probably not in the best physical condition when we started training. In fact, all the time we were in Little Creek, I had shin splints so bad that it was very hard for me to make the runs and do a lot of the evolutions. Training's a faded memory by now, and I'm like everybody else—I had the hardest training class that was ever conducted on the East Coast.

We started out with about 100 people and we graduated 28. It was a difficult training class. But I have vivid recollections of getting to a point in training where I realized that the instructors weren't going to kill us. That everything they were doing was in fact constructive. Once I recognized that I just got into training.

The way my training was broken up was that we trained

in Little Creek, and the last phase of training was done in Puerto Rico. When we went to Puerto Rico and got in the water in the warmer, milder climate, my shin splints disappeared. I started doing really well in the runs, and I think my swimming improved. By the time we got to Puerto Rico I was in really good shape, and when my shin splints disappeared I felt really good. The people who were left when we went to Puerto Rico were very tight, both officer and enlisted.

Two things absolutely stand out in my mind from training. The first is we had this huge Chief by the name of John Bakelaar who was just a commanding-size guy, particularly if he stood beside me. I remember in Hell Week on the fifteen-mile run, we were out at night. I was, of course, not running with the pack. He came up behind me in a jeep and grabbed me by the seat of my pants, by my belt. He told his driver to gun the jeep. He made me run so fast beside that jeep that I caught up with the guy in front of me.

There are a lot of stories I remember. Chief Blais, who was the head instructor at the time, has told me since then that he thought I had a little chip on my shoulder. He took that chip off my shoulder one day over in the swimming pool. We used to have this evolution where we had to swim the length of the pool with a towel in each hand. They would line half the class up on one end of the pool and the other half of the class up on the other end of the pool and on the count everybody would jump in the water at the same time. They would have to pass each other in the pool, and then the first guy out on the other end got to sit down until the last two guys came up in the pool with the towels. The slogan in class was "It pays to be a winner." Of course, the last guy in the pool was the tiredest and the wettest.

I remember being at the pool one day doing the wet towel exercises. I don't remember what caused the incident, but Chief Blais got me up in front of everybody and dressed me down a little bit and then he turned around and kicked me in the swimming pool. After that I think things went pretty well.

I remember Chief Crescini, who was a Filipino and pretty well renowned in the teams. We were doing an escape and evasion op up on the beaches of Little Creek one night and it was dark. Of course, the instructors knew which way we had to go to get to the target, and they were always out there. I remember Chief Crescini sneaking out of the brush as we're trying to sneak past him. He'd take a big piece of chalk and mark it on some unlucky guy's back and say in pigeon-tongue Filipino, "You my prisoner. I caught you." And he'd say it real loud so everybody else around could hear.

I remember almost everything about Hell Week, especially being wet, cold, and dirty. We had to go down and set up tents one night after we carried the IBSs [Inflatable Boats, Small] on our heads filled full of gear. We were going to go down in this isolated area of Little Creek and bivouac for the night. We had to set up tents made out of our poncho liners, which end up being little pup tents. No matter how many times we set those tents up we couldn't get them in a row straight enough for the instructors. Then they kept us up all night making a little bonfire.

We were always hungry. They were roasting hot dogs on the fire. We could smell the hot dogs while we were down there struggling with these tents. They probably kept us up until three or four o'clock in the morning.

At daylight they began blowing whistles. They had us up and the first thing they did was march us right straight in the Chesapeake Bay. We got cold and wet again and we had no sleep. That was the whole idea.

The funniest thing I remember is that we had this one punishment called the leaning rest, which is basically the "up" position of the push-up. When the instructor told someone to go to leaning rest he just had to get into that position and stay there with his elbows locked until they came back and told him to get up.

For whatever reason, Rick [Woolard] had to go to leaning rest on the pier in Puerto Rico one morning. One of the instructors grabbed a sea urchin out of the water and put it right under him so that if he dropped he'd fall on the sea urchin. Rick is a big, strong guy, he always was.

Of course, the rest of the class is in some sort of muster watching all this happen, and as Rick was in the leaning rest position this urchin started crawling down the pier. So they made him crawl down the pier right on top of it.

I can say that in training I never had one moment when I ever thought of quitting. I had to deal with a lot of people in my boat crew who were going to quit. The most vivid experience I had with that was, we were out on the Chesapeake Bay one night during Hell Week and it was raining and it was cold. Of course they had us take the boats in the opposite direction of the tidal flow in the Chesapeake Bay. I think we were down to maybe a four- or five-man crew when generally we would have seven.

We had to take the boats over the jetty, over the rocks. I think there was ice that night, just a thin layer of ice. We had one guy that was going to quit before we got the boat in the water. We were doing everything we could to keep that guy from quitting, because we knew if he quit the rest of us might not make the evolution. He quit.

It took us all night to finish the evolution. We had to paddle from the jetties up to the officers' beach. It's not very far. It's only a couple of miles. But when we finished the evolution they put us in the truck and the guy that quit was in there. He was apologizing to everybody, but after that nobody said anything to him.

We worked together as a class, as a team. By the time we got down to the twenty-eight officers and enlisted, everybody was helping everybody. We made our swim from Vieques back to Puerto Rico, which is over seven miles as the crow flies. But with the currents and the tidal changes, by the time a person actually finished the swim it was calculated to be something like fifteen miles. We were in the water with no food, no fresh water, no nothing for all day.

We were broken up into groups to do that, and a group can only swim as fast as its slowest swimmer. We had an individual who was not a particularly good swimmer, and in the middle of Vieques Channel he just kind of quit. This was way after Hell Week. This was maybe a couple of weeks before training ended, because the swim from

Vieques back to Puerto Rico is the last long swimming exercise that we did before training ended. We literally had to drag this guy across the Vieques Channel. I think we were the last group in.

Psychologically it's a very hard swim to do anyway, not because we couldn't be in the water all day. The psychology of the thing is that we could always see the island of Puerto Rico over there, and we were never getting there. In the afternoon I thought of everything from cotton candy to steaks on the grill.

We dragged this guy halfway across Vieques Channel and finished, we all finished. But after training was over, Master Chief Blais took all the officers over to the enlisted men's mess; it was basically a congratulatory thing for completing training. One of the things that Chief Blais asked us was, "Why did you guys let this individual finish with you?" And our response to that was, "We're a team. We would never think of not doing that."

Blais told all of us when he brought all the officers in that room together a story that I've told numerous times over my career. He got very serious after the meal was over. He said, "Now you're all going to go off to UDT. You're going to go up to the Team and you're going to run into a hundred different people who have a hundred different personalities, and they're all extroverted. You're just going to have to learn to deal with that." I've never forgotten him saying that, and I've never seen it to be untrue.

We had an extraordinary bunch of instructors. We viewed them as being constructive, not destructive. I'm sure that was the consensus of us who finished Hell Week and what came after that.

SEAL Teams were still in the embryo stages of forming. I didn't know very much about SEAL Team, I don't think any of us who went through training knew a lot about SEAL Team. Some of the adjunct instructors that came up, we knew they came from SEAL Team. When I went through training it was UDTR, UDT Replacement training.

Before any of us went up to the SEAL Team, we had

to have one or more deployments behind us. When someone graduates from training, even today, he is not a member of a SEAL Team. A person had to go through a six-to-twelve-month evaluation period by his commanding officer, and the troops of course. But the signature of the commanding officer is what made him a qualified member of the Team. And that's still true today. A guy doesn't earn his warfare designator until you go up to the Teams and prove yourself, officer and enlisted both.

There wasn't any Special Warfare officer community at that time. The officers, when I got up to UDT, were generally conceded as being the "Ivy League" clan of officers. They were guys who came into the Navy, fulfilled their obligation, did their tour in UDT, which was fun, jump, run, shoot, set off demolitions, and then they would get out of the Navy without ever having gone to sea. The people who did stay in, the Norm Olsons, the Frank Kaineses, those guys had to do a tour in UDT, go back and do a tour in the Navy, and hope to get back into UDT. Dave Schaible, for example, went EOD. A lot of them did. There wasn't any career track. He wasn't going to get promoted if he stayed in what is now known as Special Warfare.

The Special Warfare officer community was created in my lifetime, in fact when I was lieutenant junior grade. So I've benefited.

Someone would have to go back a little further than my career to figure out how we eventually convinced the Navy into giving us the officer career program. The enlisted people, as long as I can remember, always had a career program. Once they came into a UDT or SEAL Team they could spend their entire career there. Look at Rudy Boesch. He was in the teams for over forty years.

When I went into the Navy I had no desire to make the Navy a career. My thing was to do my Navy obligation. I wanted to fly high-performance aircraft in combat.

When I got disillusioned with the aviation community and went to Special Warfare, my ultimate aim, once I found out that SEAL Team TWO was going to deploy, was to join them.

We didn't have any control over which Team we went to. When someone completed training, the detailer, the placement people, basically said, "Here's where you're going to go for duty."

I did have to go to UDT before I went to a SEAL Team. But I knew almost as soon as I went up to UDT that my ultimate goal was to enter a SEAL Team, because I wanted to go to Vietnam. And the SEALs back then and the UDT guys weren't that much different. It's the same breed of cat.

The SEALs were getting specialized schooling because they had a different mission, which at that time was principally focused on the land warfare. UDT still had the fleet mission and still focused on amphibious warfare. The guys in the SEAL Teams were getting a lot of Army schools to prepare them to do land warfare. The SEALs today work almost exclusively in maritime special operations and with entry and exit almost exclusively from the water. I didn't take diving rigs to Vietnam, let me tell you that. And I didn't take parachutes either.

Once we got up to the UDT Team we understood that there were a limited number of officers and enlisted who could go to the SEAL Team, because it was only a fifty-man organization at the time. For myself in particular, I knew that was what I ultimately wanted to do.

My experience in UDT took an unplanned track. I got assigned to UDT 21 and I started in to the normal track, which was as an assistant platoon commander. I was in a platoon that was in preparation to go to the Mediterranean. That was exactly what I wanted to do. Part of joining the Navy is what the recruiting poster says—see the world. Coming from West Virginia, I had never been outside the borders of the United States, so I really wanted to see the Med. About halfway through our predeployment training cycle, a requirement came in for an East Coast detachment to go to California and learn to operate what was then called Swimmer Delivery Vehicles, and to participate in a study sponsored by the Office of Naval Research on diver performance in Swimmer Delivery Vehicles. I wanted to go to the Med, but whatever the circumstances were in the CO's and XO's deliberations, I got chosen to go to California.

So I took a six-man detachment, packed up, and went to California. I got involved in the training program with submersible vehicles in a performance study that took the better part of a year to complete. That was a particularly interesting time for me because, one, I was out on the West Coast where all the activity was going on. SEAL Team ONE was very heavily engaged in Vietnam at that point. I reported to the Naval Operations Support Group staff out there. Captain Kaine was the Commodore at the time, so I really got to know a lot of the senior officers out on the West Coast and got to interact a bit with the Teams there. Although we were in the water almost seven days a week during that time.

I stayed out there for about a year. I had made lieutenant junior grade while I was out there. UDT 21 wanted me back, because the officer who was the head of the submersible operations department was getting ready to get out of the Navy and they wanted me to come back to replace him. I didn't want to do that because I was operating and if I went back and became a department head in the team then that meant I wouldn't get sent to the Mediterranean.

Anyway, I went back under duress and became the sub ops officer at UDT 21. Less than a month later I got sent for temporary duty to the Naval Operations Support Group, Atlantic, to fulfill the duty of research, development, test, and evaluation officer, which was on an interim basis. After I had come back from the West Coast I had briefed the staff people that were there. They knew that I had a pretty thorough understanding of Research and Development, and they thought that even with my junior ranking I could satisfy the job until an officer who was deployed to Vietnam could come back and take it. I guess I did such a good job when I went up to the staff that when the officer came out from Vietnam they didn't give him the job.

This was circa 1969. The Vietnamization program had already been decided. I knew that if I didn't get to the war soon there wasn't going to be any war to get to. So I essentially went up and told the Commodore that if they would not let me free from the staff to go to SEAL Team I was going to have to get out of the Navy. And it worked.

It was an interesting arrangement for me, because the staff and SEAL Team Two had been moved into the same building. I was permanently assigned to UDT 21 when I went to the staff, and while I was on board the staff I got a permanent change of station to SEAL Team TWO. So I actually walked into the same building in the morning, but instead of going left to SEAL Team TWO I went right and went to work at the staff.

I'll never forget, it was a Friday, I was doing paperwork on Friday and the following Monday morning I was in Ranger school in Fort Bragg in North Carolina.

It about killed me. I was out of shape. I was a Navy SEAL, and these guys were looking at me to be a super top-notch individual and there were twenty thousand guys there that were in better shape than I was. The Army did things a lot differently. I could never have done the Army.

I went from the staff to Ranger school. I finished Ranger school after I got through my period of soreness and "Why am I doing this to myself?" I formed a platoon and we started predeployment to go over. Bob Gallagher was one of my instructors, especially for the Pickett portion. We had the preparatory phase, and then, boom. The airplane was there and we got on the airplane.

I didn't have the same flight path that the other platoons took. We didn't have to stop in Coronado to in-check or out-check. We had some odd route that took us in to Gulfport, Mississippi, where we got off the airplane. We had to take all the dogs that were assigned to SEAL Team back to Vietnam. So we had to care for and feed these dogs on the way over. We laid up in Gulfport, Mississippi, for three days and two nights. Those people couldn't wait to get us out of there. We landed at North Island to refuel, but we didn't stop to visit with anybody in San Diego. We went to Barber's Point in Hawaii, and then Guam, and then into Tan Son Nhut.

I landed at Tan Son Nhut, and it's like landing in any

tropical environment—the scents, the sights, the sounds. It was a very active airport. The platoon we were relieving had people there to meet us, as they always did. In traditional SEAL style they met us with igloos [ice coolers] full of grapefruit juice and vodka.

I was struck by the fact that these guys were wearing side arms. I didn't understand why they were wearing side arms in Saigon. Of course, after we got down to Nha Be it still didn't make any sense.

When we started to go through the streets of Saigon after we left the airport, and when we got out into the countryside, I was overwhelmed with how much U.S. military presence there was. I conclude to this day that the country fought the war on the terms that the Army wanted to fight. That was basically to go in and set up all creature comforts, set up officers' clubs, set up enlisted men's clubs, headquarters, all that kind of stuff. It was almost like a base in the United States. We didn't set up to fight the war.

When we got down to Nha Be, which was a Navy base down near the Rung Sat Special Zone that the SEALs had been operating out of routinely, it was a little better. It was right next to the little village of Nha Be. The Navy base itself was substantially built up, which it would have been because I didn't get there until May of '69.

Not everybody in the SEAL Teams wanted to go to Vietnam. Not everybody that went to Vietnam wanted to be there. I had extraordinary people in my platoon, but I also had some no-loads in my platoon who wanted to wear the name but not play the game. There are a lot of people who want to be SEALs, but there are a lot of people who aren't very good SEALs.

I had followed a wonderful tradition of SEALs who had gone in to Nha Be. The legacy of the platoons was pretty much that the platoons were let to do what they thought needed to be done. I was supported by extraordinary Navy pilots, the Seawolves.

Our SEALs, my platoon, carried on the tradition and didn't get along at all with the base people. The base people were there to get their little ribbons and write

Mama home and tell her they're in the war. Those guys weren't doing anything, and they did not, in my view, substantially support us as the people going out in the field.

We had to take the dogs back over, and the guys in the teams really didn't want to get rid of the dogs. We were supposed to take the dogs back and turn them over to some Air Force people in the province up above us. Being the officer in charge, whose authority is absolute and complete, when we landed I turned around and said to the Chief, "Get rid of the dogs."

Unbeknownst to me, they took all the dogs up there except one. They kept Rinnie over across from their barracks in the little hut where we stored and cleaned our weapons. Because of the hot sun, Rinnie dug a hole and he lived under the Q-hut. I never saw the dog, never knew it was there.

The way I found out Rinnie was there was I got called out of my rack in the middle of the night and the base CO was just absolutely having a cow. One of the seamen from the Vietnamese Navy had decided to take a short cut from the Q-hut to the chow hall. Our guys had taught these dogs not to like Vietnamese people. Rinnie came out and grabbed hold of this young seaman.

That created an international incident, of course. I was dressed down and told to get rid of the dog. I told the Chief, "Get rid of the dog." I got the "Aye-aye, sir," but . . .

Our guys also had a bar in their barracks. The guy who was the base CO at the time had a policy of absolutely no alcohol in the barracks. That's one of the first things this guy said to me. "I know your guys have a bar in there. If I ever catch them with that bar I'm going to court-martial everybody." I absolutely assured the guy that there was no bar in there.

Of course, every night when we came up off of an op, where did we go? We had our own bar in there.

The CO was forever, on his own, trying to catch the guys with the bar. And there was a bar in there, you could go in and see it. But when this guy went in to inspect, there was never any alcohol, nothing to be found that would indicate that it was really a working bar.

We went a long time without really making contact [with the enemy]. The Rung Sat was kind of a dead place to send a platoon during that period of time. We had a lot of trouble trying to get intel and get ops to go out on. Part of it was that people who were paying for intel had the market overinflated. They didn't give us enough money up in Saigon to pay for the intel that these people wanted, so I just quit paying for it.

We had come off of an op one night where we had made contact. After this whole period of doldrums we were just really happy that we had made contact. So when we got back to the base, without stopping to clean weapons or anything, we went in and hauled out the beer.

We were celebrating and everybody was getting into their beer and the base CO decided that was the night to make his move. He decided that he was going to do this individual little sneaky peek up on the SEAL barracks. Well, unknown to the base CO, the dog was still there.

His route of approach was to sneak right upside of that Quonset hut where the dog was laying in wait. That dog waited in silence until that guy got within striking distance of his chain. Rinnie leaped out and grabbed the CO by the leg.

I guess one of our guys had been out on the porch taking a leak or something and saw the whole thing happen. He ran down and got Rinnie off of this captain and then ran back in to tell me we were in trouble. I went out and invited the guy in for a beer.

He accepted and he was very happy to be invited in to have a beer with the SEALs. He was very jovial. He said, "I knew you guys had a bar. I knew one day I was going to catch you." He seemed very happy to have discovered the bar, and the incident with the dog seemed to be secondary. We gave him a beer. He looked down at the end of the bar which abutted the wall. I think it was Dennis Johnson who was down there drawing a stick figure on the wall, and right over the top of it, it said, "Rinnie's Body Count."

When the CO saw he was becoming a stick figure on the wall he became unglued. The joviality went away, the bar got shut down. The dog got sent out the next day. We were never in good step with this guy. Never.

I spent a good deal of time in Vietnam trying to find a different place for the platoon to go. It wasn't that we needed a huge body count or anything like that, we needed meaningful things to do. And there weren't meaningful things to do in the Rung Sat.

We went to Da Nang and operated a little bit, we were going to do a BRIGHT LIGHT [POW rescue] one time. When we were down in Da Nang we ran some neat ops. We were operating out of Nha Be on a somewhat routine basis when Tom Truxell and I went up to Da Nang, we went up to Cam Ranh Bay, we went up to Hue in an attempt to find an appropriate area for the SEALs to operate. In the course of one of our trips I ended up back in Da Nang. I went up to see the senior advisor to the first coastal team and gave him my brief on what the situation up to the north and the Cua Viet River looked like. Basically I was giving a negative report that I didn't think the platoon should be moved up there.

He said, "It doesn't make any difference—your platoon's down in Frogsville."

Frogsville was a little village that the UDT guys had set up in Da Nang. While I was gone, the Special Warfare people in Saigon had called down to Nha Be and told them to move in. I went to Frogsville, and there was my platoon, drinking and having a good time just like a fraternity party. I grabbed the Chief up and said, "Why are you guys here?"

And he said they had gotten a call from Captain O'Drain at Naval Special Warfare Group that said that I had urgently required them in Da Nang. Which was a falsehood. They had loaded up a truck, gone to Tan Son Nhut and got hold of the Navy air crew called Whitehat Airlines, and flown up to Da Nang.

I said, "Okay, where's the guns?"

They had the guns. But there were no bullets. I didn't have the piece of paper that said I could get support anywhere—boats, airplanes, ground support, all the stuff that you need to be able to go on an operation. I didn't have any Stoner ammo.

This was right in the middle of monsoons. So I took the guys back to Da Nang airport, went over to Whitehat Airlines, and talked the guy into flying us back to Saigon in the middle of a monsoon. I took everybody back to Nha Be, put the guns back in their hut, put everyone back in the barracks, and went over to see my boss, who was a wonderful officer by the name of Commander Jim Williams. He looked at me and said, "Why are you here?"

I said, "Why did this platoon leave?"

He said he got a call from John O'Drain, who wanted the platoon moved up to Da Nang. He picked up the phone and called Saigon. He talked to O'Drain for a few minutes and then he gave me the telephone.

O'Drain's first remark to me was, "Gee, I wish you really hadn't done that."

My response was, "Well, sir, I wish you hadn't done that." I got ordered up to Saigon, and that's when I was informed that the platoon had been sent up to await me, and for further transfer up to I Corps.

And I just started to go down my checklist. "Where's the orders that send me? Where's the order that tells people to support me, to provide me with air support?" I went through the whole cooking list of what you need to do an op.

They told us to go back up. I took the Stoner ammo on this Air Force plane and never told the loadmaster that we had live ammo. Normally when they're moving ordnance they don't put people on the same plane, or if they couldn't keep people off they load it differently.

So we set up in Frogsville for a while. We ran three operations on Dong Tiem island. We got the task to be sent up in there to reconnoiter, to do some intel collection. There was some intel on a two-story bunker and a whole other series of bunkers that were up there. We had two tries to get in, and then one night we did get in. The first night we got inserted in the wrong place. The second night we got pinned down very heavily by .50 caliber machine gun fire. Subsequently we found out it was friendly fire from the Koreans, who were reconning by fire.

We recovered from that and went in the third night. Our approach was a canal that was several miles long that went up almost directly to this thing. We decided, why not wade the canal instead of trying to forge across land? So we went into the canal.

I had two extraordinary point men. I had a point man named Fred Keener who made officer eventually. That guy was a consummate professional. And there was Dennis Johnson, who made E-9, also extraordinary. They found several booby traps going up.

We had not anticipated the degree of difficulty of getting up into that target. We got about halfway up in there and we saw this trail leading off to the left. We sent a scout swimmer to recon what was up there and he found a tremendous bunker complex. It was empty.

This place had mattresses, white sheets, these guys were home. They had sheets on the bed, they weren't sleeping on plywood. We realized that we weren't going to make the primary target, so we left a whole bunch of leaflets in this thing that said, "We are watching you. We see everything that you do." The Vietnamese are very superstitious.

We extracted out safely. Then we left town and went up to I Corps from there. But we learned that a combined UDT/EOD detachment went in there the next day to destroy those bunkers. One EOD guy got killed and another got his arm blown off from a booby trap.

That was the kind of stuff we were ideally suited to do. We should have done more of it. But we were off on the Cua Viet River because that's where we got sent. There was an incident that had occurred up there, where the Vietnamese sapper battalions had mined the Cua Viet River. The CNO of the Vietnamese Navy had been flying over doing a visual reconnaissance, and a ferryboat had fed him a line and exploded as he was watching, and a couple of his family members were on it.

A tasker came down for us to move the platoon to I Corps and the mission was to stop the mining on the Cua

Viet River. Now that's a big task for a SEAL platoon. That was the simple side.

Nha Be was all set up. When we got sent up to operating in the First Coastal Zone in Da Nang I had some support logged up there, so we had a limited amount of Stoner links.

We were told that when we got up to I Corps, there would be a Chieu Hoi who would guide us on a series of operations. Tom Truxell and I went out to set the whole thing up, and our take on it was that really there wasn't much that we could do. A couple of people in Saigon were being pressured by the CNO of the Vietnamese Navy to produce something.

The first day I went out to set up an op I went to the Army tactical operations center. I didn't have the Seawolves, I didn't have my own boats, I didn't have a source of ammunition. The little bit I had was still in Da Nang. I barely had a jeep to drive around in. The only way I could get around was with the Naval Intelligence liaison officer [NILO], who had wheels.

I had to depend on the Army and the Air Force for air support. I had to depend on the Army for food. I had a Navy platoon up there with little or no support.

I went over to the Army to set up my first operation based on our interrogation of this Chieu Hoi. I was a lieutenant at the time, and the Army is much more rank-conscious than we are in the Navy. I met this very pleasant Army major and he treated me very nicely. We were standing by this map looking over the area and I was pointing out to him where we were going to run our operation and the type of support I needed. He was supposed to lay on the aviation support.

In the Navy, when a senior officer of rank walks into the room, the first person that sees him stands up and says, "Attention on deck." Everybody stands up and comes to some form of attention and the senior officer walks in and generally says, "At ease," and takes his seat. In the Navy at that time, when people got promoted to flag rank they went straight to two stars. There was no such thing as a one-star admiral.

While I was talking to this major at the board, somebody said, "Attention." People got up and stood at attention. Then this guy in a very heavily starched camouflage uniform came up to where I was standing at the map with the major. He had a star on his collar, and I'd never seen one. So my response to him was, "Good morning, Chief." Because the only single stars on collars I'd seen before were Chiefs in the Navy. Of course, he was a brigadier general.

I introduced myself to him, and without greeting me in any other fashion he said, "I want to see you in my quarters now."

Everybody in the TOC was looking at me like I had poisoned his coffee that morning. The general did an about-face and marched right out. I went down to where the general's quarters were. It was typical Army. It was kind of Fort Bragg, World War Two. It was wooden structure with a little rock walkway going up and all the rocks were whitewashed. The grass was all trim and proper.

I went in and there was his gorgeous Vietnamese secretary. You couldn't find a more beautiful Oriental woman. There was a carpet on the floor and the air conditioners were all running.

The general was waiting with the door open. I went in and he closed the door, and he said, "I've heard of you SEALs. You're assassins. I know all about you and I don't want you people operating up here. This is my province and I control it. I don't want you up here."

I said, "Aye-aye, sir," which I don't think the Army guys understand.

This general was the commanding officer of the 1st of the 5th Army Mechanized Division. Which is an indicator of how the Army viewed the war at that point in time. The Marines had been pulled out, and the Marines had that province under control. When the Marines were there, nothing moved.

They put a mechanized division in there, and that province was just out of control. Then they found out that not only did we want to operate, but we wanted to operate at night and we wanted to go after hard targets. The general had a cow about that.

He put the word out to his people to shut the SEALs down. When I went in to get air support, or any kind of support, I could get it, but I had to work real hard to do it.

The other thing I recognized very quickly was that I had to clear three different areas of operations, AOs, to go in there. The Army people didn't coordinate with the Vietnamese who were in the area. There were Koreans in the area, there were Australians in the area. Also, there were spies in the area. So I had to clear three AOs and I wouldn't tell anybody exactly which one we were going into.

In fact, after a while it became so frustrating to even get an operation set up that we were basically stymied. We couldn't operate. So we became a very rowdy platoon. We lived up to what a lot of people envisioned SEALs to be. If you can't get very active SEALs out into the field, then they're going to party. They're going to do stupid things. So we did a lot of stupid things, hoping to create situations where we could get out into the field.

On the first op that we ran in I Corps, we went down to get on the Vietnamese boats and they didn't want to take us across the river. I told this guy, "But I'm defending your country." And the Vietnamese said, "No, no, no. The river is mined. Don't want to go on the river."

I had to call clear back to Da Nang to get somebody to call this guy. It took us over an hour waiting on the pier just to get across the river. Then my guys are looking at me, saying, "What are we going to do if we get the shits? Who's going to come and get us?"

We ran an op one night. They took us over there and the area we were in was a free-fire zone. Everybody moving around up there was clearly a target. We got the whole platoon across the river, and we got pinned down on the beach over there by one of these bright lights. We didn't know if we were going to get shot at or not by this Army helicopter. The other squad, not the one I was leading, engaged, and we could see the tracers. So everybody started running toward the tracers because we thought these guys were really in trouble. When we got down there it turned out that the people they had taken under fire were an old man and a young child who had violated the curfew. We immediately got on the radio and asked for medevac to come in because this kid had a sucking chest wound. All the corpsman said was, "If we can get this kid back to the hospital he'll be okay."

The first thing they asked when I called for the medevac was "Is it an American or a non-American?" I said, "What makes the difference?"

It was a very frustrating night. We were down there for about an hour. We were up next to the DMZ and we had flash tracers and light all over the place—people knew that we were there. We had a perimeter set up for protection. We didn't know whether anybody was coming in on us or not. All we wanted to do was get out of there. It took at least two hours to get a chopper.

We were used to operating with the Seawolves in the Delta. The way that we would signal the Seawolves where we were was to raise capped strobe lights and they would overfly the strobe light. We would ask them what color it was, they would respond, and they would know our position.

In this operation we were out on sand dunes. There were no trees—it was a very barren place. I don't know whether it had been defoliated or not. The Army slick got in the area and we put the strobe up. The guy swore he couldn't see it. We were aiming this strobe everywhere the helicopter flies. The Seawolves could see it through the trees. But this guy absolutely swore that he could not see the strobe light and he would not land. And he kept asking whether it was a hot area or not, and we said that we didn't know. He didn't want to land.

I told him, "You're landing or I'm going to shoot you out of the sky."

We had to uncap the strobe light to get him to land. It's like the white strobe light on the wings of airplanes. The reason we put white strobe lights on airplanes is so that you can see them for miles and miles and miles.

That's the kind of support I got from the Army. They didn't want to fight the war, didn't want to be there. I can understand that with the mind-set of the commanding general.

We went down to the hospital to visit the kid and talk to his parents. The kid was okay. We chastised his parents for letting the kids out, even though they were with Grandpa.

We didn't have good success up in I Corps either. It's not because the opportunities weren't there. We became very close with the Australians who were up there. The Australians had the artillery sites. We partied with these guys a lot and they told us all these stories about these guys who crept up on their artillery positions at night, how there was a lot of activity outside of their perimeters. We wanted to go up and operate at night outside of their perimeters. The U.S. Army would not authorize us to go do that.

We didn't do anything to stop the mining of the Cua Viet River. We did, in the sense that it was determined later by virtue of the fact that there was a SEAL platoon operating in the area, there seemed to be very little activity in the area. We were a presence, and our presence did something. The reputation of the SEALs was probably what this Army general contrived. He probably spread it. His secretary probably heard it and told her brother, who was telling it to the enemy next door.

There was so little activity that I left the platoon up there and went to the Delta to try to get our platoon moved back down to the Delta, where there was still considerable activity. I set up the area that the platoon that came over to relieve me got. That was a virgin area, and the platoon went over and had some success.

Our platoon just seemed to keep trying. In retrospect I can understand it. All I wanted to do was to do our mission. We seemed to get resistance everywhere we turned.

One of the ways the SEALs are effective, or became effective, is by creating intelligence networks. When we went in-country we were issued one hundred thousand dollars in piasters. The whole idea of that money was to pay for and build an indigenous intelligence network, our own intelligence net. If we went in behind an established platoon, the intel net was set up and working. When we had to go to a new place like Da Nang or Cua Viet it could take the better part of a whole tour for the first platoon that goes in over there to set up the net. So we were totally dependent on all the other intel sources.

I had an interpreter assigned to me in I Corps. The guy spoke flawless English. I think he was brought up in a Catholic orphanage. This was one of the smartest, most articulate Vietnamese I ever met. He was so in tune to the politics of everything that was going on that he was a real education. I always wondered what happened to that guy. They wouldn't even let him stay with us to help us meet people.

What we wanted to do was go and associate with the people in the villages. We didn't have freedom to walk around the villages up there. We had to stay inside the Army compound, we had to use the intel that came inside the Army compound, we had to interface with the Vietnamese Navy, and we had to rely on the Army and the Air Force to come in for gunship support.

When we operated out of Nha Be in the Delta, we had the Seawolves right beside us. Those guys could be there in minutes. Not an hour.

We were one of the few platoons that got to operate in and around the DMZ. I got to fly over the DMZ, and maybe into North Vietnam.

This was 1970 now. Things were winding down. The powers that be were not proactive. Here we were, we were trained, we were prepared, we were equipped, we wanted to go operate. Everything we did became so frustrating.

We had a very lackluster tour. It was rewarding in the sense that we were there prepared to do our thing. But it was frustrating in the sense that we really didn't get to do as well as we could have done. I think it was the country wanting to get out of there, everybody pushing the Vietnamization to the extreme.

It was very rare for a trainee fresh out of basic UDT training to be accepted directly into the SEAL Teams. When the Teams were first forming, some promising trainees were singled out to go into them. Several men were still in training when the Teams were commissioned and did not enter the SEALs until after they had graduated. Even though they arrived some time after the commissioning date of the SEALs, these men are still considered plankowners of the Teams, as their names were on the original Team rosters.

It was also very rare for men to enter UDT training directly from boot camp. Today, it is possible for a man to enlist into the Navy specifically to try out for the SEALs. If these people cannot pass BUD/S, they can quickly find themselves members of the fleet Navy. But in the 1960s, it took a very determined man to enter the Navy solely to join the UDT or SEALs.

Training in the UDT was hard, and in the SEALs it was even harder and more dangerous. The SEALs were performing a very difficult job in Vietnam, and performing it well. It was the training they received back in the States that most SEALs state gave them the skills necessary to survive and excel at their mission.

One mission the SEALs completed almost amazingly well was that of PRU advisors. The Provincial Reconnaissance Units were paramilitary organizations made up of Asians, but not necessarily Vietnamese, supplied and supported by the U.S. intelligence community. Each province in the Republic of South Vietnam had a PRU, whose primary target was the Viet Cong infrastructure (VCI) of that province. By capturing or eliminating VCI, the actions of the Viet Cong could be choked off for lack of effective leadership. Advisors for the PRUs came from many sources—the Army, Marines, CIA, and Navy SEALs. Among the most successful PRUs were those run by SEAL advisors. An advisor billet became a very desirable goal for action-oriented SEALs, and only the best were chosen from the many volunteers.

Because of the PRUs' standing as the action arm of the Phoenix program, their successes have been overshadowed by rumors and hearsay stories of excesses and assassination programs. The SEALs never ran an assassination program. To the SEALs, and the men they led, if someone had a weapon and refused to surrender, they were fair game. Vietnam was a war, no matter what some people might say otherwise, and a war of guerrillas at that.

The VC and NVA couldn't have been much more frightened of the SEALs, or "the men with Green Faces," as they were called, if the Teams were guilty of much that they were accused of. But to a SEAL or SEAL advisor, a captured VCI member was much more valuable than a dead one. Dead men will not give you intelligence that can lead to more and bigger operations.

LARRY SIMMONS

Commander Simmons spent his entire Navy career with Special Warfare, both in the UDT and the SEAL Teams. Volunteering for UDTR while he was still in boot camp, Simmons quickly went on to UDT 21 and then SEAL Team TWO. Later, Simmons graduated from college while still serving in the Teams and received his commission as a Navy officer. Having entered UDTR training as a low-ranking recruit, Commander Simmons later on became the executive officer at the BUD/S school in Coronado. Retiring from the Navy as the commanding officer of SEAL Team FIVE, Captain Simmons has the distinction of going from a seaman apprentice to commander during his time in the Teams.

In Slocomb, Alabama, where I was raised, just north of Panama, Florida, there was no beach or ocean. But if you spit real hard, you could practically hit the waters of the Gulf of Mexico. Much of my time as a kid was spent on the white sand beaches of the Florida panhandle. The seafood was incredible—oysters, crab, scallops, flounder, mullet, all of them were available and fresh. Not a bad life at all to grow up in.

With the ocean having been such a part of my life, when my draft notice showed up after high school, it was either Canada or the Army and Vietnam. Neither of those options really looked good, so I started investigating the other services. Going from one recruiter to another, I tried to make a deal with each of the services except the Army.

Of all the services at the time, the Navy was the only one that could guarantee me a school. They didn't state which school and tried to talk me into becoming a welder. But I knew what I wanted. I was going to be a *Frogman*.

When I was growing up, the television show *Sea Hunt* was popular. Every week I would follow the stories of Mike Nelson [Lloyd Bridges] as he worked underwater. That looked exciting and was what I wanted to do. The Navy had the training available, and I was going to do everything in my power to take it.

In 1966 I entered boot camp and was tested for the UDT. As I remember, thirty guys took the tests but only seven of us made it. After boot camp, I was sent to Norfolk, Virginia, and the Navy base at Little Creek. Class 38 started UDTR training in the fall of 1966, when it was hot in Little Creek. By the time we graduated months later, it was winter and anything but hot. There had been a friendly argument in the Teams for years as to which coast had the harder training, Coronado in the West or Little Creek in the East. I'm not sure which is hardest— it depends on your tolerance for cold. But when ice starts forming on your uniform from the seawater it's soaked in, it's *cold*.

Training was physically hard for me. All you seemed to do was run forever. And when you weren't running, you were swimming. I had been on the swim team in high school, but that hadn't prepared me for UDTR swimming. When you're swimming competitively, you use your arms to pull yourself through the water. That's where the power comes from and what I thought I was getting into at UDTR. In the UDT, the power comes from your stomach and legs, especially after you put swim fins on. I was not ready and paid the price.

Besides just the long-distance swimming, the instructors have other little tricks for you to perform. There's no way that high school swimming gets you ready for swimming while holding a bucket in your hands. Or doing laps in a pool with a face mask on. Only the face mask is blacked out with tape over the glass and it's full of water. When that water flows back into your sinuses, it's everything you can do not to choke and flail around on the surface.

We had good officers in our class, and they led us well. They also could swim a lot better than me. There was a saying at training—"It pays to be a winner." If you came in ahead during a given evolution, you won a little more rest than the guys who came in behind you. Watching this, you can put a little strategy into your training. If you paid attention, you could pick out who in the class was better than you in a given evolution. Now you didn't have an entire class to beat, you just had to beat that one man. It pays to be a winner, but only when you know you can win.

Hell Week came on me like one long nightmare. It was just a giant, miserable experience that quickly blended into a blur of physical misery. There wasn't anything particular that got me through the week except for my own tenacity. I was going to get through the course, I had committed to it, and there wasn't anything that could be done to me to force me to quit.

I'm a pigheaded, stubborn kind of guy, and when I have my front sight focused on something, I pretty much get there. At least when it makes sense to get to where I'm aiming at. And getting into the Teams made a lot of sense to me. I had no idea what I was getting into when I volunteered for training. But once I had made up my mind that this was what I wanted, they were going to have to kill me to get me to leave.

And the fact that I didn't know what I was in for during training is a big difference between then and today. The kids entering BUD/S today have a good idea about what they will be facing, and why. In the past, the unknown was a bigger enemy than people realize. It became important not to wonder why something was being done, and what was coming along later. The instructors just kept coming, and coming, and coming. . . .

There were some really great people in charge of my

training class. Master Chief Blais and Jim Cook are two of the names that come to mind. These were the kind of men who stood as an example. I would watch them and say to myself that I wanted to be just like that. They were the epitome of what I had seen in the *Sea Hunt* Mike Nelson shows, only these men were real.

After the training went on, I started looking forward to parts of it. With the incredible time of Hell Week behind me, now I could learn the skills involved in being a member of the Teams. When it came time for us to learn parachute jumping, I was very much looking forward to it. Now, I like today's high-performance canopies a lot better than what we were jumping with then. But the whole experience of flying through the air and landing under complete control is wonderful.

My class started with around 110 or 120 students. When it was all over, twenty-eight graduated, including a large number of officers. Some of our officers were just fine men and outstanding athletes. Mr. Gardner was in charge of my boat crew and was a strong leader. Rick Woolard, now a captain, was also in my class, as were Tom Hawkins and Bruce Williamson. These men went on to make a name for themselves in the Team. But for myself, I graduated UDTR as an unrated seaman apprentice, and that was my rank when I arrived at UDT 21.

Very soon after my arriving at UDT 21, Sam Bailey, who was like the watchdog of the Team, called out to me from where he sat on the quarterdeck. "Simmons!" Bailey rumbled out at me. "What are you striking for?"

What the hell is he talking about "striking"? I thought to myself. "Chief," I answered tentatively, "I don't know what you're talking about."

"Simmons," Bailey growled, "come with me." And he led me into a small back room. In the room were books, shelves of Navy books. Red ones and white ones, all different colors, assorted into sets by the cover colors. Explaining the situation to me, Bailey said, "These green ones, they're aviators. And these here red ones are engineers." And he went on about the different fields available and how I would have to pick one as my "rate" or specialty.

"You can be any one of these you want," Bailey said, pointing to the books. "Pick one of these and start studying 'em."

Looking at the shelves of books, I was more than a little amazed. I found the smallest combination of books I could find, thinking that I was going to outsmart the system. And that was how I became a Quartermaster.

Quartermaster may have had the smallest set of books, but it was not an easy rate by any means. After I made [qualified for] the rate, I soon found myself in the chart section. The skills needed to be a Quartermaster are difficult to master. On board a ship, he assists the navigator, keeps the charts up to date, and helps plot the ship's course. In the Teams, if a Quartermaster is good in cartography and drawing charts—not many are—they quickly end up in the chart shop. As it turned out, I was good at drawing charts.

The UDT 21 chart shop was run by Fat Rat Sutherland, and when I was assigned, I became his understudy. Fat Rat had a brother, Dave Sutherland, who was also a Quartermaster. Little Fat Rat, as Dave was called, was the primary cartographer on a Med cruise deployment I made with UDT 21. During the cruise I worked in the chart shop as Dave's understudy.

During UDTR training, we learned how to conduct hydrographic reconnaissance of the waters off an enemy beach. The recons would result in a number of swimmers' slates covered with numbers and notes. In the chart shop, it was our job to take the raw data from the swimmers and make detailed UDT survey charts for use by higher command. Charts like these were used during World War Two for the landings on Japanese-held islands. The job was important, but was not what I most wanted to do in the Teams.

While in UDTR, I had learned about another group like the UDT, the Navy SEALs. The stories that made the rounds of the barracks about the SEALs told me that this was the outfit I wanted to get into. It was another challenge, something different. They jumped from planes and worked with weapons, many of the things I wanted to try. Besides, we could see them walking around in camouflage uniforms—the SEALs were the only Navy unit wearing cammies then. We didn't wear cammies, and I thought they looked cool.

It was late in 1967 that I was accepted into the SEALs. Platoons had already been sent over to Vietnam, and that was something I was looking forward to. I had already heard the stories about how the SEALs were involved in Cuba and the Dominican Republic. Now I wanted my chance to see what I could do and how I would measure up.

My first months in the SEALs were spent learning the skills necessary to operate with a platoon. By the spring of 1968, I was qualified to operate in time to join a platoon that was forming up to deploy. A system had been put in place where a platoon that had just returned from Vietnam conducted the predeployment training of a platoon that was preparing to go over. It was my good fortune that Fourth Platoon, my platoon, was going to be trained by the freshly returned Eighth Platoon. Eighth Platoon officer was Richard Marcinko, already quite a name in the Teams.

The returned platoons passed along what we called "lessons learned." One thing I learned quickly from watching Marcinko was the brutality of leadership that came during war, when life or death followed your successes and mistakes. An example of that brutality and what it could mean particularly stands out in my mind.

Some of our field training took place in the Great Dismal Swamp, some of the worst countryside that could be found. John Dearmon and I had been driving around in a jeep together that afternoon. John had this jug of moonshine he had brought from somewhere and we had been taking sips from the jug. I swear that stuff must have had kerosene in it from the way it tasted, but the kick was something else. Getting over to a canal where we were going to train, we could see Rick and some of his guys walking up and down the bank shooting water moccasins.

The guys would just walk along until they spotted one of the aggressive, poisonous snakes and they would pop him with a round.

A little later, we pitched our camp nearby and settled in. I had this jungle hammock that could be hung between two trees and kept me off the ground. With the snakes we had seen that day I thought staying off the ground sounded like a real good idea. Much of the day had been spent training, patrolling, running, shooting off the guns. Now we figured it was time to sit down and talk about what we had done. That's not what Rick had in mind.

"All right," Marcinko and his crew said, "now it's time to go out." And he had us patrol along the riverbank, right where we had seen them shooting snakes that afternoon. That situation really separated the men from the boys. If you were a point man, you knew that those slithering little bastards were there. And I had point that evening. Spotting at least one of the moccasins, I just kept going. After all, guys, there are snakes in Vietnam too. The lesson sank home. We did have one guy who reacted, just a short gasp, to the snakes moving around. That was something you wanted to know could happen before you went to Vietnam. Making that kind of noise in enemy territory could get you and your teammates killed. But in the Great Dismal Swamp, with no one around but the dismal natives, you could learn the lesson without dying.

My hat's off to Marcinko. He taught us some hard-learned lessons. He was very creative, and I learned a lot from him that I took to heart. But in his turn, he learned from men like Ev Barrett and others who taught, and molded, the Teams. That is the culture of Navy Special Warfare being passed on man to man, decade to decade. So Solly day, the last day of Hell Week, is an echo from the past, from the Pacific beaches in World War Two. When I served at BUD/S later in my career, I would try to trace the historical threads of what we would teach, and where it came from.

August came and it was time for us to fly over to Vietnam. The flight was exciting, especially when we broke down in Hawaii. It seemed that the planes would always break down just where the pilots wanted them to. But we had a great time on the island, raised hell, and got in trouble. Just the sort of thing that SEALs liked to do.

Finally, we arrived at Da Nang, Vietnam, just in time for a firefight. The fight was going on all around us, and the Cobra gunships and Spooky were working the area near the base. It was quite a first impression of Vietnam, seeing the miniguns fire from Spooky, the AC-47 gunship. Spooky was a reconditioned cargo plane, a DC-3, that had been fitted with three 7.62mm miniguns that fired out the port side of the plane. Each gun could fire fifteen hundred rounds in fifteen seconds, with every fifth round being a tracer.

Watching from a distance, the effect was neat. You would see this red light extend down from the sky and lick at the ground and then disappear as its tail left the plane and went down. Then you would hear the noise of the guns firing. Not the sound of a regular machine gun. The miniguns fired so fast the sound blended together into one long WHAAAAAAA. It looked like some kind of laser tag was being played with the VC. It was strange and a very strong first impression of Vietnam.

Along with the weapons firing, there were explosions taking place here and there. I wasn't scared at all, just fascinated. We stood around watching the fireworks while the plane was being refueled. Getting back aboard the C-130, we continued on to our final destination at Can Tho.

Life became a little more peaceful for a while. The Delta was very different from up north, and large attacks were the exception. Now I was a third class Quartermaster and still the most junior guy in the platoon. The platoon was broken down into two squads, but that distinction became less important as time went on. We would work together in unit sizes dictated by the mission. Sometimes as fire teams, or squads, or platoons, or, most rarely, in conjunction with other platoons.

We had worked together for a long time by now and trusted each other. Each man knew what his teammates would do in a given situation, and we had studied each other's jobs. Positions would be moved around in the platoon as the need came up. But even though we had trained together for so long, there was still a great deal of experience some of us had yet to acquire.

We had arrived in-country well after the Tet offensive was over, and things were just kind of smoldering out in the field. Ed Bowen was a member of the platoon we had come over to relieve. Later on, when I was CO of Team FIVE, Ed Bowen would come on to relieve me when I retired. But our first meeting was a little odd.

Jim Dilley and I were with Ed down by the river where the boats were kept. Ed was giving us a talk, telling us how things were in the operational areas, and how some things were done, just an impromptu briefing. Every now and then, someone would throw a concussion grenade into the water to help discourage enemy sappers from trying to attack the boats. While Ed was talking to us, one of these grenades exploded in the water.

BOOM! That sucker went off and I went down on the deck. There wasn't much cover, but when an explosion takes place, getting flat on the ground is the natural thing to do. As I looked up from where I was lying, Ed looked down from where he had been standing. He hadn't moved an inch and just said, "You'll get used to it."

I did more than get used to it, I came to enjoy parts of what we did very much. Back home, I had never gotten into hunting. Stalking animals just didn't hold any interest for me. But hunting the enemy in Vietnam, that was very different. The level of excitement is very close to being addictive.

The first operation we went on is just a blur in my memory. What does stand out is the insertion. I remember going in on the boat and being scared. This was different than training. People were out in the jungle who wanted nothing better than to kill me. And the noise the boat made was incredibly loud to me. There seemed to be no way that anyone on shore could miss all the noise we were making. And I was sure that they were lying in ambush, just waiting for the right moment.

Then we were on the shore and settled in a few feet into the jungle. As things calmed down around us, the night became ours. The sounds of the creatures came back and told me that there was nobody else around. We own this place, was the thought that went through my mind. And from that moment on, I knew that this was what I could do. It was easy now that I knew my own senses were enough.

As our time in-country went on, we moved around our positions in the patrol. I started as the point man, walking out ahead of the others. For a weapon, I preferred the CAR-15 with the XM-148 40mm grenade launcher mounted on it. I would use the 40mm like a big shotgun most of the time. With a buckshot or flechette round in the tube, the 40mm could recon an area in a big hurry. If I walked into something, the 40mm would cut down a swath of the countryside very quickly. As I backed up, just moving my finger put the CAR up and ready.

While on point, I would concentrate on everything that was going on around me. At that time in my life, I had a very good sense of smell and used it while on point. It was a great asset. You could tell when you were near people—they just had a distinctive odor to them. And the enemy probably knew us by our smell as well.

Not all members of the platoon worked out in the slots they had trained in back in the States. I ended up as the radioman after one individual's particular actions. We were extracting after an operation and the boats were coming in. On board the boats was a Mexican-American named Moheca. He had been supporting the SEALs for five tours in Vietnam, two and a half years. He was great, and if there was anything he didn't know about working the water, it just wasn't important.

Our radioman had been talking to Moheca and told him to bring the boats into shore. The man was in his first tour in Vietnam and just didn't have much experience yet. I didn't have a lot under my belt either, but some guys pick up on things faster than others. At any rate, as the boats were coming in, our radioman decided to try and signal them as to exactly where we were.

It's possible the radioman thought the boats were going to pass us by. Maybe he figured he hadn't described where we were well enough. But while the rest of us stood waist-deep in the water, he decided to signal the boats by firing his weapon into the air!

As he stood there with the echoes of his shots fading away, the rest of us had crouched down so that only our noses and eyeballs were still above the water. The radioman just stood there with this dumbfounded expression on his face like, "What the fuck did I do?"

If it had been anyone but Moheca on that boat, we could have been in real trouble. He didn't open up on us with the boat's weapons, which would have been a very natural response to sudden fire in front of you. But Moheca knew we were around somewhere. He assumed that we might be just getting into a firefight. What was important was that he had enough savvy to notice that none of the rounds came his way.

We got picked up without any further incident, except for the radioman getting a serious talking-to. The squad then needed a new radioman, and I was volunteered. So that was how I became the frigging radioman. I never did like carrying that big box of electronics. Besides, I liked being on point. As for our original radioman, he was relegated to gear guard for the rest of the tour.

Platoons, then and today, bond with each other, recognizing the strengths and weaknesses of each member. Some guys click together and become synergistically one. By moving the men around and even culling when you have to, the platoon, and the Team as a whole, is much the better for it. Later on, when I was the commander of a SEAL Team, men would show up who had slid through the selection procedures. On the surface, these men would look good—they shot well and operated in training with the best. But when the situation was tight, they just went the wrong way. I had to release those men from the Team.

But for the most part, the SEALs I knew worked well together, and played well together. We had a constant competition with the other services, something like a friendly rivalry. But for the most part we were the rogues. There wasn't anybody in the other services we felt we could depend on as much as our own. The Seawolves and

Brown Water Navy were exceptions to that, but after all, they were Navy units.

We trusted ourselves and few outsiders. During planning, almost no one outside of the platoon would be involved. The larger forces were combined with Vietnamese counterparts, and information could easily leak to the other side. If our mission plans were put up on the TOC [Tactical Operations Center] wall, the VC would have known about them before we even left the base. This closed-mouthed attitude of ours caused some friction with the other services, but it was what we had to do to survive.

Artillery and air support we could usually get as we needed it. Other services made their combat facilities available as they could. As far as material supplies went, if we needed something, we would steal it. Some things, especially comfort items, would be in short supply in Vietnam. Being such a small unit, we wouldn't be on the larger allotment lists. But we usually managed to get what we wanted. If we needed a jeep, one would become "available" within a short time.

Our officers, even though they were relatively young, became savvy to how things got done very quickly. Part of why our officers learned fast was that we had two E-9s in the platoon, McCarty and Ev Barrett. Those two men had been in the Teams since well before the SEALs existed. If I had a Sea Daddy in SpecWar, it was Ev Barrett. That man had a way of getting you to do the things you hated the most. When I had first gotten into the Teams, I couldn't get up in front of a group of people to talk without my knees knocking together. Barrett made me do it to the point where I can now lecture to an auditorium full of people without a flinch. And he did the same sort of thing with our officers.

Besides working hard together out in the field, we played hard together in our off time. It wasn't unusual for the platoon to get together and rent a place full of booze, and blow off a couple of days. We had a good time, relaxed as fully as we could, but still managed to mess with each other as the chance arose.

I was occupied spending time facedown on a bed in

one of the rooms we had rented. Dilley and a friend had decided that they wanted my attention. Gathering up a washtub full of ice and water, they dumped it over a partition, square onto my back. That got my attention, and I don't think they particularly wanted it right then as I came flying off the bed with a .38 in my hand. I chased Dilley and his friend all over the building. They finally locked themselves in a closet to get away from me. Of course, I wouldn't really have shot Dilley. But I sure felt like it for a moment there.

The platoon moved around the Delta, conducting missions where the intelligence directed us. There was one particularly memorable op we went on near the Cambodian border. We were staying in Ha Tien at the furthermost western point of South Vietnam, just by the Cambodian border on the Gulf of Thailand. Swift boats were moving along the canal that ran near the border. The boats were getting popped a lot, and we were asked to help put a stop to the sniping.

There were these mountains right on the border that were being heavily used by enemy forces. There were caves in the mountains that had been enlarged by the VC to the point where the mountains were practically hollowed out. I was just a junior enlisted man, so I wasn't in on all the high-level briefings. What I remember is that intelligence said there were either Russian or Chinese advisors working with the VC in those caves. The mountains straddled the border, so these people could enter the cave system in Cambodia, and when they exited the other side, they were in Vietnam.

There was all kinds of shit in mountain caves, from stacks of supplies to heavy weapon emplacements. The VC had a large base camp set up in the caves, and the entire area was a logistics point where materials would get moved into that portion of Vietnam. The Swift boats [PCFs, or Patrol Craft, Fast] working in the area were disrupting things, so they came under attack.

The approach to the mountain area was heavily mined and booby-trapped. Probably my scariest time in Vietnam was when we crossed that area. After we managed to work our way through the booby traps, we climbed up on one of the neighboring mountains where we could clearly see the cave complex. Several large men were walking around, obviously much taller than the average Vietnamese. These could be the Russian advisors we had been told about. Though we could see some of the movement going on in the caves, especially these big guys, they were just out of range of our sniper rifle.

If there had been a .50 caliber sniper rifle available instead of the .308 caliber one we had, it would have been no problem to pop the advisors in the caves. Ev Barrett had the idea that we could come back later and bring a 57mm recoilless rifle with us. With a recoilless, we could wreak havoc with the VC operation.

We worked the area for several days, constantly watching the movement of the enemy. The base camp was our primary objective, and intel on it had a high priority. During one extended op, we had inserted at night and were going to run a daylight observation post. As the dawn's light got brighter, this VC came walking out of this mountain in plain sight of us. The squad had been patrolling to our OP site, and there was this lone VC just walking along the field in front of us. The field was large and flat, open except for the occasional canal and rice paddy dike.

Apparently, this one VC had just stepped out from the base of the mountain. Catching him could give us some quick intel on what was going on in the area. Fred Toothman and I were assigned to go out and try to capture this guy. Since I was acting as the radioman, I took off my radio and left it with the squad. Slipping away, Fred and I made our way along what cover was available, quietly approaching our target.

Somehow, perhaps it was out of the corner of his eye, the VC spotted Fred and me. As he spun around, he bore down on us with his weapon, an SKS rifle, and popped off some rounds at us. That was a bad judgment on the VC's part, to try and take on two SEALs with an SKS. The firefight was over in short order with no casualties on our side and one badly wounded VC on the other.

The rounds we had fired didn't finish the VC off. We

could hear him moaning and groaning from where he lay in the field. Every now and then, his weapon would go off, and that was something we had to put a stop to. The little firefight we had was enough to wake up the base camp to the fact that somebody was nearby who shouldn't be there. If our wounded VC kept discharging his weapon, we would very soon have more company than we could handle. Fred and I were some distance from the rest of the squad and were mostly on our own.

We were carrying a number of minigrenades with us. These little frags weren't much larger than a golf ball, and a man could carry several more minis for every normal-sized grenade. The little grenades [Dutch NWM V-40s] could also be thrown a lot farther than a regular M-26 frag as well, and that was the problem.

With the VC base camp starting to get riled up, neither Fred nor I wanted to expose ourselves from cover. And the wounded VC was too low for either of us to get a clear shot at him. Grabbing a minigrenade from my web gear, I pulled the pin and threw it where the wounded VC lay in the grass. Trouble was, with my heart pumping and the adrenaline flowing from the excitement, I put a little too much arm behind throwing the little three-and-a-half-ounce minigrenade.

As we watched the minigrenade whistle well over the horizon, and past the VC's spot, Fred whispered, "Throw another, throw another." I grabbed another grenade off my rig, and Fred kept watch while I tried again to nail the wounded VC. Again, I was so pumped up that little grenade just sailed off into the distance. By this time, fire was starting up around us and I had had enough of these little grenades. Pulling a standard M26 frag off my rig, I lobbed it into the wounded VC's position, and his moaning suddenly stopped with the explosion.

Now we could quickly move up to where the VC lay in the grass and grab up his weapon and any intelligence materials he might have on him. As it turned out later, that VC had been a courier and had some good stuff in his pockets and pouch. Our problem now was that we had

gotten the attention of his buddies and they were more
than a little pissed at us.

The base camp was up on the mountainside, and the
VC were shooting down at us. We had taken cover,
crouching low behind one of the paddy dikes. Small arms
rounds snapped past us, *Crack, crack*, impacting into the
water before we even heard the shots. The worst time,
possibly one of the most fearful times of my life, was
when the VC opened up on us with mortars.

There would be a fluttering whoosh and then a THUMP
as the round impacted. By the sound, they were pretty big
mortars that were being fired at us. And the geyser of
dirty paddy water, laced with steel fragments, was just
thirty yards away. THUMP—one round impacted to the
side of us. Then THUMP and another round went off on
our other side. THUMP, another round detonated behind
us at about the same distance as the first ones.

To either side and behind us? Oh God! I thought.
They've got us triangulated. Shit!

There was one tree in the middle of this open area,
growing out of the mound of a paddy dike. And we had
managed to get ourselves behind the tree's mound. And
the VC we had hit was still alive—we could hear him
gurgling as he was dying.

Mortar rounds were impacting all around us, this dying
VC was making noises again, small-arms rounds were
snapping by, and all this shit was happening at once. And
I knew that the next mortar round was going to come in
right here, where we were hiding.

Looking over to Fred, I said, "Hey, do you think we
should bag ass?"

Fred was a first class and I was still only a third class
Quartermaster—I was looking to him for leadership. And
Fred was laughing!

Toothman was cool, totally cool under pressure. He was
so absolutely under control that he was just sniggering to
himself at the situation we had gotten into. And that sort
of set me in the right frame of mind.

While we had been losing ourselves in the field, the
squad had been having their own troubles. When the VC

opened up on us, the squad put down some covering fire.
The squad had enough troubles of its own when an esti-
mated two companies of VC came out of the base camp
after all of us.

The squad managed to set up a reasonably secure perimeter, from which they called in helicopter support. Besides taking out the VC coming at the squad, the Cobra
gunships came in and bailed Fred and me out. The gunships just worked themselves out on the area, raining fire
down on the VC. You could hear the VC wounded calling
out, *"Bac si, bac si"* ["Doctor, doctor"]. The 2.75-inch
rockets and miniguns of the Cobras had changed the equa-
tion seriously in our favor.

The Viet Cong had a bad day that day, and we came
out on top. Fred and I had relaxed a bit as soon as the
Cobras started their gun runs. To make sure the birds
knew where we were—we didn't have a radio—I popped
a smoke grenade to mark our location. But we still had
to make our way back to the rest of the men. We were
way out in this field with a good bit of distance between
us and the squad. The helicopters made the linkup between ourselves and the squad easier; we could move under their cover, and they circled where the squad was. A
slick came in, lifted us out, and that mission was over.

About a week or two later, the whole Fourth Platoon
came back to the same area, setting up an observation
point overlooking the base camp. A heavy helicopter gunship strike was called in on the VC base. We may not
have been able to reach the caves with our rifles, but the
2.75-inch rockets of the gunships could fly right into the
cave's mouth.

That time in the field with those frigging mortars coming in on us was probably my worst time in Vietnam. But
it was amazing how little effect they had. If the paddies
had been dry, Fred and I wouldn't have stood a chance.
But with the soft soil of the rice paddies, covered with
mud and about six inches of water, the rounds had to
penetrate deeply before there was enough resistance to set
off the fuzes. The mud and water absorbed most of the
explosion, channeling the rest upwards. THUMP, the

round would go off, muffled by the mud, and blast a big hole in the ground. Then the water would just settle back in. The explosion would blast material into the air, and the shit, and that is not just an expression, would shower down on us. No shrapnel, just water, mud, and fertilizer. Probably this was the scariest time of my life.

Today, that situation wouldn't have the same effect on me. I would be mightily concerned, but not as scared as that young third class was. In those days, I wondered what was going to happen next. Going through the booby-trap field approaching the mountain base was probably the longest strain I felt during the whole tour. The VC had put up signs that read "Tu Dai," warning the locals about the traps.

We didn't have much choice that time—we had to get through the area. Going up to the signs, we very carefully made our way through the field. The booby traps were all over. Just looking down, there would be a trip wire connected to a grenade. Further along and there would be a punji pit. I had already encountered a punji pit while I was point man earlier in our tour.

We had jumped this guy while on patrol. I had been walking point, and when the guy took off, we shot at him. When we opened fire, return fire started coming back our way. Keeping low, we worked our way down the line. The VC we had started chasing tried to cross an opening and we popped him. Just as I took another step, I fell in a punji pit.

All my luck was with me that day. I broke through the covering and landed on the bottom of the pit, right between all of the sharpened bamboo stakes. Nothing touched me. Climbing out of the pit, I continued with the mission.

My luck held out during my whole tour, and I was never hit bad enough to warrant a Purple Heart. There was a time when, during a firefight, I caught a small fragment in my throat. The wound was superficial. The fragment was one of our own, just a piece of a 40mm grenade. It struck me square in the center of my throat and seared its way in. Our corpsman, an E-9, came over, took a look at it, and asked me if I was okay. We were in the middle of a firefight when this happened, and shit was flying all over the place as the corpsman moved to my position. When I gasped out that I was all right, he took me at my word and continued on.

The wound would have qualified me for a Purple Heart, but I just didn't want one. Earlier we had lost one of our own. Roberto Ramos had been killed during an insertion on October 23rd. The platoon had been inserting on an op and the LZ was a lot hotter than was expected. Before he could even get off of the bird, Roberto was hit in the head and knee. For being killed in action, Roberto Ramos received the Purple Heart. After something like that, I wasn't going to put in for the same medal for a little wound that didn't even need any real treatment.

And that was my one tour in Vietnam. The platoon rotated back to the States on 12 February 1969. But it wasn't just memories of combat that I brought back from Vietnam. It had been my first immersion in a foreign culture. One thing I remember vividly about the land and its people was the native food. Ba Muoi Ba, the local VN beer, was a wonderful cold drink during a hot day. I loved the food—shrimp fried rice, done Vietnamese-style, was a flavor I can still taste. Even *nuoc mam*, a pungent fermented fish sauce the Vietnamese served on almost everything, was a taste I liked. Those are the memories I prefer to recall about my tour in Vietnam.

My opinion of the VC was set early on during my tour. While looking up during a firefight, I watched a VC push his AK-47 up into the air and just wave bullets in our direction. No aiming, he just pointed the weapon in our general direction and let fly on full automatic. Not exactly the way we had been taught to shoot. Right then I thought they were not very good. And that opinion didn't change for the rest of my tour.

What the VC could do was blend in with the surrounding countryside. That's what made them dangerous. The women and children walking on the roads and in the villages, the men working the fields with their oxen, even the fishermen moving on the canals. Any one of them could attack you at any time. Most of the people were just that, people trying to survive. But you couldn't tell which one would try and shoot you in the back the moment you went by.

But the VC were tough. They were a warrior race and had been fighting for years and years. It would have been different with the ARVNs on our side if there just hadn't been so many bad leaders. The politicians bought the commissions for their sons and friends, and leadership didn't often come with the package. The VC were determined, and that's what gave them the edge. That and blending in with the people. I didn't have contempt for the VC, but they never struck me as soldiers.

After getting back to Little Creek, I trained up with another platoon that was getting ready to deploy to Vietnam. What we did over there was what I had joined the SEALs for. An opportunity opened up for me to take PRU training, so I left the platoon and volunteered for the training. I was pretty sure I could get a slot as a PRU advisor. Toothman had worked as a PRU advisor over in Vietnam, and he had told me about it while I was in Fourth Platoon. I had also watched the PRUs at work while I had been in Vietnam and was sure I could handle the assignment.

It looked good for me getting a billet as an advisor, so I went off to the West Coast and the Team ONE PRU school. When I came back from the school, a glitch was thrown into my plans. The SEAL who had told me I could take his PRU slot had changed his mind. Now I had no way to get back over to Vietnam.

That situation changed the path my life was going to take. I was still going to remain in the SEALs if it was at all possible. But I was going back to school and get my commission. Ev Barrett, before we had returned from Vietnam, had said some very encouraging things to me. Very positive words on what Ev thought of me, my leadership, and my actions on some of the missions I had led. The junior guy in the platoon—me—didn't get to lead a lot of missions, but everyone was given their chance according to their skills.

The XO of Team TWO, Stan Meston, suggested I give

school a try and stay in the Teams as an officer. So I went to college on the ROC [Reserve Officer Candidate] program. At school I pulled down straight A's in my classes and three years later had a degree and my commission.

Learning was easy, but going to school was hard. Part of my experience on the campus of Ohio State from 1970 to 1973 was bad, very bad. Groups of students were running around chanting against the war, and I had just returned from it. The protesters would block the doors to the buildings, making just going to class a problem.

For nine months out of the year, I was a social outcast. The students didn't want to have anything to do with me, and that was fine as far as I was concerned. As far as the competition in class went, the students were more interested in other things than studying. I concentrated on my schoolwork and finished a four-year degree a year early. For three months during the summer I went back to Team TWO. Those three months of camaraderie lasted me the other nine months of ostracism.

For three years, I pulled summer watches as a second class Quartermaster. On the fourth year, I was an "enswine," freshly frocked as an officer and gentleman. In September of 1993, I was relieved as Commander of SEAL Team FIVE and retired from the Teams.

There were several fundamental lessons I learned during my life in the Teams. One involved exercise. If you exercise a muscle, it will grow in size and strength. If you do not exercise something, it will gradually lose what strength it had. And this applies to more than just your muscles. If you exercise your brain, make it work hard for you, it will increase in capacity. Your thoughts will come clearer and problems can be solved more readily. The body as a whole is a great laboratory, and by concentrating an effort, any piece of it can be made stronger and better.

A lesson I learned about human beings is that most people want to do the right thing. They want to belong to good, quality organizations. The people I have had the honor of working with, and leading, were just those kinds of people. It was only a matter of taking their efforts and focusing them on a common goal that helped give the SEALs the reputation they hold today. That is also in part the difference in management and leadership. Managers look on people as a resource they can apply to a problem. That can get the job done but doesn't help the people grow.

People that are leaders and not managers go one step further. They inspire their men to complete actions that they might not feel they are capable of. Leaders also know how to stress their people in such a way as to help them grow rather than just wear them down. It is that stress, in the form of Hell Week during training, that starts making a SEAL what he is. The *esprit de corps* that comes from completing that one week stands out in the mind of every SEAL today. We all look back on that, and it helps make us alike in that one way.

The principles for special operations are simple. A small unit operating in enemy territory must not be seen, but must still accomplish their mission. They succeed at this by doing the unexpected thing. If they are going to make contact, they must do it on their own terms. And when that contact is made, it has to be done with such violence, such surprise, and such overwhelming firepower that the enemy thinks it must be a hundred or two hundred guys out there attacking them. Not the six, twelve, or sixteen men of a SEAL unit. And after the attack, the men disappear, continuing the illusion that it must have been a much greater unit than was actually there.

Those are the simple principles, move, shoot, communicate, management, and leadership, that make the SEALs so successful. Those are some of the things I learned as a SEAL that I will carry with me forever. They are the tools for life.

For the most part, the SEALs were very successful in their operations in Vietnam, but that success didn't come without a price. Forty-nine SEALs, including four UDT operators, lost their lives serving their country in Vietnam. Some of these men were killed in accidents such as aircraft crashes and other in-

cidents—the men of the UDTs and SEALs were not given hazardous duty pay without cause. But the majority of SEAL casualties were due to direct enemy actions.

Using only the most conservative estimate from available records, the SEALs accounted for fifty of the enemy for each SEAL lost. Including probable enemy KIAs and other accounting, the ratio goes up to nearly two hundred enemy dead for each SEAL loss. These numbers do not include the over two hundred SEALs seriously wounded during the course of the war. Given their very small active numbers, the SEALs suffered one of the highest percentages of casualties of any U.S. unit during the Vietnam war.

But to balance out those casualties are not just the number of enemy personnel KIA. There is also the over one thousand enemy personnel captured, the over five hundred weapons captured, and over six hundred pounds of intelligence documents captured. The SEALs were successful far out of proportion to their numbers.

CAPTAIN

RICK WOOLARD

USN

Captain Woolard is one of the few Vietnam-era SEAL officers still on active duty at the time of this writing. Having entered SEAL Team TWO shortly after its Vietnam War commitment began, Captain Woolard remained a SEAL throughout his career. While the twelfth Commanding Officer of SEAL Team TWO, serving in that position from 1982 to 1984, he developed winter warfare, sniper tactics, and combat swimming into the serious capabilities they remain to this day. He also commanded the special Red Cell unit, SEAL Team SIX, and the Naval Special Warfare Development Group. Throughout his long career, Captain Woolard never forgot the lessons he learned during his early days in the Teams.

I was born in Austin, Texas, and raised in Nyack, New York. I went to college in upstate New York at Colgate University, graduating in 1965. In March of 1966 I entered OCS and was commissioned in July that year. About two weeks after receiving my commission in the Naval Reserve I reported to Underwater Demolition Team Replacement Training (UDTR) in Little Creek, Virginia.

Two factors coincided in my life then that influenced me to become a SEAL. First, there was a war going on, and if you didn't go to grad school or get married or join the service, you were going to get drafted. The second was more influential: I enjoyed college but I was restless during that time. I wanted to do something interesting and exciting, something real. Joining the Navy and becoming a UDT man—I hadn't heard of SEALs then—sounded exciting.

A lot of guys from Colgate were in the Teams in the sixties. John Boyd, Chris Lomas, Jon Schmauss, John Huggins, and Bill Jebb were on the West Coast; Gordy Boyce, Rudy Wiggins, Ken Spaulding, and Mike Jukoski were on the East Coast. I heard about the UDT program when I was a junior from Bill Jebb, who had graduated two years before me, when he came back to Colgate for a weekend.

My first day at Little Creek is still quite vivid in my mind. I drove down from New York in my new white ensign uniform. I stopped at the front gate of the Amphibious Base and asked directions to the UDT training area. I was directed there, parked my car, and knocked on the door. It was one step up to the entrance of the instructors' hut, and so I was expecting somebody to be higher than I was, but I wasn't expecting to be looking at somebody's belt buckle at my eye level. It turned out that the guy who answered the door was a Chief by the name of John Bakelaar, six-six in his stocking feet and 240 pounds. He looked down at me with his hands on his hips and I felt like a little boy. All I could see was his bright, shiny UDT belt buckle in front of me. When he saw I was an ensign and heard I was starting the next UDT training class, he just kind of chuckled. The instructors were routinely nasty to trainees, but I wasn't quite a trainee yet, so he was quite civil. He got me later, though.

I went through UDTR Class 38, the late-summer-to-early-winter class in 1966. At that time we were still running UDTR courses on the East Coast, three a year. Training was quite difficult, but even after the toughest days I usually had a little left in me and remember remarking that it could have been harder. I was certainly glad it wasn't. It was tough enough.

In retrospect, having been the training officer for the last four East Coast classes before the training units were consolidated in Coronado in 1971, I'd have to say my training class was unremarkable in most respects. We started with about a hundred and finished with twenty-eight. We didn't lose too many officers; only two out of eleven dropped out.

One thing that was remarkable about Class 38 was the number of people who made a career of the Navy. Amongst the officers, I'm the only one still on active duty who was an officer when we went through training. Mike Jukoski retired as a captain in 1991, Dawson Richardson is a captain in the Reserve, Bruce Williamson and Tom Hawkins retired as commanders. Many of the enlisted troops later got commissions. Commander Sonny Simmons relinquished command of SEAL Team FIVE in 1993 and is retired now. Ed Bowen is the CO of FIVE now, and Jim Dilley is at Naval Special Warfare Group TWO. Both Ed Bowen and Jim Dilley are commanders. In fact, Ed and Jim were in my boat crew all through training. Ron Rodgers is now a warrant officer. Mike Bailey, Chuck Fellers, and Tom Shoulders all made good as Chiefs in the Teams.

I really wanted to finish training. It's a matter of attitude. I tried to find out as much as I could beforehand, but fortunately nobody would tell me any of the details. Subsequent to that, I found the more you tell someone about the daily routine, such as what's going to happen on such-and-such a day of Hell Week, the more you really do that person a disservice. The thing that's going to get a trainee through is not knowing what to expect each day in detail, but just knowing that it's going to be very hard and he's going to have to put out max effort. If you tell people the details and they're expecting something to end at a certain point and it doesn't—say they're expecting a two-mile run and the instructors take them on a four-mile run, a mile swim, and run them through the O-course twice—that can be demoralizing.

I just made my mind up that whatever the instructors wanted me to do I was going to do as well as I could. There was no way they were going to get me to quit.

The Sunday before Hell Week began, I don't think anybody got much real sleep. I had foolishly gotten my head freshly shaved as a sign of dedication. After a couple of days carrying a rubber boat on my head, I was still dedicated, but I also had a huge sore on my unpadded scalp.

We came to hate the sound of a whistle, because it signaled to stop whatever we were doing and start doing something more painful. If we were walking, it meant hit the deck. If we were on the deck, it meant crawl. If we were crawling, it meant get up again. I hate the sound of a whistle to this day.

I was lucky with my boat crew. There were two officers, myself and another ensign named Dave Purselle. He was senior to me, so he was the coxswain, steering the boat from the stern. I was up front in number one paddler position with Ed Bowen number two. Leigh Barry, Jim Dilley, and two other big strong guys were behind us. We had a highly motivated and capable boat crew. We won most but not all of the boat crew events in Hell Week. I say this not because I'm proud that we won the events but because that was when I really learned that it pays to be a winner. If you won an event, let's say the Around the World trip or the Thirty-Mile Paddle, or another of the evolutions that you had to do as a boat crew, that usually meant you had a little extra time to sleep or eat.

One of the evolutions I remember best is drownproofing, which is staying afloat for long periods even with your hands and feet tied. I was not a college swimmer and I wasn't the best swimmer in the class. Ensign Hugh Dunseath, who had swum for Syracuse, was the best swimmer, but I was good in the water and I've got big lungs, which are a real advantage. When I take a deep breath, I just bob to the surface, while guys with really dense bodies sink like rocks, so at first I wasn't too worried about drownproofing.

Before the final drownproofing test, Chief Bakelaar had us tied up alongside the pool waiting our turn. Everyone was sweating the evolution, including me. What the hell, you just might drown. I'm lying on the cold tile with my hands tied behind me and up comes Big John Bakelaar. He's in a jovial mood. "Okay, Mr. Woolard," he says, "it's your turn now," and picks me up by the lines tying my hands and my feet. I give him a sickly smile, and so as he throws me into the pool he says, "Smile in the face of adversity, Mr. Woolard." I passed the test, but I didn't smile again until it was over.

Some of the instructors were dreaded by the trainees. A guy named Harry Mattingly, who came over from SEAL Team TWO just for the first part of training when the class was still large, was one of our most feared instructors. He had absolutely no mercy. He was a good Teammate, though, as the guys who knew him can verify. Later he was killed in Vietnam.

Another instructor named Gene Fraley was also subsequently killed in Vietnam. Fraley was a mind-game guy and a good runner. He liked to smoke cigars while he was leading a run so the trainees had to run in the smoke. Fraley used to quietly tell us about how many airplane crashes he'd survived and how lucky he was. I believe he had been the sole survivor of at least one airplane crash. He loved to mess with people's minds about how everyone around him had died and he hadn't. Fraley was blown up by a booby trap about two years later in Vietnam, so I guess his luck ran out.

The instructor who sticks in my mind, because I would have done anything for this man, was a Senior Chief at the time, Tom Blais. He had a way of projecting righteousness, high expectations, and integrity, and he instilled real fear in the trainees. It was a good kind of fear, because we were afraid of disappointing him. He had such strength of character, such force of personality, that most guys would have done just about anything for Tom Blais. He was a real leader. He still is. I'm proud to call him my friend. His son is an officer in the Teams now.

One of the more remarkable guys in our training class was Ensign Bruce Williamson. This was his second time through training. He had started training two classes before mine in Class 36. During Hell Week he had somehow broken one of the bones in his lower leg. He figured it was about Tuesday of Hell Week when he was running the boats.

The boats were old World War Two landing craft. Six to eight of them were lined up abeam of each other in a big field. Trainees had to race over these boats, up one side, down into the welldeck, then up and over the other side, sprinting from one boat to the next. The winner of each heat got to sit out. This was tough and it was dangerous. It was a real "pays to be a winner, hurts to be a loser" type event. All the trainees really competed hard to win each heat, because they didn't want to run these boats at all. Someone was always getting hurt; they just beat the hell out of you.

When the doctors X-rayed Bruce, nothing turned up, so he kept going. He finished Hell Week and went a week or two after, but finally he just couldn't walk or stand up on the leg anymore. At the hospital, the doctors thought it was bone cancer. Remember, this was in pre–sports-medicine days when they thought ballistic stretches were good for you and you took salt tablets, never water, on long runs. It wasn't until Bruce's leg started mending that they could see the break on the X ray and realized that he had gone through all this with a broken leg.

At any rate, he came back through our training class. He was one of the hardest guys in the class, and he had the sense not to tell us in advance what was going to happen. But the thing that impressed me about Bruce was that he had the option to not go through Hell Week again. He'd already done it once, so Tom Blais told him he didn't really have to do it again. I suspect Blais told him, ". . . but if you want the Program, of course I know what you'll do. . . . " So Bruce Williamson went through the entire UDTR course again, including Hell Week. This was very unusual in those days. I was pretty impressed. Later, I found out that Tom Blais himself had gone though Hell Week twice, put through the second time by instructors who had been trainees when he was an instructor. They really packed it to him.

I wanted to go to SEAL Team TWO ever since I first heard of the SEALs, but at that time [1966] they were not taking guys directly from training into the SEAL Teams. Guys had to go to UDT first, go on a cruise, get a year or so experience, and then they could volunteer for SEAL Team. I volunteered as soon as I got to UDT 21 after training. While in UDT, I was an assistant platoon commander for a good lieutenant named Dick Draper. After about five months I took over the platoon with another ensign named Louis Herman Boink III. Lou and I took the Third Platoon of UDT 21 to the Caribbean with the Amphibious Ready Group for a four-month deployment in 1967.

The chain of command in the UDT platoon on that cruise was Ensign Woolard to Ensign Boink to a first class Gunner's mate by the name of Clyde Albert Thomas. Thomas was a legendary character, one of the original UDT guys who had trained at Fort Pierce in 1944 and gone off to clear the beaches for the big Pacific landings in World War Two. A large number of those first Frogmen were volunteers from the Scouts and Raiders, the bomb and mine disposal school, or from the Construction Battalions [Seabees]. It turns out that Clyde Albert Thomas had been in the Construction Battalions before becoming a Frogman, and the "Seabee" nickname stuck with him for the rest of his life.

Seabee was my leading petty officer. At the time he seemed ancient to me, but he still went out and did PT and all of the platoon training events every day. Having broken his leg in jump school, and having made his fifth qualifying jump with that broken leg, Seabee wasn't keen on jumping, but he would do it four times a year to maintain jump status for pay.

Seabee was already a legend in the teams. I looked through his service record with great interest. It was one of the old types with handwritten entries. This man had graduated from training with the Naval Combat Demolition Units in Fort Pierce, then he had been sent out to Maui to do advanced training with the UDTs. He had been a UDT swimmer in many of the major Pacific amphibious operations in World War Two. Tinian, Saipan, Iwo, he was there. The UDTs swam close in to the beach and did a recon, then came back and put explosives on the obstacles and blew them, often while under heavy enemy fire.

Seabee was one of the few World War Two combat UDT men left in the Teams in the late 1960s, at least one of the very few who were still operational.

Despite this, Seabee Thomas wouldn't be able to join today's Navy. Not because of poor character or incompetence. Quite the opposite—Seabee was a fine, upstanding fellow and one of the best demolition men I have known. The problem was, Seabee Thomas didn't know how to read or write.

He was just a great UDT man. I really enjoyed being around Seabee. He was humorous, a real morale builder, never downcast. I suspect that no matter how tough things seemed, he'd always seen worse. He wasn't a natural leader, but he knew how to give orders, and people respected him just because of what he had done.

Seabee scared the hell out of me for a while. Nothing to do with the job, but because he got deathly ill during our cruise. He was really sick and not responding to medication. Here I was, a new-guy ensign entrusted with this living legend, and he's about to croak on me. I was really afraid that I would go down in Team history as the ensign who killed Seabee Thomas. We knew he was going to pull through when he told us that he wanted to be buried at sea from an aircraft carrier on a Sunday so as to screw up as many men's liberty as possible.

He did get better and carried on in UDT 21. Seabee retired as a Gunner's mate first class in the early seventies. He was a crusty old character from a different age, and I was really glad to have known him.

I got the word that I was going to SEAL Team TWO when the skipper of UDT 21, Lieutenant Commander Joe Heinlein, met us at the pier as our ship docked after that cruise just before Christmas of 1967. It puckered my grommet a bit, but I was happy that I had the chance, that I had been chosen to go to SEAL Team TWO. I was still all acclimated to the warm weather of the Caribbean when I went to Army Ranger school on the 3rd of January 1968.

If you were in either SEAL Team in the late sixties, it was taken for granted that you were going to Vietnam. I was told that I was going over in a platoon later on in

'68, but I wasn't told exactly when. A new batch of ensigns had come on board around the same time I did. Three of these new officers were all from one training class, the one that graduated in the summer of '67. We went to Ranger school together: Rich Kuhn, who's a captain right now at Special Operations Command Europe; Tom Murphy, who retired as a captain a few years ago; and a wonderful guy named Bubba Brewton. The four of us went off to Ranger school together, and I got the word later that Bubba Brewton and I were taking a SEAL platoon to Vietnam in June of 1968.

At the Team I was treated as a new guy. Everyone was when we came on board. We were just FNGs; nobody paid much attention to us, nobody talked to us. We'd gotten this treatment when we were in UDT training until the day we graduated. We went to underwater swimmers school and were the new guys there, and then we graduated and went to jump school and were new guys, and we went to UDT and were new guys, and then a few of us went to SEAL Team and were new guys there.

I was tired of being a new guy.

What I remember is walking around SEAL Team TWO, going to PT, attending musters and whatnot, and nobody said anything to me. It seemed like I had been doing this for weeks. The first guy who said anything to me was a Chief who stopped me in the passageway and said, "Hey, you're new around here, aren't you?"

I said, "Yes," expecting some old guy/new guy crap.

But he said, "Welcome aboard. Good to see you." Then he asked me my name and shook my hand. It turned out to be Bob Gallagher, one of the Teams' most decorated SEALs. He was one of two men in SEAL Team TWO awarded the Navy Cross during Vietnam. They still call him the Eagle, and with good reason. He's one of the most remarkable fighting men who ever came out of the Teams.

Here he was, he'd been in Vietnam twice by that time and was already a legend in SEAL Team TWO, and he could stop and say hi to a new guy. That always impressed me. I took his example and I always tried to do that myself later on.

Another thing I remember is Jocko. He was a Vietnamese monkey that one of the early platoons brought back in '67. This monkey was the most vile, disgusting, evil-tempered creature that ever walked, climbed, or crawled the face of the earth. Jocko was kept in a big cage right on the quarterdeck of SEAL Team TWO, though people occasionally let him out for sport. Jocko may as well have been a new guy, because everybody who went by would harass him.

He was so foul-tempered that they would stake him out in front of the entrance to the Team, even during the winter. This was a tropical monkey from Vietnam. Maybe that's why he was so mean, he was cold. Jocko bit. The duty section would stake him out on a long chain with just enough range so that if a visitor walked all the way around him and hugged the side of the building, he could just reach the door without being bitten or scratched. Jocko would be jumping up in the guy's face the whole time but he couldn't quite reach.

At first I thought it was disgraceful how these nasty SEALs were treating poor Jocko. They would tease him unmercifully. I was nice to him and brought him pieces of fruit and other food. Until . . .

One time Jocko got out of his cage during afternoon Quarters. I was standing there in my ensign uniform along with a hundred other guys. This beastly monkey was scampering about like a live gargoyle in the exposed overhead piping, under the rafters in the old Team building. He singled me out of this whole sea of guys who all looked the same in uniform, jumped down, and bit the hell out of me right through my shoulder padding. No more Ensign Nice Guy with Jocko after that.

Finally somebody had a lick of sense and figured out they had to get this monkey out of this military command. A guy named Jerry McClure volunteered to take him home. McClure was married, with a houseful of kids. He liked having Jocko around; he was a soft touch. McClure deployed with me to Vietnam on my first tour. I had to send him home early when Jocko somehow got hold of a lighter and burned his house down, killing himself in the process. I always thought that was Jocko's final revenge on SEAL Team TWO for taking him from his happy home in Vietnam.

Anyhow, the four new-guy ensigns completed Ranger school in March of '68. We all earned our Ranger tabs. Bubba Brewton and I were Ranger buddies and had many interesting and miserable times together, but that's another story. Back at the Team, Bubba and I formed up our platoon. We did some additional training in jungle and riverine ops and field medicine, a lot of shooting, some demolition work, and a lot of patrolling. In late June of 1968, the fourteen men of Third Platoon flew across the Pacific to the Forest of Assassins.

Our new home was Nha Be Naval Base, in the northwest corner of the Rung Sat Special Zone, not far from Saigon. Rung Sat means "Forest of Assassins." SEALs had been in Nha Be for several years, but it had always been SEAL Team ONE. We were the first East Coast platoon in there. I think the West Coast guys were happy to be moving on to different places, because they'd had some bad luck there—guys killed in ambushes and in accidents. Nha Be had not been kind to SEAL Team ONE.

Our job was to keep the Long Tau shipping channel open. At that time the Long Tau River was the main route in from the South China Sea and the rest of the world to Saigon. A lot of the war material was being brought into the country through this shipping channel, which in some places was quite narrow as it wound through the Rung Sat.

Since Tet of '68, the VC and the NVA had been trying to sink a ship in this shipping channel, which would effectively block it for some time until the wreckage could be removed. Our job was to hunt the VC and keep the Long Tau open.

At that time the VC were rocketing ships and putting mines in the shipping channel. Minesweepers were going out every day and every night, sweeping the channel to keep it open. And every night they were coming back shot up. Even though we had river patrol boats [PBRs] there running interference and Seawolf helo gunships on call, the minesweepers were getting hit hard. Those guys in the Brown Water Navy really earned their combat pay. They were taking a hammering, but they kept the channel open.

Before we deployed, I remember getting direction from Lieutenant Commander Ted Lyon, who was commanding SEAL Team TWO. He said, "Rick, it looks like you're going to have to do some patrolling in the Rung Sat. SEAL Team ONE's been setting a lot of canal ambushes and not having much luck, so you're just going to have to figure out some new tactics."

With this in mind, our first op was a fairly long platoon-sized patrol, four or five thousand meters. The plan was to insert by helicopter and then patrol around and see what we could see, set up an ambush, and then move on and set up a second ambush. The helo landing zone was in an area that had been defoliated. The banks of the Long Tau shipping channel had been sprayed with Agent Orange so there would be no place for the VC to hide when they snuck toward the water to put out mines or set up rocket attacks.

As we came in to the LZ, I was standing on the skid of the lead helicopter regarding myself in my mind's eye as I imagined John Wayne would go into a hot landing zone. The slick came to a hover at about eight feet, and at about four feet I jumped, all set to charge off into the bush to set up a perimeter. Well, I jumped off the helicopter and sank into about two feet of mud and didn't budge.

The helicopter set down beside me and everybody else stepped gently out and calmly walked through the mud while I was still trying to pull myself out. That was the first lesson I learned: Mud sucks and gravity makes it worse.

Patrolling through this defoliated area was really bad. Living vegetation sucks up moisture, but where we were, everything was dead and the mud was really deep. I doubt we had gone more than fifteen hundred meters before we were all on the verge of heat exhaustion. So that was the second lesson: Don't bite off more than you can chew before you find out about a place.

We didn't see or hear a thing all night. The third lesson was that if you set up an ambush in a bad spot, you won't make contact.

After that, we modified our tactics to include less patrolling. We patrolled where we could, but in places where we couldn't patrol, we came up with a tactic called the underway insertion to get in undetected.

There were several ways to get in and out of an operational area at that time. We could come in by helicopter or boat, sometimes using false insertions so the VC or the NVA wouldn't know from the auditory pattern where or if we were on the ground.

If we went in by boat, we had a choice of PBR, minesweeper, or occasionally a Swift boat. Also available in Nha Be at the time was a Mike boat, a heavily armed and armored landing craft that could accommodate the entire platoon plus others. But the Mike boat was loud and slow and a big target, so we didn't use it much. We eventually got some Light SEAL Support Craft [LSSC], which we liked much better.

I'm not sure my platoon was the first to use underway insertions, but we were the first that I knew about and we didn't learn it from anyone else. Instead of having a PBR nose into the bank during a series of false insertions, we would have the boat cruise fairly close to the riverbank without changing the throttle setting and we would just jump off. A whole patrol of SEALs, a squad or a platoon, could jump off into the water, get up on the bank, and clear weapons of water, and no one would know that they were there.

We'd been in-country about two weeks and had conducted a few operations without making contact when my squad made an underway insertion into an area a few kilometers due east of Saigon. There had been a spate of 122mm rocket attacks launched from that area into Saigon. The VC would hump these big rockets into position, set up, fire them into the city, causing random death and damage, then fade away into the night.

The night we got our first hit, we did a night underway insertion from a PBR and crawled up on the bank to drain our weapons and listen. We were down on our bellies facing inland with the river behind us. Just as I was about to give the order to get up and move out, right next to me Julius Ramos most urgently got my attention. I turned around and there was a ten-meter sampan slowly moving up the river with four or five guys with AK-47s in it. They were about thirty feet behind us in the very spot where we had jumped off the PBR, and they didn't know we were there. Ten minutes before when we went by them in the PBR, they must have been right alongside the bank, pulled in under some nipa palm. We must have passed almost within touching distance of these guys and hadn't seen them.

So I rolled over and faced the enemy. There wasn't time to alert the squad, but I did get the attention of Chuck Detmer, who was right next to me with a Stoner light machine gun. Those VC were moving right through our kill zone.

I just aimed and without a second thought put my M16 on what I thought was full automatic and pulled the trigger. It went pop. A single shot. I'd put it on semiautomatic. Instead of this horrible carnage that my awesome weapon was going to wreak on these guys there was just one shot. I think I hit one VC, but I don't know for sure. Chuck Detmer opened up right away with his Stoner, and then the rest of the squad saw what was happening and they opened up as well. The sampan capsized, and so we came back the next day and dived for the weapons. I think that was one of the few times SEALs did any diving in the Mekong Delta. It wasn't attack swimming by any means. It was just strap on a bottle and go down and see what you've got. Turns out that what we got was one of the 122mm rocket squads.

We had some pretty good operations and we had some bad luck. Nobody was killed in my platoon, but a couple of guys were wounded, including me twice. The first time anybody got wounded in my platoon was in a kind of tragic accident. Not even an accident, but a mistake.

There was a program to emplace sensors where the VC and NVA moved so that technicians could hear or otherwise sense them coming. We worked with the PBRs to put in the sensors. When their batteries wore out and had to be replaced, we went back to get them. We put them right near the water's edge, but they were in VC territory, and while the PBR sailors could have done it themselves, they felt better having us SEALs do it.

One afternoon I was racked out after a night op when Bubba Brewton came in and said, "Rick, I have some bad news for you. Couple of guys have been hurt, one of them pretty bad."

Bubba had taken his squad out to recover sensors. They had booby-trapped one of the sensors before they implanted it with a special zero-delay hand grenade. When the pin was pulled and the spoon [safety lever] was released, the grenade would immediately detonate. Just the thing for a quick booby trap. Recovering a booby-trapped sensor was tricky. Our technique was to find the sensor, tie a long line around it, tie the other end to the PBR, and get the PBR underway with us in it. This would just pull the sensor out of the mud and into the river. The grenade would go off somewhere along the way and no one would get hurt.

This time the grenade didn't go off. It stuck to the sensor in a clump of mud. They pulled it all the way up to the PBR. The lieutenant who was in charge of the PBR fished around and got the grenade from under the flange of the sensor. The spoon was still held down by the mud, so it wasn't going to explode. Everybody gathered around to see what was happening, some of the PBR guys and some of our guys as well.

The PBR lieutenant had the grenade in his hand and he knew it had a zero-delay fuze. All he had to do was hold it or tie the spoon down and it would have been safe until we put the pin back in.

I don't know why he threw it, but he did. The spoon came up, and as advertised the thing went off immediately. He lost a good part of his hand. He had a flak jacket and helmet on; otherwise he really would have been shredded. Brewton, who was standing right next to the lieutenant, didn't get a scratch. He was lucky. One of our guys, Skip Isham, lost an eye. He was our first casualty. He eventually had to leave the Navy because of this. Lesson: Leave ordnance to those who understand it.

Third Platoon's next casualty was me. The T-10 area, in the northeastern corner of the Rung Sat, was a very heavily forested, swampy, impenetrable area where the intel people figured the VC and NVA had many base camps. This was where a lot of the trouble on the Long Tau and around Saigon was originating. It was a free-fire zone. Anyone out at night was fair game. Few U.S. forces had gone up into this area. It was nasty. The Long Tau shipping channel ran through it. The PBRs got shot at whenever they went in there, and the Seawolves would take fire when they flew over. Third Platoon started running patrols there in October 1968.

The first time we went up into the T-10 we had a hard time getting in. The waterways were so small, so intertwined, and so poorly mapped that it was difficult to tell where we were. But we knew there was some high ground back up in there, and that was probably where the VC had their base areas.

We figured instead of trying to come in the way the Army had been doing from the high ground to the north and the east, we'd come in from the south and the west through all the muck and slime. We took our boats as far as we could on a high tide, then got off and worked our way in to the high ground. We set up an ambush along a road outside a village. A guy came by with a gun. We hailed him, he ran, we shot him. After recovering his AK-47, we set up a perimeter nearby, knowing there were more VC in the village and they would come looking for him and us.

We had a perfect ambush set up. It was great. We had claymores covering the approaches. Everyone had a good view and clear fields of fire. We had our rear protected and nobody could see us. We were down in the tall grass and we just knew we were going to wax these guys when they came out after us.

Sure enough, up the road came ten or fifteen guys with AK-47s. I'd left the ambush position to crawl up to the road to see if anyone was coming. They came up the road pretty fast, and I just had time to crawl back to our perimeter when they reached our kill zone.

"Claymore!" I whispered. The VC were right there, thirty feet away. We would have had them cold. We wouldn't have had to fire a shot. Only the damned claymores didn't go off. We cranked them two or three more times and they still didn't go off. I couldn't believe it. Still on all fours, I said, "Open up!" to Bill Garnett, and the whole squad started shooting. We dropped a few of the VC right away, and the rest of them retreated, taking us under fire. That's when I got shot in the arm and leg.

We searched the area collecting enemy weapons and documents while waiting for the Seawolves to arrive. They took a fair amount of fire from the village and treeline. I couldn't walk well enough to get back to the boats—it was about a mile—so we called in slicks and left in style, guns blazing and the Seawolves roaring over and hosing the place down. We tried the claymores one last time before the slicks came in. The damned things went off. Lesson: Explosives can be unreliable, so you'd better have a backup plan.

About ten days after this it was Brewton's squad's turn to go out and they were doing a boat operation. We had a new boat at the time, the Light SEAL Support Craft. We really liked the LSSC, because it was extremely quiet. There was room on board for the Boat Support Unit crew of two and seven or eight SEALs, and there were pintles for mounting weapons up to M60 machine guns or even grenade launchers. It was low, fast, and so quiet you could hardly hear it coming.

Bubba decided he wanted to take his squad back into the T-10 area and try some waterborne ambushes with his squad in the LSSC. Occasionally, I would go out with his squad. My rules were that when we ran platoon ops I was in charge, and when he ran his squad ops he was in charge, even if I was along as a guest patroller. The gunshot wounds in my arm and leg were still open, but it was going to be a dry op, so I decided to go along with them. I really didn't have anything better to do.

The tactic was to motor at high speed to the target area, then go really slow and quiet and ease into a good ambush site. If we could, we'd plan it so the tide would just drift us up to where we wanted to be. We wouldn't even have to turn the engine on in the ambush area. Then we'd just sit there in an inconspicuous spot where we weren't silhouetted, maybe up against the bank under some overhanging bushes. We'd wait and keep our eyes and ears open. Even on a dark night, and this was a dark night, it's amazing what we could hear and see.

Before long, we heard and then saw some VC crossing the river in a sampan, so we eased out until they saw us, then shot them up and captured their weapons. Good deal—here it was, not even midnight and we had a hit and were still dry.

We then went to a different area and set up another ambush. It was a dry hole, so Bubba decided, "Let's go back past the first place and see if anybody's turned up to check it out."

We went back to the first ambush, and we didn't see any sign of the enemy. Everything was quiet. The LSSC had a small windscreen forward of the cockpit, and I was sitting with my back against it so I could see and hear better. The rest of Bubba's squad and the boat crew were in the cockpit behind me. I was sitting on the starboard side and Brewton was to my left.

We were idling quietly downstream about fifty feet off the right bank. I don't recall having heard anything, but all of a sudden I just knew we were in danger. I had this bad feeling . . . I must have subconsciously heard something. I turned to Bubba and said, "Let's get out of here," then told the boat officer, Lieutenant [now Rear Admiral] Jay Prout, "Jay, floor it, now!"

The helmsman rammed the throttles all the way forward. The boat surged forward for a second, then slowed down to about three knots. BAM! From the riverbank on the right, they were firing rocket-propelled grenades at us.

After giving the order to move out, I had turned to the

right, because that's where I felt the danger. We were close to the riverbank. I was turned half facing that direction when I saw the first rocket coming at us.

It's quite impressive to see an RPG fired at you on a dark night. It hit the water about ten feet short of the LSSC and made a big orange-red blast underwater.

The explosion blew me to the left slightly, and I remember feeling a light touch on the back of my right shoulder where I now have a thick five-inch scar. I had a shotgun that night. Regaining my balance, I emptied that shotgun at the spot where I thought the RPG had come from. After hearing that RPG-7, the shotgun sounded like a pop gun.

I was expecting the rest of the guys in the boat to open up. Nothing. There was an M60 man amidships on the starboard side who should have been firing back. That was Al McCoy, a fine Texan from my UDTR training class boat crew. He had caught a piece of shrapnel in the gut and was down inside the boat.

A couple of other guys had Stoners. I wondered why the hell they weren't shooting back. The blast from the rocket had blown them almost out of the boat. They were hanging on to the outside of the hull, clambering back in, as we were trying to get out of there. Another man grabbed the M60, but the RPG blast had blown the ammo belt right out of the feed tray.

This was not good. I yelled, "Get this thing under way," but the boat couldn't go any faster. Upstream artillery fire had blown a lot of branches into the water. Leaves were clogging the intakes and the Jacuzzi propulsion couldn't get any water to push. There we were, engines going like hell and we're doing three knots in the other side's kill zone.

Then the VC fired another rocket at us. I thought it had to be a dud, because I could see and hear it coming but there was no explosion.

It turns out that the VC must have been in as much of a hurry to reload as we were to get out of there. They didn't properly arm the second RPG. It hit the boat broadside about four inches above the waterline and left a big dent in the ceramic armor, but it didn't detonate. If it had, the boat and us would have been sunk.

We eventually got out of there after someone jumped in the water and cleared the intakes by hand. We called for Seawolves to hose down the VC and a medevac helo to meet us at the nearest village. Al McCoy went to the hospital, and so did I after Doc Burwell took a look at my shoulder. A piece of frag from the first rocket had blown up right into the forward part of the boat. If I hadn't been sitting exactly where I was it would have taken Brewton's head off instead of tearing up my shoulder. Lesson: It's better to be lucky than good sometimes.

Jay Prout, Al McCoy, and I were hit by shrapnel, but everybody else was just hit by the blast. They were singed, their ears were ringing, and their feelings were hurt, but they weren't damaged. Jay got a little piece of frag in his throat. Not many guys can say that they got a Purple Heart with an admiral, but then not many admirals have been on SEAL ops.

So Al McCoy and I were dusted off to Third Field Hospital in Saigon. McCoy went right into surgery and they got the shrapnel out of his guts. He had medical problems afterward that eventually resulted in him being evacuated to the States, where he was surveyed out of the Navy on a medical disability.

I spent a miserable night at Third Field Hospital. They cleaned up the wound, leaving it open to heal from inside, and put a bandage on it. The shrapnel missed the bones, but the wound was deep and I was really hurting. Doc Burwell had given me morphine in the boat, but morphine doesn't do much for me. I didn't feel the medical staff was paying attention at the hospital. It was a big open ward and I could hear wounded men moaning and crying out all night. Some guys in this ward really were badly injured. They needed care and they weren't getting it.

From what I could tell when I got up and gimped around, the nurses were off in a back room having fun with the doctors. This deeply infuriated me. Wounded men weren't getting the treatment they deserved. I couldn't sleep, so I wrote a letter to my sister Moira.

The next day I called down to Nha Be to my platoon. My cammies had been ruined and the nurses had taken them away from me. A couple of my guys drove up with another set of cammies and I just limped right out of Third Field Hospital and into our vehicle. Back in Nha Be, I turned myself over to the care of the doctor there, who cheerfully closed the wound with over a hundred stitches, the last twenty or so being quite memorable as the anesthetic had worn off. I was back in action a few weeks later.

I don't want you to have a skewed impression of my opinion of the nurses in Vietnam. True, my experience at Third Field Hospital in October 1968 was not positive, but I gained a lot of respect for some of the nurses there after Bubba Brewton was wounded on his second tour a year later.

He ended up in the renal ward. Renal wards are where people who have malfunctioning kidneys go. In Vietnam, it wasn't for people with kidney stones or urinary tract infections, it was for young men who were going to die soon, because when you're going to die soon your kidneys shut down. That was the last ward he was in, and he was in that ward for a long time.

At the time—late 1969—I was at the other end of the Delta with another platoon on my second tour. Whenever I could I jumped on a helicopter to Saigon to see him. Every time the same nurses were there. Sometimes Bubba was asleep or incoherent, so I went around the ward talking to the young soldiers and Marines who were shot up and dying.

If two weeks or so went by between my visits, a whole new cast of characters was there. The other guys all were dead.

Going around the ward, I talked to the guys about home and all, joked with them, young men I never knew before. Didn't matter. These boys couldn't have their relatives come over from the States, and most of them knew very well without being told they were never going to see them again. It was one of the saddest places I have ever been.

I got to know the nurses, and they were wonderful people. They went way beyond the call of duty to treat those wounded men as well as they possibly could. I don't see how they did it, a whole year putting all they had into taking care of fine young men who they knew were going to die.

During my first tour while my wounds were healing, I remember going on one nontypical SEAL operation. That was the All Officer Operation. Binh Thuy, further down the Delta than Nha Be, was where the in-country SEAL headquarters was based. For a few days in late '68, there was a bunch of SEAL officers down there for a meeting. So we all decided, let's run an op. Let's run an All Officer Op. The idea may have come up when we were drinking. We scrounged up some gear, those of us who were not based in Binh Thuy, and out we went.

We had an intel report of a VC communication station being in a certain place. We decided to go there and get the communicator. We patrolled in, watched the place, and we found this guy and got him and captured his codes. I don't recall everyone on the op—there were eight or ten of us from both coasts—but Chuck Le Moyne, Bob Gormly, and several other prominent SEALs were there.

In general, when my platoon got into firefights, we could tell if we were up against the VC or the NVA. The North Vietnamese were organized. They would maneuver, they would engage us. The VC would just shoot, and then run away and snipe at us. Their tactics weren't too good.

We were entitled to take R&R. Some guys went to Australia, some to Hong Kong or other places. I didn't go anywhere my first tour. Nha Be was right near Saigon. There was an exciting war going on and decent liberty, and I saw no reason to leave Vietnam.

I had gotten married in September 1969, two weeks before I left for my second tour, so I did take R&R that time. I went off to Hawaii, where Sandie and I resumed our honeymoon. That's where our daughter Jen came from.

In 1968, my platoon's routine in Nha Be was not too arduous. Every night a squad would be going out, unless some really hot intel came in. If this happened, I'd scare

up who I could, we'd throw on our gear, sprint to the
helicopter, and go on in. But normally we'd plan our ops
three days to a week in advance. Specific hard intel on
enemy targets was very scarce then, so we were left to
our own devices. Typically the patrol leader—myself,
Bubba, Warrant Officer Sol Atkinson, or Chief Bill Garnett—would go up in one of the Seawolves for a visual
recon and fly over an area he thought had potential for
getting us into some sort of scrap. We'd plot our routes,
where we wanted to go in, where we wanted to come out,
where we wanted to set up. After we flew over an area
we'd leave it alone for a while so the enemy on the ground
wouldn't be suspicious. Then we'd go in a week or so
later.

We'd have six or eight operations in mind at any given
time. We didn't go to the Tactical Operations Center and
start clearing the area until shortly before the op. In case
there was a leak we didn't want the op compromised.

Some of the troops would go out every night. They
didn't have anything else to do and they wanted to get as
much operational time as they could. We liked our job.

It was a fairly convenient way to fight a war. We
wouldn't be out in the field for more than twenty-four,
forty-eight hours at the longest. Often we could go out,
run the op, and get back in time to have breakfast. I always made sure I sent my SITREP [situation report] off
to the Team and higher headquarters before I went to
sleep, and I insisted that my other patrol leaders did the
same. If you put it off until later in the day you forget
details, or something else comes up. So no matter how
tired I was, I'd finish the SITREP, and then I'd have some
chow and get my head down for a while.

After a few hours' sleep, I'd check on the troops, do
admin stuff, coordinate with the base, Seawolves, and
PBRs, have a platoon meeting, then maybe get some more
sleep and take it easy that night. Go hit the club—there
was an Officers' Club in Nha Be—have a beer with the
Seawolf pilots and the PBR guys—then the next day try
to get some more sleep before going out that night.

The Nha Be Naval Base was a good place. We even

got freshwater showers by the end of my first tour. There were only saltwater showers when we first got there in June '68, but it would rain about three o'clock every day, so everybody would strip down, go outside, and stand under the overhang of the roof with some soap and get clean in the runoff. This amused and entertained the hooch maids no end. As far as life in a combat zone went, compared to a lot of field operators' experience in Vietnam, Nha Be was the lap of luxury.

Nha Be was a Navy show. We had the SEALs, the patrol boats, the minesweepers, and the Seawolf helicopters all on base, so we were nearly self-sufficient.

We didn't have anything directly to do with the Air Force. We never saw the Air Force people, we only saw their planes. If we really got in trouble the fixed-wing fire support craft we'd get would be Air Force. They were cordial if somewhat detached on the radio if we had to call them in.

The Army 9th Division was operating in our area of the Mekong Delta. We got along okay with those guys. Their tactics were to go in large groups and conduct big sweeps of an area. It seemed odd to us that they would go in such large numbers and make so much noise that they minimized their chances of surprising the enemy.

The only time we worked directly with the Army was when we needed extra helicopter gunships, a dust-off, or slicks for infil or exfiltration. Those Army helicopter pilots were great. They'd come right into hot LZs and get us every time. I can't say enough good about the courage and the competence of the Seawolves and the Army helicopter pilots of that war.

We didn't see much in the way of Marines. There was a Marine advisor to the South Vietnamese troops in the Nha Be area, and we would share intelligence when we could.

All the SEALs in my platoon were good operators. Bill Garnett, Jerry Todd, Bo Burwell, Chuck Detmer, and, of course, Bubba Brewton stand out in my mind after twenty-five years. We ran our ops the way we wanted to. We carried out the tactics, techniques, and procedures that we'd been taught in training. They worked just fine.

All in all, Third Platoon had a successful tour. We ran a lot of ops, more than most platoons. In those days, body count was the measure of success, though I always thought weapons captured was a better measure. We did well in both departments. We didn't have anybody killed, and only two guys were seriously wounded in my platoon. I brought everybody back alive, and I felt pretty damn good about that.

Regarding equipment and weapons, overall we were adequately supplied. One thing about an operator, he's never totally satisfied with his equipment, and he absolutely can never have enough good intelligence. In retrospect, I have to say we had pretty good gear. We were one of the first units to have camouflage uniforms. That was a morale thing. When it's midnight in Vietnam and you're wet, it doesn't make any difference whether you've got cammies on or a leisure suit.

We got the XM-148—the over-and-under 40mm grenade launcher—when it was still experimental. That was a good weapon. I carried it on my CAR when I wasn't using a shotgun.

We had full-automatic shotguns [Remington Model 7188s], but they were intolerant of the salt water and dirt. For myself, I used an old-fashioned pump-action shotgun [Ithaca Model 37] with a duckbill modification. The duckbill would spread out the pattern of shot, flatten it and elongate it sideways to give wider coverage of the kill zone. It was especially useful for water ambushes.

We used a lot of SEAL innovation and ingenuity in cutting down the M60 machine gun for our use. The bipod legs would be removed, saving about a pound and a half of weight. The bipod mount was removed and the barrel was cut back to the gas cylinder, in the process removing the front sight, and the flashhider then was reinstalled. Doing all of that work would take another couple of pounds of weight from the weapon. All in all, we could take the M60's weight down from about twenty-three pounds to around nineteen. That helped make the weapon much handier for one man to use on patrols. By just putting on a complete barrel assembly, the weapon would be returned to its original condition. The work we did adapted the M60 to be an individual rather than a crew-served weapon.

The Stoner was a light machine gun firing linked 5.56mm ammo, the same caliber as the M16. The ammo is about half the weight of an equal amount of M60 [7.62mm] ammo, and the weapon itself is much lighter. Again it was officially a crew-served weapon used as an individual weapon by the SEALs. That design was good, although we did have a couple of embarrassing moments with the Stoner barrel disconnecting from the receiver when you needed it most.

Although we were pretty well equipped, at the time it seemed that we couldn't get gear as fast as we wanted. We wanted boats faster, we wanted certain types of ammunition faster, we wanted automatic grenade launchers faster, we wanted starlight scopes, more and sooner and smaller. I remember being hacked off enough so that I vowed that I'd do what I could in the future to make sure the operators would have everything they need. As a young lieutenant, I didn't want to be in an office doing admin and supply-type stuff. But I realized that someone has to do that sort of thing—otherwise the troops on the ground are not going to get the kind of equipment and other support they deserve. Ever since 1968 I've remained sensitized to the fact that you'd better have some good people back at headquarters with operational experience, who understand operations and know what the operators need and how to get it.

My most poignant memories of Vietnam are of my assistant platoon commander, Bubba Brewton. John Cooke Brewton. He went through UDTR eight months after I did, but we went through Ranger school together. You get pretty close with your Ranger buddy in the wintertime, and we were in a winter class.

Bubba was a big strong guy and a fast runner. He was from Mobile and graduated from the University of Alabama; Bubba was always interested in how the Crimson Tide was doing in football. He'd been a cheerleader at

Alabama. Some people look askance at male cheerleaders, but I think he liked the part about getting to hoist women around by their off-limits areas.

This guy was an outstanding operator and tough as nails. He also had a great sense of humor. You couldn't hurt him. At the same time he was very stubborn and you couldn't tell him anything, either.

Before we deployed to Vietnam that first time, if he didn't have a date for the weekend he'd put on his uniform and just fly somewhere, anywhere, and he'd meet the stewardesses. Guys in Navy uniforms were quite acceptable in those days, and he was a good-looking man. He would just get women.

When his training class was in swim school in Key West, a bunch of them had gone up to Miami and had fallen in with some young ladies from all over the world who were training to be stewardesses with Pan Am. He knew a lot of stewardesses. We'd be doing the morning run at SEAL Team TWO and a plane would take off from Norfolk airport and Bubba would get this wistful look in his eye and say, "Yeah, there goes Cheryl on the seven forty-one to Atlanta."

In Ranger school they couldn't faze him. In our platoon he was very aggressive, quick-thinking, and courageous. He was a hard guy and a very strong leader.

He was lucky, too. Even though he was right next to the booby-trap grenade when it exploded in the PBR, he wasn't even scratched. The first time I got shot, when I was on all fours in that field and the claymores didn't go off, those AK-47 rounds would have hit Brewton if they hadn't hit me first. Ten days later in the LSSC, if I hadn't been sitting just the way I was when the first RPG went off, the frag that ripped my shoulder would have taken Brewton's head off.

We used to joke about it. I'd say, "Hey, Bubba, what's going to happen to you when you go back to the States and I'm not there? You're going to have a safe fall on you. You're going to get run over by a truck." He'd just laugh. He was twenty-four and thought he was going to live forever.

His fatal flaw was that he got so used to being the ambusher that he figured he would never make contact except on his terms. So he blew off the possibility that the enemy could catch him by surprise.

When I went out on his patrols, I noticed that after he'd break ambush, it was almost an administrative patrol to the LZ or the boat pickup point. I'd say, "Bubba, don't go admin yet. This is still tactical."

He'd say, "Yeah, but we've been here all night and there's nobody around to catch us."

His luck held during our tour in 1968 but ran out a year later when he was on his second tour. His platoon had set an ambush all night in the T-10 area. No contact, and when it got light they moved out toward the extraction point and walked right into a VC base camp. Several guys got shot up pretty badly, though I think they inflicted as much damage as they suffered. Bubba's quick reaction when the VC opened up on them helped save the rest of the platoon. He got the Silver Star and Purple Heart for that action.

He was wounded on Thanksgiving Day, 1969, and died of wounds in Saigon on 11 January 1970. His father and his fiancée, Cheryl, came over to be with him while he was in Third Field Hospital. The Commander of Naval Forces–Vietnam, Vice Admiral Zumwalt, presented Bubba's medals to him in the hospital and took Mr. Brewton and Cheryl under his wing. The doctors said Bubba wouldn't make it to Christmas and then not to the New Year, but he had a strong heart and hung on until the second week in January. He was in the renal ward I talked about earlier, and he was in great pain for a long time. Admiral Zumwalt did everything he could for Mr. Brewton and Cheryl during their vigil. Later that year, when he became Chief of Naval Operations, he saw to it that a new Destroyer Escort was named after Bubba. I was present when Mrs. Zumwalt christened the USS BREWTON, DE-1086, in the summer of 1971. Right after that, I put in my request to transfer from the Naval Reserve to the Regular Navy.

The BREWTON is no longer in active duty, but Bubba's name is on the Wall. Every time I go there I put my hand on it and I think of him and all the other fine young men in the renal ward at Third Field Hospital.

Not all of the SEALs' combat in Vietnam took place in the jungles or swamps. The 1968 Tet offensive by the Viet Cong put the SEALs in the position of fighting wherever they might be. Buildings and barracks were fortified and careful watches were kept to alert the platoons about any incoming VC. Some combat took place in the cities and towns of Vietnam. Squads and platoons coming in from extended patrols in the countryside could find themselves in the middle of fierce house-to-house combat. This kind of fighting was more familiar to the veterans of World War Two in Europe than to the counterinsurgency experts in the Teams.

Though the '68 Tet offensive was a resounding defeat that decimated the ranks of the Viet Cong, it was somehow misinterpreted back in the United States. To the American public, it was reported as a loss for the U.S. and South Vietnamese forces. But no individual unit was more successful in defeating the Viet Cong during Tet than the SEALs.

★ ★ ☆

FIRST CLASS DRAFTSMAN

HARRY HUMPHRIES

USN (LEFT 1969)*

Harry Humphries was one of the SEALs in Eighth Platoon who entered the city of Chau Doc during the Tet offensive in 1968. This was one of the rare incidents of the SEALs conducting house-to-house and street-to-street combat in a style reminiscent of World War Two. Rick Marcinko was the officer in command of Eighth Platoon during this and other actions.

The PBRs arrived off of Chau Doc while it was still dark. Rick had them lay off shore until first light, so they went into their RPG defensive maneuvering mode to help avoid incoming RPG rocket fire. Rick had been in intermittent contact with the Army Special Forces C-Team's TOC [Tactical Operations Center] in Chau Doc. He was trying to learn what conditions ashore were like before we landed. By now, Rick had established a radio relationship with the OD [officer of the day] lucky enough to have had the duty during the Tet offensive. We knew that the city was overrun with VC, but that was all.

At first light we landed and zigzagged towards the TOC as quickly as we could. We received a few stray sniper rounds that came our way that could very well have been so-called friendly fire. We did tend to look like VC from a distance.

*Dedicated to Maggie Franckot.

251

When we arrived at the TOC, the scene there was dismal. The OD was lying on a bunk with his hands behind his head staring up at, or through, the ceiling. I remember being impressed with his matter-of-fact coolness as he listened to the radio reports of massive VC movements that were coming in from various outposts throughout the province.

There was one semifrantic voice coming over the radio shouting an ever-increasing count of VC troops coming into his view. I believe that report was coming from one of the Special Forces A-Team troopers camped on top of Ngui Gai mountain, a piece of expensive real estate that those guys fought for on a daily basis. Rick and I were later going to observe the situation on Ngui Gai firsthand while on a recon of the area. The mountaintop offered an excellent view of the entire area and served, among other things, as a spotting position for the local artillery batteries.

During our return trip down the Bassac River towards Chau Doc, Drew Dix, the provincial PRU advisor, was in contact with his safe house in the city. Drew, along with a few of his PRU scouts, had accompanied our platoon on the border LP [listening post] operation that we had just completed. Getting off the PRC-25 radio, Drew came over to me and said that all of the American civilians in Chau Doc were in VC-held sections of the city. He was concerned about the American nurses there, who had no way of defending themselves. The people at Drew's safe house suspected that the nurses might be captured by the incoming VC. There was no doubt that Drew had close friends in there who were in danger of becoming victims of the Tet offensive. We both agreed that we had to go in there and get them out.

While the platoon hit the TOC, Drew went to get the jeep he had left at his compound the night before. When Drew came back to get me, I asked Rick if I could break off from the platoon. Rick agreed that I had to go with Dix to give him some backup. There was a pleasant surprise waiting for me when I got to Drew's vehicle. Mounted on the rear bed of the jeep was a .50 caliber machine gun. A nice piece of firepower to go traveling with.

Drew knew the route to the safe house where he wanted to link up with his people, company men. He told me that his people were surrounded and that I should stand by for his warning that we were entering the danger area. When Drew gave me the signal I would be free to use the .50, which should have a tendency to suppress any enemy sniper fire.

Jumping up on the back of the jeep, I checked out the .50. Opening the cartridge box on the mount and the feed tray cover on the weapon, I loaded a belt into place and jacked a round into the chamber. Test-firing two short bursts, I knew the .50 was ready. Wally Schwalenberg, Eighth Platoon's dog handler and one hell of a good man, jumped into the jeep carrying a Stoner. They were both something that I was glad to see. Then Frank Thornton climbed into the front shotgun seat armed with an M16. Now we were ready to go.

As we were pulling out, Rick looked directly into my eyes and, for one of the few times I can remember, was dead serious. With noticeable concern in his voice, Rick said, "Keep your head down, asshole, and be careful." I was abundantly aware of his sincerity and couldn't help but smile back when Rick added, "Maybe you'll get laid."

As I gave Rick a thumbs-up, Drew laid rubber all over the street pulling out of the compound and into the battle zone of Chau Doc. With Frank and his M16, Wally with his Stoner, and me on the .50, Drew was racing at the jeep's top speed through the narrow VC-held streets. As we approached the safe house, Drew gave us a heads-up, since it was inevitable that the sturdy building had been fortified.

Sure enough, as soon as we came into range, the shit hit the fan. Our small-arms fire wasn't very effective, as most of us had to hold on to the jeep with one hand as we fired. Without hanging on, everyone would have been thrown from the jeep because of Drew's swerving to make us a difficult target. Standing up in the back, I returned fire with the .50. The large tracers helped me aim the weapon like a big fire hose. With the stability of the mount, I was able to direct streams of fire near and through the windows that the VC were firing from.

Poor Drew was in a hell of a predicament while driving. Sitting where he was, practically right under the muzzle of the big .50, Drew had to take his hands off the steering wheel to protect his ears from the thunderous concussion of the muzzle blast not three feet away. Naturally, Drew couldn't slow down, and the jeep swerved drastically, almost hitting the parapet of an upcoming bridge.

Seeing Drew's trouble, I stopped firing so that he could drive the vehicle. By then the enemy fire had stopped anyway. Finally, we reached the safe house. Pulling up to the heavily barricaded complex, we waited for the steel door to be opened.

Westie, the O [operations] officer, opened the gate and waved us through. Carrying a submachine gun in one hand, Westie was waving with his free hand as the gate swung open. The people in the compound had been under a lot of fire and appeared to have done quite well for themselves. No small amount of credit was also due the help given by the detachment of Hmong and Chinese PRU guards assigned to the safe house. Drew and Westie exchanged information quickly, then Dix introduced the rest of us in the jeep. We discussed a brief patrol order for our insertion to the American nurses' house.

The plan was for us to penetrate the VC-held area with three jeeps and either immediately extract with the nurses or take control of the house and hold it until we could be relieved. We could only hope the nurses were still alive, as we were going to try and get them, no matter what.

Both Drew and Westie knew the layout and location of the nurses' house—we couldn't have gone without that. I stayed with Drew in his jeep, and the others went with Westie and Jim Moore, the P [Provincial] officer. We took off trailing each other, racing at the jeep's top speed. We rocked over on two wheels as we turned corners in Chau Doc's back streets, receiving fire from pockets of VC too surprised at our sudden appearance to get a decent shot as we rushed by, or through, them.

There didn't seem to be any central command or control on the part of the VC. Mostly we encountered them in scattered, disorganized pockets. By the time we were discovered and identified, we would be out of sight, thanks to the densely packed housing in this section of the city. The insertion became one long firefight as we encountered one small group after another.

My memory fails me for much detail about the run. It was a blur of split-second situations coming and going in rapid succession. Sometimes, during a quiet moment or in a dream, I get a flashback of specific detail on our harrowing run through Chau Doc.

Before I knew it, the jeeps were screeching to a halt—we had reached our destination. Our advantages of surprise and speed were now gone. We were clearly in the middle of the largest concentration of VC we had found that day. And they had time to coordinate their efforts and zero in on our position. Their incoming fire sounded like Chinese firecrackers, cracking in rapid succession around us. Jumping out of the vehicles, we dove into defensive positions in the courtyard before the front door of the house.

Along with Westie and Drew, I was lying on the ground next to the house's folding steel grating, an accordionlike affair that was drawn across the open doorway and securely locked. The others had, true to their training, set up a half-moon defensive circle in the yard, anticipating an attack by onrushing VC. Looking through the grating, we could see about three VC scrambling for cover in the kitchen at the far side of the house.

The incoming fire seemed to let up as we took cover ourselves. We hid behind a porch wall made up of concrete columns about six inches apart and three feet high. Apparently the VC lost visual contact with us for a moment. Looking back now with time to think, the lull probably lasted only a matter of seconds.

Drew yelled out something like "Maggie, are you there?" His call having shown our position, the VC opened up on us again. Bits of concrete wall, pavement, and tile shingles were flying through the air as bullets exploded all around us. I remember being relieved to hear a frantic, sobbing, female American voice loudly whisper from inside the building, "There's a bunch of them in the kitchen!"

"Where are you?" Drew called out.

"Under my bed!" she returned.

"Stay there," Drew answered as we turned our attention to the building. The doorway we were looking through faced into the living room of the house. Maggie was hiding under her bed in the bedroom, to the left of where we were looking. Drew directed us to fire straight through the grate and told us that the bedroom was to the left. That was all we needed.

All our weapons opened up on the door, sweeping fire back and forth from the ground to the ceiling and back again. Inside, I could hear the VC scattering and screaming. Drew stopped the firing, then told Maggie to open the door and stay close to the ground. I didn't notice any fire coming from the VC who had been in the house. But the intense fire coming at us from the surrounding buildings reached a peak. Those guys wanted our asses bigtime.

The locked grate seemed a problem. Drew called out to Maggie, "Get the key and unlock the door." We could see Maggie as she came into the living room and started searching for the front-door key. The VC had piled up all the furniture in the center of the room, and it was in this mess that Maggie was frantically searching for the key. Apparently our luck was still holding, as she opened a drawer and stood up with the precious key in her hand.

None of us were thinking very well at the time. If we were, we would have realized that we certainly had the firepower with us to shoot the lock off the door. Between the Stoner, M16, shotgun, and Swedish K submachine guns we had, the lock would have been nothing but scrap in a moment. Of course, that action would have taken some thought, something that was in short supply with us at the time.

Maggie unlocked and folded back the grate and then collapsed, sobbing, on her knees. That poor kid had been through some moments of stark terror. As she was still too high and exposed, I grabbed her, throwing her down on the pavement and landing on top of her. The others started diving back into the jeeps. This place was far too hot for us to stay. Everyone knew that we had to take our chances fighting our way back out. Not one word of directions came from anyone.

Pulling Maggie up by her shoulders, I threw her into the rear of the jeep, under the .50. As Drew started to pull out and follow the other vehicles, I dove into the jeep, landing on Maggie. The incoming fire remained at its peak intensity as we pulled out and turned the corner. Again under the relative safety of speed and surprise, we headed back to the TOC area.

More firefights took place as we headed back, the same as when we went in towards the house. There was still no indication of command or control on the part of the VC. As we pulled into the TOC area, I hustled Maggie over to our corpsman, Doc Nixon. During the extraction events, Maggie had gotten cuts on her knees and legs. Doc examined her and administered stitches where needed. Strangely enough, I remember looking down at her leg and finally realizing she was a girl.

This is one of many scenarios from that time that still pops up in my mind. I don't remember if I have all the players right except for Drew, Westie, Jim Moore, and Wally. Frank Thornton and I were together on so many intense situations during those days that it is difficult to remember exactly which ones they were. There is no question that the situations brought out the finest in everyone involved. It was an honor to be a member of this group of SEALs, Company men, PRUs, and civilians.

14-18 FEB 68 1500-1822 WS018548 SEAL Element 8th PLT (2 men). Task: Collect intelligence in 7 mountain region. Inserted and extracted by SLICK. Terrain was mountains. Weather clear. Verified with US eyes VC strength, movement, strongholds and tactics. Observed a total of over 400 VC. No engagement. Dressed in black pajamas and sterilized equipment element passed and was reported as two Russian Advisors. Bold actions as this can net worthwhile results. Enclosure (2) SEAL TEAM ONE Command and Control history for 1968.

As SEAL Team ONE had the primary commitment to Vietnam, it fell upon it to record as much of the actions that took place there as possible. This resulted in interesting situations such as the above operation, conducted by SEAL Team TWO personnel, being reported in the Team ONE history. But the SEALs were action-oriented operators who excelled at most of their duties, record keeping not being one.

What the above operation does indicate is the audacious manner in which the SEALs got their job done. By the second full year of combat duties in Vietnam, an experienced cadre of seasoned veterans was available on both coasts. These men had learned what it meant to fight in an unconventional war. Now they were learning even more about the enemy they faced and the people they were defending.

COMMANDER

RICHARD MARCINKO

USN (RET.)

*A man who joined the Navy and soon developed a
determined intent to become a frogman, Richard Marcinko went through UDTR training as an enlisted man
and earned his place in the ranks of the UDT. As he
learned of the Navy SEALs, Marcinko became just as
determined to become one of the new breed of operators and to join their ranks, which he did after a
detour to earn his commission as an officer. As a
"hard charger," Marcinko moved through the ranks
of the Team quickly, earning himself a reputation as
a maverick officer, but one who always got the job
done. That job included becoming the eighth Commanding Officer of SEAL Team TWO as well as the
founding officer and first CO of SEAL Team SIX and
later the Commander of the special Red Cell unit.*

This story really started just after the Tet offensive of
1968, while I was in Chau Doc with my men, the Eighth
Platoon of SEAL Team TWO. We had been through some
really hairy times during the offensive, and the fighting in
Chau Doc had been house-to-house for a while and costly.
We lost one of our own, Clarence Risher, to a sniper the
last day of January.

While in Chau Doc, the platoon hooked up with the
local Special Forces C-Team, who were running all of the
A-Team outposts along the Cambodian border and

throughout the area. While with the C-Team, I met some of the players from the A-Teams in the area. Along with the Special Forces soldiers we had met we were also getting along well with Drew Dix and Westie. Drew Dix was the provincial PRU advisor and Westie was the operations officer for the local American intelligence contingent. After the ruckus had died down from Tet, we were living out of the safe house with Drew and Westie.

The safe house was right on the river so we could keep our PBRs within easy reach, and Westie's Nung team was just up the street for backup. The Nungs operated under Westie as part of his action arm and Drew managed the team. Technically, I think the Chinese Nungs were hired as part of the CORDS [Civil Operations and Revolutionary Development Support] program to have a self-defense group for the villages in the south. At the time, Drew was a Special Forces sergeant E-6, and he would use the Nungs to collect intelligence in the area. Part of the fringe benefits for the Nungs was that they were able to turn in enemy weapons for the bonuses [bounty] that they would bring from the Agency people.

In the process of running these operations, Drew's people would move along the Vinh Te Canal where it was part of the Cambodian border. Their ops would go all the way out to and past where an A-Team had set up their camp in the Seven Mountains. Personalities being what they are, Drew liked the officer out at the A-Team, a first lieutenant, I think, better than he did the light colonel in charge of the C-Team. One was a hustler after my own heart and the other wasn't. But Drew managed to get us—myself and Harry Humphries—an invitation to go out to the A-Team's camp.

Catching a ride in a helo, we went out to the A-Team and spent a couple of days with them getting the lay of the land. What I wanted was to get a good feel for what action was taking place in the region and whether it would be worthwhile to bring my platoon out here. If there was enough action, perhaps several SEAL platoons could start operating the area.

The A-Team had been in place for a while. Among

their duties they ran a four-deuce [4.2-inch] mortar pit for local fire support and would put out small recce [reconnaissance] patrols to keep an eye out for enemy activity. Mostly what the A-Team did was watch and report on the flow of activity coming across the border from Cambodia into Vietnam.

The Viet Cong trained on the Cambodian side of the border and could be seen from where the A-Team had set up. Or at least the cloud of dust raised by the VC could be seen. When the dust cloud came up, out would come the big eyes to see what was happening over there on the far side of the fence. As the VC would cross the border, the men of the A-Team, as well as other observers, would try to see where the VC were hiding their weapons caches.

Army spotter planes, 0-1 Bird Dogs, would fly over the area trying to make out what was going on down on the ground. The planes were almost always shot at by Chinese .50 calibers in the hands of the VC in the Seven Mountains area. The pilots got pretty weird ducking all those bullets in what was not much more than an unarmed wood frame covered with cloth. One of the guys would try to get close enough to the VC to roll his wheels on the mountains—he did his best to give something back to them for shooting at him. Not being able to get any bombs, this guy would drop grenades, stuck into coffee cups and their pins pulled, down on VC locations. When the cups broke, or spilled out the grenades, the levers would fly, starting the fuse. That gave the grenades enough of a delay to get to the ground before they went off. Besides his java bombs, this pilot had strapped an M79 to his plane so that he could dip the wing down and make a clear shot. Flying over the area, this Army nut would sucker the VC into taking a shot at him. If he managed to see the flash of firing, he'd go back and raise merry hell with the VC from what was an "unarmed" aircraft.

The Army A-Team had a few quirks of their own with the way they operated with their higher echelons and support. Harry and I stayed with them a few days, and the lack of support appeared the most obvious problem. The team would put in for a resupply mission and a C-7A Caribou would make a supply drop right outside the camp. The area around the camp was basically open terrain, not flat, but there was little in the way of vegetation between the camp and the Vinh Te Canal. This made it an easy thing to spot when a load was coming in.

I saw some of the requisitions, and what was dropped wasn't necessarily what was ordered. Ammunition had been asked for, and the supply drop contained orange soda. The PX and not the bullet run had come in. But that wasn't the only odd thing about operating in the bush with that A-Team.

Here we were, basically at arm's length from the enemy, and little in the way of aggressive operations could be done. The mentality or psychology, if you will, of the situation was incredible. We could see the enemy training across the canal in Cambodia and just watched them go past us. The Army had tried to get further down from the Seven Mountains area and into the Tranh Forest, but they had never been able to sustain their operation. Mostly this was due to their light armament and lack of heavier fire support.

When the Army Special Forces units went into the Tranh Forest, they would very soon be out of range of any available artillery support. Because they were such a small unit, they didn't get the helicopter support the bigger units had available out of IV Corps in Can Tho.

So what the Special Forces did was run a lot of patrols through the area, keeping an eye out for enemy activity on the Vietnamese side of the border. The A-Team also spent a good deal of time keeping their force of locals trained up in operating the four-deuce tube and pushing for a more aggressive attitude toward operations.

What stood out to me was how the American Army spent so much time listening to and running down rumors, and then writing reports on the results. They worked more on that than they did on invading the enemy's territory and taking the fight to him. The real fighting the Americans did was when they were being overrun by the enemy.

And the overrun mode was almost becoming a graduation exercise for the VC training across the canal. All the American forces could do was watch the moving clouds of dust in Cambodia and think, "Well, shit, we're next."

Harry and I were watching all of this and talking to the troopers who were doing the eyeball-to-eyeball stuff. This was how we were able to fill in the blanks on our own assessment of what Charlie was doing.

What we had figured out was that the VC who staged much of the Tet offensive had come into Vietnam through the Seven Mountains region. We [the Eighth Platoon] had been up on the west side of Chau Doc near the canal prior to Tet and had run into the enemy on their way in. The word from intel was that this was a normal traveling route for the VC. If that was the case, and everything we had seen supported that hypothesis, then the VC had to be caching their supplies and weapons in the Seven Mountains region.

As SEALs, we could call in the Seawolves for air support. That advantage would allow us to call in air support much more easily than the Special Forces units could. What we needed to know was if there was enough activity to make the missions worthwhile. That was the situation that had gotten Harry and me out to the A-Team base, but now it seemed we had to go even further to see with our own eyes just what was happening on the ground. Everything we had heard from the A-Team seemed to point at there being some really worthwhile targets in the area. But this was just shortly after the Tet offensive had ended and the area was still pretty hot.

All my wandering around was partly an orientation tour, meet and greet, see who was there, what was going on, and what support was available. Bringing up a platoon for operations was what I wanted to do.

Operating with Westie and his people had been a good run for us as well as for them. When Westie's people came up with intel on a target, he had a hard time getting the C-Team in Chau Doc to react and get a real offensive going. There was a mentality in the leaders at the C-Team that they were there to help the Vietnamese fight and that there wasn't going to be a U.S. eyes-only mission. That mentality made it hard to get POL [petroleum, oil, lubricants] support and all of the other things it takes to really push an offensive ahead. The Army commander absolutely didn't want any of his people doing operations outside of the screen of his artillery. So if you couldn't drag a cannon or two along with you, no Army units would be taking the fight to the enemy.

The enemy held the high ground and could see everything that was happening on our side of the border. That situation would keep you from hiding a tube or two in a town and springing a surprise on Charlie. And even if you did get a forward base set up, Charlie's intel was so good that they would know everything a major unit did before the dust settled from the choppers.

As SEALs, we didn't operate with that mentality, and taking the fight to the enemy was our bread and butter. Drew and Westie were fun to work with and the Nungs they led were real fighters, but Chau Doc had taken a pasting during Tet. The fuel farm was a smoking ruin, and the hospital had been shot to shit as well. It wasn't like there was any way of saving grace anymore—we had been hit and hit hard.

It was time to nail the swimmer before he got into the water. The cache system the VC had in the Seven Mountains region gave them the ability to move lightly when crossing the canal and the border and still be sure of a good supply stockage in Vietnam. That was a situation that was going to change, and Harry and I were seeing just what we could do about it.

We still wanted to get out into the country and see what we could see. Getting out to the A-Team and looking at what was there had been a start. And now an opportunity for getting further into the bush was offering itself.

There were other Special Forces units even closer to the border. Some of the units weren't very large, not much more than a fire team or even just an advisor or two. The A-Team we were with had been supplying one of these forward units, an advisor in Tri Ton. Mail and stuff would come in to the A-Team by helicopter, and they would pack up what was needed in Tri Ton and send it along overland, usually by jeep. The situation had deteriorated pre-Tet, post-Tet, and during Tet. Ambushes had become so common that the team couldn't get permission from the higher-ups to make the mail run. Enter your friendly Navy mail carrier.

Harry and I volunteered to take the mail up to the advisor's post—actually an Army major in charge of the subsector, in Tri Ton. This would give us the opportunity to get a good feel for the land and the people who lived in it. The first question from the Army people was, just how were we going to get there?

"We'll walk," was my answer.

After all, no helicopters were going into the area, and the team didn't have a vehicle they could give us. The distance was only about twenty kilometers and the roads were good, at least good for Vietnam. The Army guys must have thought we were more than a little crazy, but they accepted our offer to go.

As we followed our SEAL traditions, uniforms for the mission were casual. Harry and I wore black pajamas and sandals, not exactly standard issue but nothing that would stand out much either. For weapons, I was carrying a 9mm Swedish K submachine gun, and I think Harry had a CAR-15 that day. The chest pouch I wore carried four magazines for my K. Along with the submachine gun I had a couple of grenades and a hush puppy.

The hush puppy was a suppressed Smith & Wesson Model 39 with a special slide lock. Though a holster was available for the weapon, I usually carried it hanging from my neck on a lanyard. From the lanyard, I could put the hush puppy into action faster than by pulling it from a holster, and speed could be important. Others may have had different experiences, but my hush puppy was used mostly for the very reason it had been given its name, silencing yapping village dogs. Very seldom did I use the hush puppy against a person. Dogs and ducks raising an alarm were a much more common target. And even hitting the dog didn't always silence it right away—a few yelps would get out.

But the pistol was quiet, especially with its slide held shut during firing by the slide lock. I always used the weapon as a single-shot anyway, as the subsonic ammunition we had then wouldn't work the slide reliably for semiautomatic fire.

For this short op we wouldn't carry any packs, and the mail was just in a small sack easily slung over one shoulder. Being the masculine sorts we were, Harry and I sported full mustaches, had a few days' worth of beard, and were generally in a nicely scruffy condition. I was tanned brown, but Harry Humphries would tan dark, almost black, under a tropical sun, and we had been in the sun for some time.

That was our gear, not intentionally sterile in that we wouldn't carry any American-made equipment, but we sure didn't look like Joe Grunt. The little mail sack our mission had been centered around didn't seem like much, but when you were out in the field for a long time, any news from home or the world in general was worth a lot. Having breakfast with the A-Team, we shot the shit and picked up on what they considered the problems in the area and what they were facing in the way of enemy forces. What we learned was not what we had heard from Westie or had shown up in any reports we had read from the American intel community. What we were told was the personal, judgmental, gut feeling kind of intel that a soldier doesn't put down in official documents but that he might say in a face-to-face with a fellow warrior. Stuff that could be very valuable to a SEAL platoon thinking about moving into an area.

Finally ready to go, we paid our farewells, and our bar bill, which was pretty small, orange soda not being my favorite potable, and set off on our mail run.

It was one of those real hot days Vietnam could have, dry and dusty. We had left early in the morning, but at that time of year there really wasn't much in the way of a cool time of day. Having been given directions to Tri Ton, we were just walking along the road trying to watch everything at once. Enemy scouts were in the area along with VC in the hills. They were the ones who had been ambushing the earlier runs. Scouts would see the vehicles and report to the forces in the hills. When a vehicle hit a choke point somewhere on the trail, the ambush would be sprung.

But two guys walking along don't raise the dust or make the noise of a vehicle. They also get footsore and tired of walking after several hours. Harry and I had decided that we'd just about had enough of this infantry work and that there had to be a better way when we heard the sound of a vehicle coming up the road behind us. It was just the chug-chug-chug of a little Vespa cyclo bus, not much more than a motorbike with delusions of grandeur. But it was transportation, and local transportation at that, so it wouldn't stand out.

Stepping out from the side of the road, we ambushed the bus by intimidation more than anything else. There were only about six Vietnamese aboard, but when Harry and I clambered in, we filled half the little bus all by ourselves. Pointing ahead and saying "Tri Ton," we made our desires known to the driver as he nodded and got us all going.

While moving along, Harry and I watched everything around us as well as the people aboard the bus. What little talking we did between ourselves we did in Spanish in case we were overheard. It wasn't that we expected the locals to understand English, but the bus had probably come from the market in Chau Doc or something like that. The locals might not understand English, but they had probably heard it and knew what it sounded like. If anyone did report the two fat-assed foreigners who took up so much of the bus, they would also say they didn't talk like Americans.

With the locals being between the VC and NVA on one side and the ARVN and American forces on the other, playing both sides was just a way of surviving. Nothing to hold against anyone, but nothing we would forgive either. What Harry and I spoke about was what to do if anyone got goosy and looked as if they were going to sell us down the river at a VC checkpoint or something.

Mostly what we did was look at the terrain around us

and watch the people on board the bus watch us. The locals would give us more information than anything else by the way they acted when we passed crossroads and trails along the way. People would get nervous and glance around when we passed certain places, places that Harry and I would make a mental note of. During our walking phase, Harry and I had also seen glints of light up in the hills, such as would be made from sunlight glancing off glass. Foot trails were around that were obviously well used, but in locations that no legitimate villager would have any use for.

Coming to a break in the road, the driver stopped the bus and pointed down the other trail. Calling out "Tri Ton" in that singsongy voice a nervous Vietnamese tended to have, the driver made it obvious that if we wanted to get to Tri Ton, we would have to walk the rest of the way. The bus had skirted the town, and we had about another thirty-minute walk ahead of us. When we climbed out of the little bus, a very relieved driver and passengers moved along their way, leaving Harry and me to our own concerns.

The place didn't seem like an ambush site, just another turnoff in the road, so Harry and I continued walking into town. The village wasn't very big at all, and we made a bit of a stir when we walked in. The Special Forces sergeant who was one of the advisors came out of a hooch to see us dressed only in his pants. We had arrived about fifteen hundred hours, siesta time, and they had definitely not been expecting visitors.

That didn't mean we weren't welcome. In fact, once the surprise wore off, we were soon seated with a cold beer in our hands. Delivering the mail, we received an intel dump from the advisors, along with a number of questions such as: Where had we come from? How had we gotten there?—they hadn't heard a helicopter. And what did we mean, we were sailors?

The situation we walked into in Tri Ton was one I would see again and again in Vietnam. The Army major was getting replaced in a few months and was preparing his end-of-tour report as well as doing all the political things necessary in Vietnam—going over to the subsector chief's house and kissing the ring, seeing all the other local politicos, and filling out reams of paperwork so there would be an easy turnover to his replacement. All of this since he had gotten back from his R&R.

That gave us a kind of an attitude feeling as to how effective the Army's one-year-on-station system for advisors was. The first three months of a tour would be spent learning just what the hell you were there for. By the fifth month maybe you had earned the respect of your Vietnamese counterpart and could operate effectively. The seventh month was your R&R, and by the eighth month you started saying your goodbyes. Not the most effective use of time in-country.

For Harry and me, our little tour around the countryside proved worthwhile. After we had gotten to the outpost in Tri Ton, we spent some time with the advisors, learning from them what they had seen and thought. On our way into town, we hadn't seen any weapons, but more than a few signs of VC activity. All the movement and indications pointed to a large number of VC moving about the area. The situation looked good for bringing a good dose of "doom on you" to the VC, SEAL-style.

The trip back to the A-Team and then Chau Doc was much the same as the trip out—plenty of signs of activity. What was probably more interesting than what we had seen ourselves was the intel reports that came in about seven days later through the regular Navy channels. The big story was about the Russian advisors working in the Seven Mountains region. Was the report about Harry's and my wanderings or did we actually have Russian advisors out in the field?

My questions weren't as farfetched as they might appear. Though the information in the reports fit what Harry and I had been doing, there were other possibilities. The info from the A-Team and the Tri Ton people had told us about possible Chinese advisors working with the VC in Cambodia and probably Vietnam as well. What the Special Forces guys had seen were big Orientals working with the VC units. Guys as big as Harry and me, too large to easily write off as VC or North Vietnamese. And they couldn't be Cambodians, because one, the Cambodians weren't friendly to the Vietnamese. And two, the Khmer Kom Cambodians who were in the area didn't even look much like Asiatics; they were dark, almost ebony, in color.

It had been good that Harry and I had not been reported as Americans, but I had mixed emotions about the situation. There was the question of could there really be Russians around or was this an indicator of how screwed up our intelligence reporting program was. It didn't matter much who you were working with, locals, PRUs, scouts, or whatever. Eventually they all learned what it was we wanted to hear, and that was what they sold us. Whatever other information they might have just didn't get reported sometimes. A good example of this is Nick Rowe, the Special Forces officer who had been captured by the VC. I don't know how many reports we heard about a round-eye in the Delta—far more camps would have had to be around than we could ever have walked to. I wasn't on the op that chased Nick down, but I had talked to him since then. Nick figured that he was moved from camp to camp probably about two days before anyone could learn where he was. So we had gotten the information we wanted to hear, but always just a little too late.

That was one of the situations that made our eyes-on investigation of an area so important. It was interesting just how much you could see once you got up high in the terrain. It was like looking out over the plains out West in the States. To the south you were looking out over the Tranh Forest, where you couldn't see shit except for the top of the Tranh. Towards the Vinh Te Canal and the Cambodian mountains in the distance beyond, the situation was different. That direction you could see everything—it was wide open and like watching maneuvers in Arkansas.

For the Special Forces guys, their primary bit was to watch these groups, try to pick up on who they were exactly, and track their movements into Vietnam. For us, it was obvious that there was more than enough activity and targets to be worth our coming into the Seven Mountains in some force.

As a Navy Team, we had a much different system going for us than the Special Forces units had. All of the support I would need for operations in the Tranh Forest and Seven Mountains was available from the Game Warden Task Force, which we were a part of. For helicopter support I could call in Seawolves or Cobras out of Can Tho to cover us. The birds would do sixty-mile runs or whatever was needed to get to where the battle was.

Eighth Platoon had come into the Seven Mountains region to operate, and there was more than enough going to keep one SEAL platoon busy. That one little wandering operation Harry and I did led to at least three more successful ops for us in the area. On one night op, the platoon was surrounded by a VC company who were crossing the Vinh Te for liberty or whatever in Vietnam. The situation allowed us to witness the level of training reached by the new VC coming out of Cambodia.

At one point, we were fighting off a surrounding group of VC while taking cover in an old graveyard. The macabre surroundings were overshadowed by the actions of the VC we were facing. For the first time I was watching the VC act like regular trained soldiers. When we fired on them, the VC would drop down and return fire while trying to outflank us at the same time. It was almost like watching an old World War Two movie except it wasn't blanks being fired. While pulling our own chestnuts out of the fire, we would see the VC break left or break right, move, drop, and fire just like conventional forces. All right! Too bad they were on the wrong side. We did manage to get out of that one with nothing more than a good impression of the local VC, but it looked like another SEAL platoon would be a nice thing to have around.

Henry J. [Jake] Rhinebolt was the officer in charge of Detachment Alfa, the Team Two SEALs in Vietnam, at the time, and he came out to lead a second platoon on ops with us. Going out on one op in the Tranh Forest, Jake probably figured he should have stayed back where he was.

We were going in on a two-platoon sweep of an active enemy area. I was leading the Eighth Platoon and Jake had the other. Right from the start, Murphy's Law seemed to be taking over. One of the Cobras out of Can Tho that was going to give us cover blew off his canopy during the flight in. The squadron commander wasn't about to let his bird fly about in possible combat without a hat on, so he called it back to Can Tho, and the wingman went with it. We still had Seawolves on call, so that wasn't too bad.

Then we inserted into the grassland near our target. The slicks came down to just above the grass and we jumped out. Expecting to hit the ground and move out, we fell through the tall grass. And tall was the word for it. We just kept falling and falling, finally landing after a much longer fall than we expected. Magazines would whip up and smack you in the face because you weren't ready to hit the ground, it was so far away.

Nobody was hurt, though, and we moved out into what was almost total darkness. Once we got under the canopy of the forest, you couldn't see anything. The treetops were so closely interwoven that very little if any light got down to the ground. It was so dark that I walked into a hooch. The traditional little Buddhist light was burning, but I never saw it until I bumped into the building.

We had night vision equipment available to us, but the stuff was really too heavy and cumbersome to bother with. The starlight scope, the AN/PVS-1, was a neat toy and a new thing but just too much to mess with on an op like this. The AN/PVS-1 was too heavy, so fragile that it could easily break if you hit it, and the draining batteries were a real pain in the ass. Besides all of that, using the scope left a green ring around your eye that made you look like Ricky Raccoon as well as ruining that eye's night vision for at least an hour.

There was a division-sized operation going on some-where, so our slicks were called away, leaving us on our own. Jake Rhinebolt's platoon was only a few hundred meters away and completely out of sight. In the high grass we couldn't see anything anyway, and when we got into the higher vegetation, it was too dark to see the other platoon. The hooch I had walked into was fair-sized, not just a lean-to but a building large enough to be an aid station or something like that.

Working from the building, we spread out, looking for anything that might be around. And there were some VC nearby and Jake found them. A VC patrol had been coming into the area, and Jake's platoon ran into them while out in the open. The firefight was short and fierce; by the time we got there it was over. We didn't get away clean, though—Jake had been hit.

An AK round had struck Jake on his rig, smashing into his magazines. The bullet itself didn't do much damage to Jake, but the spalling from his magazines really ripped up his gut. Though messy, the fragments of the magazines were light metal and didn't do near the damage an AK round could have. Problem was that we didn't have the Army birds on call anymore for a medevac. We were able to call in a Seawolf extraction and got Jake out all right.

The Seawolves didn't have enough lift to take us all out of there, so Jake's group pulled out with him. Deciding to continue with the sweep, we moved out and came across a camp with ducks set out as watchdogs. We had seen people moving around the Tranh with ducks and didn't think anything of it, but around this camp they were a real problem.

Whether they were ducks or geese I don't really know. What I do know is that they were big noisy honkers, better guards than dogs would have been. This was the first time I had seen the ducks staked out the way they were, but it wouldn't be the last. Up till then, I had just thought the locals were dragging along chow with them until I saw them around the camp. The hush puppy can take out a duck as well as a dog without much noise, but somehow calling the weapon a "hush duckie" doesn't have the proper SEAL ring to it.

What we found after the camp was a real surprise. Following along the many trails that crisscrossed the area we stumbled over a weapons cache, a big one. In the cache were M1 Garands encased in Cosmoline and wrapped in protective brown paper. Exactly the condition they were in when they had been issued by Uncle Sam to our allies. Along with the Garands were B-40 rounds, Mark 2 grenades, ammo, and all sorts of ordnance. What it looked like was that the VC had overrun some kind of ARVN supply dump or armory somewhere. If the stuff had been captured or bought on the black market wasn't important to us just then. What did stand out was the condition of everything, especially the rifles.

Unwrapping the paper and tape from the Garands showed us that even the leather slings were in good condition. These things just had never been exposed to the harsh environment of Vietnam. Buried in the ground and sealed in boxes the way they were made the supply cache invisible from the air. If a helo had flown over the area, they would have seen nothing out of the ordinary. You had to go in on the ground and search around like we did to locate the cache.

We brought a number of the weapons back out with us, mostly just to prove their condition more than anything else. There was more stuff than we could pull out with us, even with helicopter extraction. And blowing the stuff in place would just deny it to the enemy until they brought in a resupply. What we did was far more devious than any of those answers.

At that time there was a program going on back in the States to take care of these little caches we would find. I think the program was called POOR BOY, but I may be mistaken about that. What the program did was manufacture enemy ordnance modified to explode when it was used. All sorts of things were made and packaged in regular Chicom and Russian packaging—B-40 rounds, mortar rounds, grenades, even small-arms ammunition filled with explosives instead of propellant powder. By salting the caches with these materials we denied them to the enemy and screwed up his supply system at the same time.

Not all of the ammunition in the cases we placed was doctored. What the ratio was I don't know. But the VC could use the hidden supplies and suddenly notice that things were exploding when used. Rumors of that sort of thing happening would spread through the VC ranks like a disease. Personally, I thought it was a great way of attacking the problem.

Even if you took the stuff out in Chinooks, it seemed that all we did was store it for Charlie's later use. They would steal it back, as they could. But salting the cache in place would frighten the VC into not using what they had. And the supply record keepers up in Hanoi or wherever would receive the requests from areas like the Seven Mountains and have supply dumps on their books. That would hold up any replacement material from coming in as soon as it could. Instead the supplies would be held as a "last resort" by the local commanders.

We had checked out the materials we were placing earlier. Setting up a VC mortar tube and dropping a salted round with a remote rig was all it took to convince us of the efficiency of the program. There was nothing left of the tube after the explosion, which would have wiped out the crew and any VC who might have been nearby. Careful records had to be kept by us as to which caches we salted, but the results were worth the trouble.

Before leaving the cache site, we set out a few more little toys the brains back home had made for us. We had been given pressure-fuze mats that looked like olive-drab bath mats. There was an anti-handling device in the mat that, along with the pressure of anyone stepping on the mat, would fire any explosive device we hooked into the system. Putting some of the mats out along the trails and rigging them up to claymore mines made sure that Charlie couldn't get back to his camp too easily.

There wasn't any question that Charlie was around in numbers. During the nights you could hear firing in different parts of the forest. The VC could have been test-firing weapons or hunting some of the game that was around. At the time there weren't any American forces in on the ground except for us.

After that operation, we moved further along. Starting from Chau Doc, we had gone on to the Seven Mountains, then the Tranh Forest, and ended up in Rach Gia on the western coast of South Vietnam, facing the Gulf of Siam. A nice line of operations from Chau Doc almost straight south to Rach Gia with activity all along the way. Enough activity was going on for the higher-ups to try something new, and they sent the PACVs into the area.

The Patrol Air Cushion Vehicles were real monsters to the superstitious Vietnamese. Skimming across the marshlands on their cushions of air, the PACVs could swoop in on Charlie where nothing had been able to move before. Of course, you could hear those things coming from a long way off. And it didn't take Charlie long to learn that you could "shoot out the tires" on a PACV by punching holes in the rubber skirts. But for a while the roaring beasts were neat to have around.

The PACVs had a psychological gain for a while, as did many of the things we used against the VC and NVA. If you took the time to study the Vietnamese people you could learn about them and sometimes use their superstitions against them. Putting the painted teeth and eyes on the front of the PACVs is one example of this. Other things you would pick up the longer you were in-country.

I used to think that when we went through a village and the little kids would come out, reach up, and touch us with both hands, they were just being nice kids. What the action really meant was that they were trying to pass their "evil spirits" to me and I would carry them off out of the village. When I learned of that I played my own game back at them. If I was cammied up, I would reach up and gather some of the green paint from around my eyes on my fingertips. As the kids reached up to me, I would quickly smear a little of the paint on their foreheads. That got a reaction. The kids would just scream at the top of their lungs and run back into their hooch. Don't try to pass your devils onto me; devil god give you some of his.

But unless you talked to the people, you just didn't learn about what was going on in their lives. If you went back to Dong Tam or wherever after a patrol with your TVs, air conditioning, and Yankee civilization, you couldn't know what was going on. And some of that information might save your life. The U.S. compound was not where you went to talk to the locals. They had their own way of life.

Chau Doc during Tet of '68 is a good example of how the Vietnamese acted towards what we tried to teach them. The medical teams in Chau Doc were trying to instruct the local midwives on what were the modern techniques for delivering babies. The ladies would agree with the instructors and do as they were shown. When the Tet offensive opened up, the medical community in Chau Doc was inundated with casualties. Everyone with medical training soon found themselves involved with major trauma and surgeries. In the meantime, as the bodies were being brought in the babies paid no attention and kept on coming. And the midwives went back to slapping the women on the stomach to expedite delivery and get their engines started, just as they had been doing since before Christ was a mess cook. The methods the Vietnamese had been using for years worked for them. They would pay attention to what we tried to show them and as soon as we weren't looking, go right back to the old ways.

Chronologically, my platoon was the first SEAL unit to try and find sources from where Charlie was getting his support and replacements. The situations for SEAL operations varied according to the area. In the Rung Sat, the ambush was the way to go, because of the terrain and how the VC operated. In the Delta, the breadbasket of Vietnam, movements were more conventional and we were always being watched by somebody—the population density in the area saw to that. It wasn't a matter of good guy/bad guy to the locals. It was a matter of who held the biggest gun to your head.

All the local Vietnamese guy with a family wanted was a hooch, some chickens and ducks, perhaps a pig, a water buffalo, his paddies, and some frogs and fish in the water. Out of all the groups in South Vietnam, it didn't matter if that one guy was a Buddhist or a Catholic. He had the landlord in Saigon taxing him, and the VC were taxing him as well and taking his kids to boot. The VC weren't raping and pillaging as much as seems to be remembered now, at least not in some areas. And on top of all this, along comes the clumsy, round-eyed American with his size twelve boots knocking down the farmer's fences and blowing the hell out of his dikes, the defensive barriers he had built against nature.

The average Vietnamese probably suffered as much from the Americans as he did at the hands of the VC. Now this is just the average guy; the situation for villagers, and especially village leaders, could be very different. We supplied the Vietnamese with tractors, chickens, and grain, but we didn't give him the land. We helped him plant his crops, but we didn't hold the land secure so he could harvest them.

Training, be it UDTR, UDTB, or BUD/S, is the single most common factor in the Special Warfare community. The thread that binds all SEALs and UDTs together, past and present, is the shared experiences of training and the infamous Hell Week. But the SEALs are unable to perform their missions without support. Specialist ratings are found in the Teams today performing valuable services. But these same ratings are considered "nonquals" (nonqualified) by SEAL operators. The only "quals" are those individuals who have passed through the forge of training.

To be a SEAL operator and serve with the Teams in combat meant that you had passed training. But there was a very small group of men who served in combat with the SEALs as Teammates and operators, even though they had never gone through the same training as the SEALs. These men were the Teams' corpsmen.

Because of the interpretations of existing regulations and accords at the time, corpsmen were not allowed to take the full SEAL or UDT course of training in the 1960s. This interpretation has changed now, but then, as noncombatants, corpsmen were not allowed to take the demolition training that was so much a part of UDTR training. Weapons training, for self-defense, was allowed to be given to corpsmen, as well as tactical combat instruction. Corpsmen in the Teams who were qualified to operate in the field were expected to carry "their share of the boat" when on ops.

Many corpsmen developed a reputation as operators. These men are accepted as close equals by one of the most singular fraternities of fighting men in the world—The Navy SEALs.

SECOND CLASS HOSPITAL CORPSMAN

GREG McPARTLIN

USN (LEFT 1969)

Greg McPartlin is known in the Teams for two reasons. By the older SEALs he is known for having been a corpsman in Vietnam. To the younger SEALs he is the owner of McP's, a popular bar on Orange Avenue just down the road from the SEAL base at Coronado. McP's demonstrates the old SEAL style of having a good time by a warning printed on the back of the bar's menu: "If you don't like crowds, don't come on Thursday night." When a waitress was asked to translate this, she said, "That's when the SEALs show up."

Greg was one of the more unusual SEALs—he was accepted as an operator but never went through UDTR or BUD/S. The Teams had requirements for trained specialists as support personnel, especially corpsmen who would be expected to serve in combat. Corpsmen who had completed the rigorous UDT training were very few in number. During the Vietnam War, regulations prevented corpsmen, who were considered noncombatants, from going through the full UDT training course when they were assigned to the Teams. That situation wasn't changed until after the war was over. A separate, special course was set up for these individuals, and Greg was one of the first men to complete it.

The SEALs were not at all what I was thinking of when I entered the service in 1967. I had been driving an ambulance in the Chicago area, specifically Lake Forest, Illinois, while my brother was already serving in Vietnam as an A-4 pilot with the Marines. When my 1-A draft notice arrived, I decided it was time for a change. Going up to the Marine Corps recruiter in Waukegan, I said to him, "I'm 1-A and I don't want to be drafted into the Army. I'll be a Marine."

This didn't seem to be a problem to the recruiter. "Son," he said to me, "what is it you do now?"

"I drive an ambulance."

"Well," he said, "we need corpsmen in the Marines."

Sounded good to me. "Okay," I answered, "I'll be a corpsman."

"Well, you'll have to talk to that man over there," and he indicated a Navy recruiter in the next office.

"But that man's a squid!" I protested.

"Yes, but the Navy trains all of the corpsmen we use." The Marine continued, "We'll guarantee on your contract that you'll be able to go to the Marine Corps right after your training."

So I signed up with the Navy. Right after I completed boot camp, I went on to A school and from there to field med. When I had completed my training and was a qualified corpsman, I was sent over to the Marine Corps. And not your regular Marine unit either—I was assigned to the Third Marine Force Recon. As a field corpsman, I would be going into the bush with my fellows in Force Recon, so I certainly received my share of a very rugged training regimen.

By early 1968, my unit and I were deployed to Vietnam, just in time for the '68 Tet offensive. The fighting was hot and heavy in my area, but I was pretty much a noncombatant type. Though I didn't do any frontline stuff, I did receive a lot of on-the-job training, mostly in how to put guys in body bags.

After only three months in Vietnam, my recon platoon was called back to the States. We were just too badly off in terms of casualties to be a functioning unit. My adventures in Vietnam with the Marines had taken the gloss off my image of the Corps. Now, getting away from the Marines had a great deal of appeal for me. Once at Camp Lejeune, I approached the Chief corpsman and asked him if there was anything else available. "Have you ever heard of the Navy SEALs?" the Chief asked me.

"Yeah," I answered after a moment's thought. "They're some kind of UDT unit."

"Can you swim?"

"To get away from the Marines?" I answered. "I can walk on water."

And with volunteering came a series of tests, both mental and physical. My training with Force Recon had toughened me even more than my time in the Chicago area had, so I didn't have a great deal of trouble qualifying. Now I found myself in a new program called Special Operations Technician. Though I didn't know it at the time, corpsmen were not allowed to go through BUD/S then.

By August of 1968, myself, Steve Elson, and about seventeen other corpsmen found ourselves in Key West, Florida, reporting for special operations technician training. Meeting us were Joe Kazmar, Dick Ray, Roger Moscone, and other SEAL instructors. The program was a new one, and the instructors didn't quite know how to handle us corpsmen. But they knew we were going to be operators and going out into the field with regular SEALs. That they knew how to prepare for.

The instructors put us all through three weeks of the worst PT you could imagine. Only five corpsmen, myself included, lasted that training. Trouble was that I had already been to Vietnam and the instructors didn't want to drop me from the class. Every time I wanted to quit, the instructors would find something else to have me do. Joe Kazmar had me doing flutter kicks in the water, kelp around my legs, for what seemed like hours. "I quit!" I would say.

"Doc," Joe answered, "you can't quit. We've already gotten rid of the rum-dumbs. We're not going to let you quit."

And that was how it went for weeks. I suppose that my first meeting with the instructors should have given me some warning about what was coming. It was on a Sunday, when I had arrived at the school to be checked in. August in Florida is hot, and I could feel the heat abate a little as I entered the school building. On the quarter-deck, Joe Kazmar was one of the instructors checking us in. "Hey, guys," I said cheerfully. "I'm here to check in."

Looking at me disdainfully, Joe said, "Gimme fifty."

And I just got here, I thought to myself as I dug into my pocket. "I've got two twenties and a ten," I said as I handed him the money. "Here."

Then all the instructors were laughing like crazy, but that didn't prevent Joe from taking the money. "Now drop and give me fifty push-ups," he said, pocketing the bills.

I had just started training. "That's no way to treat . . ." I started to say.

"Pardon me!" Joe exclaimed. "What are you trying to say? You puke! You ain't gonna last, I'll see to that."

The instructors just started giving us all a ration of hard times from the moment we arrived. And I had no idea what to expect. This was a new program, and none of us had really known what we were getting into. By the time our first three weeks were up, the few of us who were left were getting in pretty good condition. Just having completed their parachute training at Fort Benning, the newest class of UDTR students from Little Creek arrived in Key West to receive their dive school training. We joined the class at this point, and we all took the SCUBA session together.

The only portions of the normal UDTR training that we missed were Hell Week and the demolition training. We had been run around, worked on, and pounded into the sand so much that we could hold our own with a good deal of the normal duties of a SEAL. Which was the whole idea behind the course in the first place. To meet with regulations and international accords, corpsmen could not receive the regular course of instruction, especially not the demolitions. That has changed now, but back then it caused us a few problems when we arrived at the Teams.

There was a stigma attached to us as nonquals. Even though we had taken a great deal of training, we had not completed UDTR and Hell Week, so we were all just pecker-checkers. By November, the regular trainees went back to Little Creek and the four of us corpsmen who were left went up to Lakehurst, New Jersey, to get parachute training at the Navy school.

Jump school was something else. There was just the few of us, so we kind of got an accelerated course of instruction. We had one day of ground school, one static line jump, and then fourteen free-falls. And all the jumps were done in two days. We were jump-qualified and had the Navy gold wings to prove it, and we still got home in time for Thanksgiving!

Now it was time for some fun. I checked in to UDT 21 right after the Thanksgiving holiday, and my gold wings immediately caused a stir. "Doc," I was asked by some of my earlier dive school classmates, "where in the hell did you get the gold wings?"

"Hey," I answered, "I'm free-fall-qualified." And that allowed me to jump with the East Coast Jump Team. Soon it was time to go down to Roosey Roads in Puerto Rico with UDT 21 for winter deployment. When 21 returned to Little Creek, I continued basking in the sun at Roosey Roads with UDT 22. Since they were short a corpsman, they asked me to stay. When I finally got back to Little Creek—by this time it was almost the spring of 1969—there were some new traveling orders for me.

Fred Kochey was the XO of UDT 21 at the time, and he called me into his office. "Doc," he said, "you've got to go over to the SEAL Team."

"Super," I said. "I'll get my stuff."

"You don't understand," he continued. "You're going to the West Coast and SEAL Team ONE."

There had been a constant but fairly easygoing rivalry between the East and West Coast SEAL teams since the first day of their commissioning. Each Team, ONE at Coronado and TWO at Little Creek, considered themselves superior to the other. Since I had taken my training with mostly East Coast instructors and students, I had picked up their tastes.

"Hollywood UDT!" I exclaimed. "West Coast pukes! No way. I want to stay with the Apollo splashdown crew." I had been training with the UDT men who had been picked for the Apollo capsule recovery team. All of the incoming space capsules, from Mercury through Gemini, and Apollo, were first met in the water after splashdown by specially trained UDT men.

"No, Doc, you can't," Kochey said. "Your counterpart got killed. You have to report to Team ONE no later than June 1st."

There's no arguing with orders or the Navy. "I don't have any leave or anything, and it's already May," I said. The Navy wouldn't ship the personal effects of anyone under the rank of E-5. When I had first come to Key West and then Little Creek I had driven in from Chicago. There was no way I would be able to afford to have my belongings sent to the West Coast.

"No problem," Kochey said. "You can leave now." And he authorized me some basket leave so that I could take my gear out to the West Coast myself. After a long cross-country drive, I arrived in San Diego and reported in to Team ONE at Coronado, just across the bay.

The Chief Master at Arms of Team ONE at that time was a corpsman named Blackburn. Chief Blackburn hated other corpsmen, especially low-ranking corpsmen such as myself. Since I had arrived at Team ONE in time to check in on a Friday, Chief Blackburn thought that a perfect reason to give me the weekend duty.

Dick Wolfe, a corpsman who had been with me on the East Coast, had checked in with the Team a week earlier. Dick had already been assigned to Kilo Platoon, and was quickly involved with their training. "God, are you lucky," Dick told me one day. "You get to deploy in October."

Going to Vietnam with a—to me—brand-new SEAL platoon didn't exactly strike me as the best kind of luck.

"What the hell are you talking about?" I said. "I just got here."

"My platoon," Dick answered, "is already in predeployment training. They're all out at Niland [the Team ONE training area in the desert near Salton Sea, California]. I'm leaving before the summer's over."

Team ONE moved fast. As they had the primary Vietnam commitment, SEAL Team ONE had more men incountry than Team TWO and so was increasing in size and adding more platoons at a greater rate than Team TWO. But I still had some time before I would be deploying. And I found an interesting way to fill some of it.

Jess Tolison was a plankowner of Team TWO and had spent more than a few years on the East Coast. When he had taken his commission as a warrant officer, Jess was transferred to the West Coast and Team ONE. Jess knew me as a recent East Coast transfer and approached me one day in late June. "Doc," Jess asked, "Are you free-fall [qualified]?"

"Yeah," I answered.

"Well, we need you for the Fourth of July demonstration. We're practicing tomorrow. Have you got a paracommander?"

"Hell," I answered, "I don't have anything."

"Let's go over to the loft and see if we can't fit you up."

Going over to the parachute loft, we were able to fit me out with the gear I needed to be able to jump with the demonstrators. It was the end of June and the jump was coming up soon. The next day, I was out on the field with the other jumpers getting ready. It was June 30th, my birthday, and it looked like it might be my last one.

There was a little cloud cover over the jump zone when we exited the bird. Perhaps I had exaggerated my experience just a bit. We left the plane at about 10,500 feet. I had put my reserve chute on upside down so my stopwatch and altimeter were on the bottom of the pack. Looking over the pack, I could read both instruments but I misread the altimeter. Because of the cloud cover obscuring the ground, I opened up at about six thousand feet. Trying to read my instruments upside down I thought I had passed one thousand feet when actually I was just going through seven thousand feet.

Since I had opened so high, I drifted all the way across San Diego Bay, finally landing at the National Steel boat-yards. Sending a jeep to fetch their wandering parachutist, the guys harassed me unmercifully. "I thought you said you knew what you were doing," one of them said.

"Well, I'm sorry. I just need a little more practice."

With some more practice jumps, we were getting the feel for each other and starting to look pretty good. On the Fourth, we would be jumping over Glorietta Bay, next to the Amphibious Base. There is a large area on the shore where most of the audience would be, and right across the bay was a yacht club and large golf course where we could land. The day of the demonstration, we had a large audience celebrating the Fourth and watching our show.

When it came time to jump, we exited the plane in good order and formed up on each other. Gathering up, we fell through the air while holding hands and forming kind of a ten-pointed star. Breaking the formation apart, we separated to pull our chutes. I'll show these sons of bitches, I thought to myself as we broke away. I'll be the first one on the ground and make up for opening so high in practice a few days before.

As we hurtled towards the ground, you could almost hear the collective gasp of the crowd as I came closer and closer without opening my chute. I was keeping an eye out for the new Bay Bridge that spanned across the water from San Diego to Coronado. The bridge was so new it hadn't even opened yet. As soon as I reached about six hundred feet, I would pull my chute and open up lower than anyone else in the team. I'm going to be the first on the deck, I thought as I saw the bridge and released my chute. The audience got a better show than they had bargained for, but I was comfortably in control of my chute when I passed the bridge, which is about 250 feet tall. I was on the edge of the golf course in a moment and bundling up my chute.

It took no time at all for Jess to explain to me his thoughts on my jumping style. "You're never jumping with the Jump Team again!" he fairly shouted in my face. Funny thing, that kind of jumping didn't go over real well on the East Coast either.

In July, I went out to Niland, where Alfa Platoon was doing their training. A VC village had been set up to train the platoons for Vietnam. There was some time to kill before I would be able to join the platoon proper, so I went into the little club near the camp, the HiHo Club, to relax. Inside the club was Wayne Bohannan, the leading petty officer [LPO] for the platoon, along with some others sitting there shooting pool. The LPO's opinion of what he considered a nonqual corpsman was not long in coming.

"That's all we need," Bohannan said. "Some goddam fleet pecker-checker in our platoon. Jesus Christ, nonoperators going into the field with us. As if we didn't have enough to watch out for."

On and on he went, just putting out a line of garbage and giving me a hard time. And his platoon didn't have a corpsman. This was one of the guys I would have to go with? My grip got tighter on my pool cue as I played my game, with Bohannan putting it on heavier and thicker as he went along. Finally I had had just about enough. Slipping back with the butt of my pool cue, I nailed Bohannan right in the crotch. Turning around and grabbing his head while he was still bent over, I got a good grip on his hair. "Do you want your face smashed on my knee?" I asked pleasantly.

Bohannan indicated that he did not think that my continuing along those lines was a good idea as he kneeled down on the floor. The two other platoon members sitting nearby were satisfactorily impressed. "You're all right, Doc," they said. Bohannan got up in a moment, shook my hand, and I was accepted as being an operator.

During training, I was issued a Stoner as my weapon. This was not exactly the sort of thing a corpsman normally carried, but I didn't mind. "Cool," I said as they handed me the weapon. "This is neat!" I hadn't been able to hit the broad side of a barn during training, so perhaps they thought if I put out enough firepower I could at least keep the enemy's heads down.

And it would be soon enough that I would find out if the theory would work. In October, Alfa Platoon deployed for the sunny shores of Vietnam.

Lieutenant (jg) Dick Flanagan and Ensign Bill Moody were our platoon's leader and assistant leader respectively. Following them were the twelve enlisted men that made up Alfa Platoon. As the platoon's corpsman, I was in Alfa squad. John Mitchell was in the other squad, and I had given him some cross-training in field medicine.

I tended to stick with our senior officer and his radioman most of the time on ops. The LT liked it that way. In fact, when there were times that only two men would be staying on the deck, only so much room in a helicopter, the LT would have me get the radio and stay with him. That way he had both a radioman and a corpsman.

It was an active deployment. I did about sixty-five ops and received a Bronze Star and a Navy Commendation. I also delivered over one hundred babies for the native South Vietnamese around our base.

The op that stands out the most in my mind is probably our first one. It isn't memorable just because it was the first, it was also a costly operation. It was a break-in op with another platoon working with us, against standard procedure. The op was a hammer-and-anvil ambush, one platoon, the hammer, patrolling through an area hopefully driving the enemy in front of them into the second platoon's ambush, the anvil. That type of ambush can be very destructive to the enemy, as you can get them in a deadly crossfire. But communications between the two platoons must be top-notch.

This time, the communications between the platoons wasn't working and things went badly. The hammer unit walked into our ambush, and we opened fire on what turned out to be our own men. Lieutenant (jg) David Nicholas stood up as he recognized what was happening and tried to stop the firing. The shooting stopped, but it was too late for Nicholas.

We had hit Nicholas and two of the scouts from the other platoon before we realized what had happened. Dropping my smoking-hot Stoner, I ran over to where Nicholas lay and immediately started to work on him. While I knelt there at Nicholas's side calling for a dust-off chopper to come in to the side of the canal where we were, I knew it was too late. Nicholas was dead, but my training wouldn't let me give up. For close to forty-five minutes I continued giving Nicholas CPR until heat exhaustion threatened to make me a casualty myself.

Another SEAL was trying to give Nicholas morphine while I worked on him, but I stopped him. "Let me see if there's a life here to save before you do that," I said. But the lieutenant had one round right through his sternum; there was never a chance.

Finally we medevacked out and returned to our base at SEAFLOAT [a semi-portable river base built on pontoons] that night. We didn't have a doctor on hand at the base, and I had to pronounce him dead. "There's no sense in trying to medevac him out now," I said to the officers at SEAFLOAT. "There's no life here for us to save." Risking a medevac chopper to a hospital for an obviously dead body just didn't make any sense. Now I followed procedures I had learned with the Marines—tag and bag the body, collect his personal effects, and send him home.

Within a couple days of that first disastrous operation, Lieutenant Commander Dave Schaible, the CO of Team ONE, came down to SEAFLOAT accompanying Admiral Zumwalt for an inquiry into Nicholas's death. While they inspected our facility, I was asked what we needed. "A doctor would be good," I answered. Inside of three days, down from Saigon came a brand-new Navy doctor, who seemed only a few days out of his residency, complete with his flak jacket and helmet. The doctor was absolutely scared to death about being with us on SEAFLOAT surrounded by miles of enemy territory. But a bunch of good supplies had come along with him.

That doctor may have been qualified, but he absolutely wouldn't leave the barge. Nothing I could say would make the man move off what he considered the only secure location around. A Vietnamese scout of ours came in one day saying his wife was in labor and having trouble. Bringing the woman into our medical annex, I quickly examined her. She had been in labor for thirty-six hours and was not doing well. After seeing what the situation was, I went and got the doctor.

"Doctor," I said, "we've got a problem here. This birth is going to be a breech."

"Send her to the VN hospital," he said.

"Sir," I said, struggling with the word, "it's three days by sampan. Her BP is down to about eighty over forty. I put her on O_2 and started an IV. Let's do a C-section."

"I'm not going to do a cesarean on a Vietnamese."

"Well, I'm not going to let her die."

With that, he stormed out of the room. I went ahead and did the C-section. A small incision, what is called a bikini cut, and the head was right there. The baby was all right, and the mother was going to do okay herself. Turning to the doctor, who had come back into the room I said, "Why don't you go ahead and close?" as I removed my gloves and walked out of the room to tend the baby. I received a Lifesaving Commendation Medal from the Vietnamese government for the incident.

As far as the local Vietnamese were concerned, I was the doctor, the *bac si*. I would go into the villages and bring along the pHisoHex soap, penicillin, whatever I needed, and treat the people. And the little I was able to do paid off big in terms of intelligence. I could speak pretty good Vietnamese, but an interpreter would also come along on my "house calls." It was a pretty hot area we were in. There would be women and children in the village, but very few men unless they were very old or very young.

The area we were in was called the Annex, new Nam Can. Where SEAFLOAT was anchored, the barge base we lived on, was where the old city of Nam Can had been on the Cua Lon River far down on the Ca Mau Peninsula. Nam Can had been captured by the VC early on during the Tet offensive the year before. Further fighting had just about destroyed the city, and heavy enemy activity prevented rebuilding the city. The whole area had to be secured, so the jungle was defoliated. Agent Orange defoliated most of the area, and Zippo, an Army M132A2 flamethrower on board an armored Monitor boat, took care of the shoreline. Without any cover to use, it was much harder for Charley to operate against the SEA-FLOAT base. The people who had been moved out just went about five miles downriver and set up their village again. New Nam Can was a fishing village, as the old one had been, and we tried to do what we could for the locals.

There must have been eight to ten thousand people in the area, between the villagers, fishermen, and peasants living in the countryside. But there wasn't one motorized vehicle around. There were no roads, none. All the transport was done on the water by sampan. I wouldn't see a jeep unless I went up to Can Tho or Binh Thuy, the bases where we got most of our supplies.

The Annex was VC-controlled at night and controlled by us during the day. That situation was changing. SEAL PRU advisors would go to the Annex at night and capture individual VC. Occasionally, I would go along with the snatch teams. Working with intelligence that I could gather from the villagers, we could target a VC when he came in to get supplies or see his family. Interrogation would often Chieu Hoi the man, turning him to our side. Once we had him in, he could supply us with further intel. If the intel worked out, we could pay the Chieu Hoi, sometimes giving them captured sampans or motors. Within five or six months, we controlled the area almost completely. There was even work starting to rebuild old Nam Can at its original site. Just a shore facility for SEAFLOAT at first, but increasing construction was an obvious sign that the VC no longer commanded the area.

The situation for me changed suddenly after an op. The other SEAL platoon's corpsman, Dick Wolfe, was killed on an op in late November, leaving me the only SEAL corpsman for two platoons. There were plenty of other corpsmen around with the support troops, but I was the only one available who was qualified to go out on ops. The op where Wolfe was lost was a parakeet op. The insertion bird had landed on a hooch rooftop for lack of a better place to put down. Wolfe was the first one out of the bird just as the helicopter's skid went through the rafters. The Army pilot started putting power to the blades to keep the bird out of the building and he just lost control. The chopper tilted over and the rotor struck the corpsman right in the back of the head, leaving only his face left and throwing him into the bushes. The bird ended up collapsing the roof and impacting on the ground. Several men aboard were injured, Lieutenant (jg) Prouty dislocated his shoulder, and the door gunner was thrown out and had been badly burned.

Back at SEAFLOAT, we did a rapid deployment op as soon as we learned of the situation. Jumping out of the helicopter as soon as it was close to the ground, I ran over into the hooch. Taking care of the door gunner, I was looking around calling out, "Where's Doc?"

The rest of the men were out looking for him as they secured the area. Coming back into the hooch, one of the guys said quietly, "Doc, go help Doc."

When I was shown where Wolfe was, it was obvious that there was nothing to be done for him, at least not while other men were still injured. "Just leave him there," I said. "I'll take care of it later." And we pulled his vest over his head. Reaching into his gear, I took the sodium pentothal out of his pocket and the Rolex watch from his wrist. His watch would have been stolen as soon as the body reached Saigon, so this way I could return it. The net result of all this was to make me the only SEAL corpsman for two full SEAL platoons.

In a way, it was pretty good for me. I could select my ops. I didn't have to sit in a lot of long-term ambushes but was able to move around a lot. Mostly, I did parakeet ops after that. One op resulted in my getting wounded and refusing a Purple Heart for it. The injury had been a minor flesh wound to my right shoulder. No one in the platoon had gotten a Purple Heart up to that point, and we decided to keep it that way.

We had real good intel for the op. Our target was a district level province chief. Going in on the target, we

grabbed him after a stunt worked for us. I think we were
the first West Coast platoon to start using the fake extraction method of ambushing our targets. As soon as we
had come in to the target hooch, the chief di-di-maued,
running from the back of the building. With the target
gone, the platoon made a rather noisy show of leaving,
grabbing a few prisoners who hadn't gotten away. Throwing the prisoners on board one of the birds, the rest of the
team climbed on themselves. The two insertion helicopters lifted off and, escorted by the Seawolf gunships that
had been circling, left the area. Silence soon settled back
in.

Within five minutes or so, the VC who had run away
returned from where they had been hiding in the bush.
With their weapons held by the barrel across their shoulders, the VC would be talking, laughing and grinning at
each other at how they had beaten the ''green faces'' this
time. Going back into their hooches, they relaxed. Even
the province chief had returned and went about his business.

That was when the five of us who had stayed back got
up from where we had been hiding. The M60 man, the
radioman, myself with my Stoner, and two of our scouts
were the stay-behinds on this op. With the radioman calling back the birds that were just over the horizon, we took
out the guard on the chief's hut and barged in. Spraying
down the other people in the hooch, we grabbed up the
province chief. Now the extraction bird was coming in
and it was time to leave.

During the short firefight, the target had been gut-shot,
so I immediately went to work on him, starting an IV
with serum albumin and dealing with the wound. There
had been some VC who hadn't come back with the rest
of the group, and now fire started coming in on us as we
headed for the extraction bird. The fire was coming from
a treeline off to our side, past a rice paddy. The situation
happened so fast that the door gunner for the bird was
still snapping pictures with his camera when the incoming
started.

As we started putting out return fire, the man to my

immediate right opened up. As I spun around, I was struck hard in the shoulder and went down to my knees. Apparently, I had been hit by friendly fire. The wound wasn't too severe, just a clean hole through my shoulder. But it hurt like hell and I wasn't a happy individual. We pulled back to the chopper and climbed aboard after our prisoner. Still putting fire into the treeline, we lifted off and moved out.

Getting back to SEAFLOAT, I had my wound treated and saw to our prisoner. The chief recovered nicely and was soon able to answer questions. The intel we received was good—in fact, the operation had been much more important than I had known. Admiral Zumwalt was on SEAFLOAT along with a camera crew.

That little fact almost caused an incident for us. When we landed in the bird, I wasn't in bad shape, so I paid attention to our wounded prisoner. As we were taking the man down to sick bay, I had slung my Stoner over my shoulder and went past one of the cameramen. Coming back out of sick bay a short time later, the cameraman came up to me and asked how the prisoner was doing.

"Fine," I answered. One of the other guys called out to me, asking, "Doc, do you want to take the other prisoners back?"

As I was turning to walk away, the cameraman asked, "What's that on your back?"

"That?" I said. "That's my Stoner."

"What's that?"

"It's a machine gun, 5.56mm, belt-fed, gas-operated, with a rate of fire of around one thousand rounds a minute." I had come a fair way since they had first handed me the weapon back at Coronado.

Now the cameraman was really interested and started to interview me. Not really thinking anything of it, I talked to him. "What's your rate?" he asked.

"E-4."

"No, no. That's your rank. I asked what your rate was."

"SEAL Team ONE. I'm a SEAL operator."

"Are you a corpsman?"

"Yeah."

"But isn't it against the Geneva Convention for a corpsman to carry more than just a sidearm for his own protection?"

"Are you nuts? Who the fuck has heard of the Geneva Convention out here?"

Just then Admiral Zumwalt came up. "Excuse me," he said to the reporter. "Can I have that tape?" As he took the recorder out of the protesting man's hands, Zumwalt continued, "You know you're not allowed to be back in this area. You can't speak to these guys. As a matter of fact, you've never met them. They don't exist for you. Do I make myself clear?"

Given the fact that the man was surrounded by SEALs and deep aboard a Navy installation, he hadn't much choice. Besides, we liked Admiral Zumwalt and wouldn't have cared to see anyone give him any shit. Especially not a civilian. I must have been a little more shook up from having been hit than I thought—otherwise I wouldn't have spoken to the guy. Turning to me, Zumwalt made that situation abundantly clear. "Doc," he said, "don't ever speak to a reporter again." And with that, he walked away, a thoroughly cowed reporter in tow.

Stowing our weapons away, a number of us decided to get some chow. Dave Langlois, our M60 man, was with us. Dave was a real banjo-playing redneck and not one to keep his thoughts quiet. Going in to the mess area, we stopped as soon as we entered. There were tablecloths on the tables and steaks on the grill. "Jesus," Dave said. "What do you think this is?"

None of us cared—it was food, good food by the look and smell of it. As we went in, a guy all dressed up in whites came up to us. He was really done up, had the rope over his shoulder and everything. "Gentlemen," he asked us, "would you mind waiting until after the officers have been fed?"

Not quite the thing to ask several guys who had just come in from an operation. "Yeah, we fucking mind," I said. Though we didn't have our weapons with us, we were still pretty much a sight. Mud was caked on our camouflaged uniforms and our faces were smeared with camo paint that had started to wear and run together. In general, we stank, just the sort of thing to add color to an admiral's reception.

The cook, who knew who we were, just looked at us and said, "Come on in."

We tracked in through a side door, picked up our food, and sat down to eat. While we were hitting the chow line, Admiral Zumwalt came in to meet us. Walking along the line, he introduced himself and made small talk with each of us. Until he got to Dave.

Going up to Dave, the admiral asked him his name. "Dave," Langlois said. "What's yours?"

Without losing a step, Zumwalt answered, "Elmo."

"Hey, good to meet you, Elmo," Dave said, shaking the admiral's hand enthusiastically. "You gonna eat lunch with us?"

We always kind of liked Admiral Zumwalt, and he apparently thought the world of us. His son, Elmo Junior, was operating with us as one of our Swift boat drivers. The operations at SEAFLOAT later on had a great effect on Admiral Zumwalt. The area had been heavily defoliated with Agent Orange, long before we knew there was any kind of danger attached to it. Zumwalt's son, exposed to the agent, later on died of cancer suspected to have been caused by Agent Orange. Zumwalt always took personal responsibility for what had happened, and his son's death hit him hard.

A lot of guys from my platoon have suffered since the war from cancer. I have some skin rashes, what we called jungle rot, myself that match what they say can show up after exposure. I don't know myself, but it seems that what is said now about the agent could be very legitimate.

Elmo Junior was really a very nice guy, and he was in quite a spot fighting what seemed to be his father's war. The other officers harassed him a lot, but we really liked the guy. He always wanted to be a SEAL, but he wasn't, though he did operate in support of us sometimes.

Now, I was considered a SEAL, just one who had never gone through BUD/S. I operated with the guys, supported them, I even think I may have been shot by one, accidentally, of course. No one argues my qualifications, and I was able to wear the Trident when it came out. Today, corpsmen can go through the full BUD/S program and operate in all the Teams. In fact, if you look at some of the top graduates, as well as the students who are considered to have the "stomach" or "fire in the gut" it takes to be an exceptional SEAL, very often they are corpsmen.

While on ops in Vietnam, I already carried a lot more than just bandages. The Stoner that was noticed by the reporter was my favorite weapon, but not the only one I carried. Along with extra ammunition for the M60, I would carry a LAW rocket when it was necessary. And I always had a sidearm, usually a Smith & Wesson Model 39, whenever I was on an op, and often when I was off duty as well.

All the men on an op carried standard medical supplies and were trained in their use. Serum albumin, a blood expander, was carried by all of us, secured in a metal can along with the materials to administer it. About the only thing I carried different from anyone else was additional morphine. Before an op, I would issue everyone a morphine Syrette. Drugs weren't a problem with us, except for once when a mistake was made.

On a long, boring op, such as an extended OP [observation post] or ambush, I would have Dexamil tablets I could issue. The tablets, an amphetamine, were stay-awake medicine to be used when we needed it. Properly dosed, they wouldn't adversely affect a man's performance. When I issued the pills, I would also give the men instructions to take one tablet every four hours.

On one op, a man took four pills in one hour. When he started seeing elephants going by, it was time to go home. The op was compromised, so we called in extraction and went back to SEAFLOAT. Getting back to our bunks, we all stayed up for two days waiting for the pills to wear off. Little incidents like that made me extra careful about issuing meds. And the guys wouldn't abuse the meds on purpose. That would just get them killed and maybe take someone else along with them.

My job on an op was primarily that of prisoner handler and interrogator. If anyone was injured, I immediately took over as the platoon's corpsman. During patrols my position was normally rear security. My rear security slot led to my getting the Bronze Star on one op.

While on patrol, an ambush was about to be initiated behind us. I noticed what was going on and interdicted the ambush with my Stoner before they could open fire. Sometimes, I would end up being point on a patrol when we were leaving an area. You can't always maneuver the squad the way you want to, so you just reverse the order. When you do that, the rear security man suddenly gets to take point.

I was pretty much the good guy on operations. I would search the bodies and took care of the wounded after a hit. During the initial fire phase of an op, I usually wouldn't fire unless I was in a position on the ambush or interdicting something. That didn't mean I wouldn't carry a full load of ammunition for my Stoner. I carried 450 rounds—two boxes holding 150-round belts in pouches on my web belt and one full belt box attached to my weapon.

When the firing was over, I would go into the hooches and search them, paying attention to any wounded I might find. The platoon was very, very good in placing their shots. I don't think we ever killed a kid. We did wound some, but wouldn't leave an area until everyone was treated.

And that's something that you just don't read about much. We were a compassionate platoon. Many of the SEALs were. We just weren't killers who would go in and strike everybody down. We wouldn't shoot women and children. Hell, we didn't even shoot the pigs that were running around. But we did let the Kit Carson [native] scouts do that.

Some of the scouts and almost all of the Chieu Hois were different. They were merciless. We would have to hold them back or they would kill anyone in sight on an op. They would be standing there cutting down people until we told them to stop. And these would often be fishermen, not VC. There wasn't any way they could compromise us after an op went down.

If we found a wounded woman or child on an op, whenever we could, we would take them out with us. After getting them treatment, we could sometimes put them right back in the area where we got them. We would go back into a hot area and drop them off. Those parents and other Vietnamese would see that and things would change for us. Our intel would increase and the VC would lose a little more of their hold on an area.

As far as intelligence went, we had a never-ending source of up-to-the-minute quality intelligence. The platoons could have operated round the clock, seven days a week, if it wasn't for the terrible strain it would be on all the operators. But if you wanted an op, the intel would be available. And we always operated on fresh intel, a luxury not everyone had.

This resulted in some funny ops. One time we took out some tax collectors without firing a shot. Setting up ahead of time, we were well in position before the targets came into the area. As our scouts were talking to the tax collectors, they waved our sampans over to where they were. The tax collectors were at their ease, weapons held loosely in their hands, not pointed at anyone. As our sampans were paddled over by other scouts, we lay hunched over in the bottom of the boats, our weapons at the ready. Getting over to the tax collectors' sampan, we just raised our weapons and had them.

That op netted us about four thousand dollars in piasters. Taking everyone up to Can Tho, we got all our scouts drunk and happy. Another time, one of our SEALs stopped a junk full of Buddhist monks, who were anything but supportive of our part in the war. As the SEAL started taking the monks out into the bushes, I called out, "Hey, what are you doing?"

It looked like he was taking them into the bush to kill them. I knew none of us liked the monks, but this was a little severe. I felt relief when the SEAL called back, "I just want their clothes."

He came back a moment later with an armload of red

and yellow silk robes, which he proceeded to stuff into his pack. Getting back to the base, he put on one of the outfits and got into the chow line. All of the natives who were working there backed away and refused to serve him. He did make a pretty dangerous-looking Buddhist monk.

Our platoon leader was Dick Flanagan. We called him Radical Dick because he would get so hyper on an op when we made contact, screaming out orders and generally hollering. Dick had the best camouflage on when we went out. It was like he had a makeup artist do his face. The only problem was he would stick a pack of Pall Malls into the sweat band of his hat. That little four-cigarette C-ration pack would look just like a little red target, surrounded by the white box. And it would be stuck right to his head. "*Dai-uy* [Lieutenant]," I said, "you've got a nice target on your head there."

"I'm trying to keep them dry," was his answer.

Trying to stay dry was a losing battle in Vietnam. The VNs had these little bridges across canals and muddy areas, not much more than a fallen log. We called them monkey bridges because you needed the agility of a monkey to stay on one all the way across. With all the mud and everything the guys would smear on the log before I got to it, there wasn't a chance I could cross the thing. I just got into the water and waded the canal—I was going to get wet when I fell off the log anyway.

This "staying in the other guys' footprints" bit looked good in print. But when you're the last man in a patrol, the area in front of you is so churned up, there's no place that isn't slippery. There isn't a neat line of footprints. It looks like a herd of horses went down the path. It seemed I was never on exactly the same trail as the rest of the guys, I would walk alongside the churned-up mess. I'm surprised I never hit a booby trap, as I was almost always to the side of the trail by a yard or two.

We loved to operate in the rain when we could. After all, we couldn't get much wetter in the Southeast Asian environment. But rain could be the best cover in which to operate. You can move fast, even break silence and talk. Set up situations and move into villages quickly. When the monsoons started up, it would be hard to see ten yards in front of you. With the sky just opening up and rain pouring down, hitting the trees and ground. Any sound short of a gunshot would be just absorbed. On top of all that, the rain would also clean you up, washing the mud and sweat off. Another simple blessing was that the bugs wouldn't be flying when the rains came down. And Vietnam had more bugs than anything.

We didn't get much R&R while in-country. Any long enough stretch of time off would be spent up in Ben Thuy or Can Tho. Finally, in March of 1970, our tour in Vietnam was over and it was time to rotate home.

After returning to Coronado, I was given a choice of assignments. I could either join up with a platoon that was going over to Vietnam within a month, or I could go to instructor school. I picked the school. After graduation, I came back to Team ONE as a cadre instructor. With my two tours in Vietnam, one with the Marines and one with the SEALs, I had some experience to pass on to the men.

As an instructor, I taught two major subjects, medical and small weapon tactics. The classes would be held either at the base in Coronado or out at Niland. It worked out to my spending about two weeks at Coronado, then a week out at Niland. Niland was where our range facilities were, and the area was being improved. A new camp was being built, Camp Kerry, named for Lieutenant Bob Kerry, the first SEAL to win the Medal of Honor.

Niland is a lot of open area, plenty of room for our VC village and all the other facilities we needed. The land had been an old Navy gunnery and bombing range, so with all the ordnance lying about, we pretty much had the place to ourselves. A camp was set up on the banks of the All-American Canal, and in general, the conditions were pretty primitive.

The training we gave, which used to be called cadre training, was SBI, SEAL Basic Indoctrination. Guys who came over from UDT or had just graduated training came over to us to get their introduction to SEAL methods. The course was about eight weeks long, and we gave the students weapons training, field medicine, tactics, and techniques. Since then, the course has been phased into BUD/S. At that time we were not BUD/S instructors but cadre from the Team.

The medical training I gave included advanced first aid. I also told them about the medicines we carried, how to start IVs, give shots, CPR. More than just the basics but enough to give them a start when they got to a platoon.

Out on the ranges, I acted as one of the safety officers. Normally a simple job, but once it got fairly busy for a moment. The students generally listened closely and did exactly what you told them. My real exciting day happened when one of the officers dropped a loaded M60 machine gun. We were all out on the firing berm, completing an exercise, and had just secured from firing. As this one officer stood up, he either tripped over the M60 or dropped it hard. At any rate, the gun broke its sear and just started firing uncontrollably.

When I looked over to where the weapon was firing, there was no one near it. There was just this gun jinking across the ground spitting out bullets. The students went over the berm line, and the man who had dropped the weapon was nowhere to be seen. Diving at the weapon, I twisted the belt, popping the links and stopping the gun. Not exactly what I most wanted to do that day, but the recoil was driving the muzzle of the weapon over towards where people were standing. That was quite a safety violation.

Jess Tolison was the warrant officer in charge of training, and he and I came to be pretty good friends. I had been an instructor about eight or nine months and it was becoming time for me to go back to Vietnam with another platoon. I had extended my time in service but hadn't shipped over yet. It was looking like the service was going to become a career for me until something happened.

A few of us, Jess and myself included, had been working on the pop-up range all day one weekend. There was a class of students coming in on Monday, and we wanted the range set up before then. A number of students were out helping us get the work done on a very hot day in the desert.

That evening, Frank Bomar, Jess Tolison, and myself were at the HiHo Club after work having some burritos and a pitcher of beer. We had worked late but got most of the job done. By about ten o'clock, Mr. Tolison decided that he was going to head back. Giving him the keys to the six-by-six, I said, "We'll be right behind you."

It had been a fourteen-hour day in 108-degree weather, so we were all a little dehydrated. Instead of drinking a lot of water for the heat, back then the proper thing was to take salt tablets. Each of us just had a couple of beers, and that was enough for the evening. Jess took the six-by and left for camp. What we didn't know was that he missed the turn going into the camp.

The road into camp was just a loose gravel road with the turn leading into camp having a high bank on either side. The truck went up the bank and rolled back down on its side. Bomar and I came up to the scene of the accident just a few moments later. It couldn't have been long since the truck had rolled, because the wheels were still spinning.

Pulling the car up to the rear of the truck, I grabbed my medical kit and flashlight and jumped out. The back of the truck was right in front of me, and I wanted to know if any students were in it. Quickly checking the rear, I found it empty. Turning to Frank, I said, "Go back into town and get some help."

As Frank drove off, I went up to the front of the truck and found Jess. He was still in the cab but had fallen partway out of the window, and his head was under the frame of the cab. Seeing the situation, I climbed over the cab to where I could reach Jess and checked for a pulse. There was hardly any pulse and his skin was sweaty, cold, and clammy, strong signs of heat exhaustion.

Seeing he was having trouble breathing, I pulled up my medical kit and got ready to perform a tracheotomy. As I reached around to the back of Jess's head, I could feel where the doorpost had crushed his skull. Again, I was back in a situation where there was nothing more I could do.

Bomar got back with the Highway Patrol in about an hour, but it was far too late. Jess was dead and there had been nothing I could do about it. When they reached me, I was sitting there in tears. There just hadn't been anything I could do to move the truck or help Jess. The coroner came out, and immediately we had a jurisdictional problem. The turn down into camp was on Navy property, and I told them so. The cops said that I was drunk and that the accident happened on a civilian road and they were responsible. Just being twenty-two and having watched a friend die, I didn't feel like arguing with them.

A civilian funeral home finally sent a vehicle to pick up the body and take it in to town. I went along with Jess. Somehow the Highway Patrol officer, who knew who we were, got it into his head that the accident was alcohol-related and wrote it down as such. It was a time when the SEALs' reputation for heavy drinking really worked against us.

Finding out the next day what had been reported, I bellowed, "No way!" I was fit to be tied. I grabbed Frank Bomar and went to report to the CO. It was a Sunday morning, and there was nobody else in the office but Hendrickson, the new CO.

"So," he said, "you boys had a little party last night, eh?"

With that, my last shreds of patience burned away. I called that man every name I could think of in several languages. "What the fuck are you talking about, 'a party'?"

"Well," he said, "the police report reads the accident was alcohol-related."

"Mr. Tolison's dead," I ground out. "The cause might be criminal negligence, but not because of any booze."

"Yes, well, that remains to be seen."

"Whose word are you going to take?" I shouted. "Mine and Frank Bomar's? He was our Teammate."

"Son, you just calm down."

"Don't give me any of your 'son' shit," I said as I

turned and walked out of the office. Going home, I slept until the next morning.

The next day, Monday morning, we were supposed to report to this big hearing they were going to hold over the accident. The next thing I knew, Frank Bomar wasn't anywhere to be found. He was now with X-ray Platoon and was on his way to Vietnam. I went across the street to the SpecWar group and asked to speak to Captain Kaine. He was the head of the group, and I wanted to tell him my side of the story. Jess was a highly decorated SEAL and my friend. I didn't want his death to look like he died a drunk. Kaine listened to me but said that things were out of my hands and not to worry about it. But he did believe me and was not too happy with the CO of Team ONE.

Going back to the Team, I asked if I could escort Tolison's body back to the East Coast for burial. The CO told me that he would be doing that himself. My understanding was that Hendrickson was not well received by the men at Team TWO. They had been Tolison's close friends and he wanted to be buried back there with them.

When the autopsy had been done the Sunday morning after the accident, I had been in attendance at the hospital. They did a blood alcohol test but commented on the fact that the body was very dehydrated. In fact, the pathologist said I was looking pretty bad and told me to get some liquids inside of me. The blood alcohol test on Mr. Tolison showed a bare trace of alcohol in his system, and that matched up with the story I had been telling them.

When Hendrickson got back from the East Coast, he called me into his office. The general gist of the chewing out he gave me was how dare I go over his head and that I was out of there [the Team]. I had less than six months to go, so I left the Team and the Navy. But one thing I wanted to do was set the record straight about Tolison. And this story now does that.

By 1969, Vietnamization had begun. In the Vietnamization program, the responsibility for operations against the enemy was to be put more and more into the hands of the South Vietnamese forces. By the early 1970s, the end of U.S. involvement in the Vietnam War was in sight. The last SEAL direct action platoons deployed in 1971 would end their tours without relief and return to the States.

But the SEALs were still needed for missions in Vietnam. Special detachments performed rescues of U.S. personnel downed behind enemy lines. Advisory duties were still performed by individual SEALs in assisting the Teams' South Vietnamese counterpart, the LDNN.

But duty in Southeast Asia was becoming harder and harder to secure in the Teams—something that was of great concern to young officers who still felt they had to test themselves in combat. And the few duties available in Vietnam were becoming even more hazardous. With the pullout of U.S. ground forces, fire support and medevac facilities became less and less available. Something that made even hardened veteran SEALs shudder was the idea of no Seawolves available or, worse still, medevac dust-offs or extractions taking hours to arrive instead of minutes—if they arrived at all.

The few SEALs left in Vietnam by late 1971 and early 1972 performed their hazardous duties well. No small measure of this is the fact that two of the Teams' three Medals of Honor were for actions that took place after most of the SEALs had left Vietnam for the last time.

CAPTAIN

RYAN McCOMBIE

USN (Ret.)

Captain Ryan J. McCombie was the fourteenth Commanding Officer of SEAL Team TWO, serving in the position from June 1986 to September 1988. During his time with the Teams, he saw them evolve from the combat of Vietnam, through the debilitating cutbacks of the postwar of 1970s, and finally to the buildup of the Special Operations Forces in the 1980s. He served four assignments in SEAL Team TWO—platoon officer, training officer, Executive Officer, and Commanding Officer. He was the first U.S. SEAL to serve a tour of duty with the French Commando Hubert (SEALs) and the first military attaché to the Communist People's Popular Democratic Republic of the Congo. As a young ensign, fresh to the SEAL Teams, McCombie struggled for his chance to see combat in Southeast Asia during the waning years of the Vietnam War. He succeeded and was the last man from SEAL Team TWO to be sent to Vietnam.

Jerry Waters was killed in a parachuting accident near Suffolk, Virginia, in November of 1971. We found Jerry on the drop zone with one leg extending out from his chest and the other exiting under his shoulder blade. Later, we stopped at the Three Cats, a bar near the Suffolk drop zone, on the way home to do a postmortem of the accident. Doug Ellis would soon do a full investigation. In the meantime, all we knew was Jerry's para-commander parachute had not deployed from its sleeve. Pulled too low?

Upon hearing of Jerry's death, the team naturally migrated to the Acey-Deucey Club [now the All Hands Club]. We sat about having drinks and telling stories about Jerry. Stories about his previous night escapades were especially noted. As we bought drinks, we always bought one for Jerry. At one point I bought a round for my table; it probably cost three or four dollars in 1971. I gave the waitress a twenty-dollar bill and went to the head. When I returned and asked for my change, Tom Keith told me he'd tipped the waitress with it. Oh, well, I guess even lieutenant jg's deserve some harassment.

Almost the entire Team took the day off for Jerry's funeral. We drove down to Savannah, Georgia, to the orphanage where Jerry was raised. At the cemetery all the SEALs, including me, placed our new Trident breast insignia on Jerry's casket before it was lowered into the ground. He was the first SEAL we lost after the insignia was issued, and it just felt like the right thing to do.

After the formal ceremonies we went to the local watering hole. Like all the other SEAL combat vets, Jerry had left money in his will for a party. Before leaving for combat, each SEAL would see to it that there was money left for his teammates to have a party, a wake if you will, in the man's honor for his memory, and for a last gesture for his friends. When a round of drinks were bought, you had to buy a drink for Jerry. After all, it was his money. We were all drinking, but there was this growing pile of drinks sitting untouched. "He'll be around," we told the waitress when she inquired about the untouched drinks. "Don't take them away, he'll be here, don't worry about it." There wasn't any trouble to speak of. The locals mostly left us alone. The SEALs had said goodbye to another one of their own.

I guess this story began on 20 January 1948, in a little coal-mining town called Spangler, in western Pennsylvania, where I was born. My father was a welder/steamfitter, so my family moved about some in my early years. We lived in Brownsville, Texas, Pittsburgh, Pennsylvania, or wherever the work was. By the time I entered second grade, the family had settled down into the house that my mother still lives in today in Barnesboro, Pennsylvania.

So, I had a small-town, country childhood. A childhood quite different from today. Mother had gone to college on Saturdays to get her degree and continued her teaching career after the fifth son started grade school. Much of my youth was spent in the woods, hunting and generally walking about. The woods had become a second home, and my family didn't worry about me being "up on the hill." I eventually became an Eagle Scout. There was real trust in my family, and my parents always believed we boys were doing the right thing. It was not unusual for me to come home from school, take my .22 rifle or my bow and arrows, and be gone until suppertime.

My father loved hunting. From a very early age, he took my brothers and me to the woods. Crow and ground-hogs were the game we stalked, when I was too young to have a license. As I got older, small game—grouse, rabbit, squirrel, and an occasional pheasant—then deer were taken for the family table.

Going out in the wild with my dad taught me marksmanship and instilled in me a respect for the woods and all its creatures. A respect that is with me to this day. Another skill I learned quite early was to know my location and directions at all times. Sometimes in the early fall, before hunting season began, we would go crow hunting. Being very young, I would often fall asleep in the warm afternoon sunshine while my father was calling in the crows. When it was time to return home, my father would awaken me and have me show him the way home. Even though I was no more than five or six, tired and sleepy, if I went in the wrong direction, he would let me walk on until I realized my mistake. Before I was old enough to start school, I had a strong sense of direction and location. That sense of direction has stayed with me throughout my career. My wife would say that either it doesn't carry over to roads and highways or I've become a bit rusty in recent years. But then maybe she isn't working hard enough as my copilot/navigator?

By the end of my senior year in high school, I had received an NROTC scholarship. I decided to take it at Penn State. A small article appeared about me in the *Barnesboro Star*, a local weekly paper, telling all about how I wanted to make the Marine Corps a career. I do not remember telling anyone that I wanted to make a career of the Marine Corps. I have and, even then, had the highest respect for the leathernecks, but I wanted the Navy and to be a Frogman.

While at Penn State, I continued in sports, mostly lacrosse and wrestling. The freshman wrestling coach, George Edwards, encouraged me to try out for the team. Though I had never wrestled before, I had lifted weights with discipline and constancy throughout high school and was consequently strong for my weight. I was proud of being asked to try out for the team until I practiced against Danny Kholhepp, a Pennsylvania state champion, who introduced me to the mat in a rather violent fashion. Then he kept me in close proximity to that mat for the entire session. I was to learn there was more than sheer strength to this sport.

I never did win a match, in practice or otherwise. On the other hand, my neck rapidly passed seventeen inches as I spent many minutes on my back bridging. I was never pinned—a small compensation! After being tossed about for a time by true wrestlers and dislocating my shoulder and ripping my sternum amongst sundry minor injuries, I decided to give up something I really wasn't very skilled at doing. Nevertheless, my impressions of the discipline of the sport stayed with me and so also the physical conditioning and combativeness.

Of course, college meant the schoolwork of reading and study. I had always been a voracious reader. One day a story made a particular impression on me. It was an article in, I think, *Reader's Digest*. It told all about a special Navy unit called the SEALs. I remember part of the story told about the men hiding in the mud and water, breathing through reeds, waiting for their opportunity to ambush the

Viet Cong. Wow! I thought. Now, that's really something. That's what I want to do. If there had never been an indication that I was mentally deficient, now there was one. Staying in the mud while the enemy creeps around you? C'mon, you gotta be brain-dead. Not for me. From then on, I wanted to be a Navy SEAL.

In my second year at Penn State, I was offered a slot at Annapolis, the Naval Academy. Although that had been my dream during high school and a good friend of mine, Jerry Wood, had gone to West Point, I now liked my life and turned down the Academy. Maybe I turned it down in part because there weren't any girls there yet, maybe because I was in a hurry to graduate and go to Vietnam, maybe . . . maybe . . . In any case, it's just as well. I was always a bit of a renegade. Not like Dick Marcinko or some of the other legends in the teams, but I always had my own mind and an unwillingness to bend to something I disagreed with, regardless of who said it. Probably a Pennsylvania Dutch trait from my mom.

Anyway, the Naval Officer Training Corps was fun— at least some of the time. I would do anything to get out of some of the training, but other parts I loved. My first summer cruise as a midshipman was an adventure. My ship was the USS R. A. OWENS DD-827. We went to San Juan, Puerto Rico. We took a bus to Roosevelt Roads Naval Base, where we flew backseat in F-9 Cougar jets. This was all to give us a taste of naval aviation, and the pilots did their best to ensure that we left our lunch in the cockpit so we could clean it up the remainder of the afternoon. I was one of the few whose stomach muscles sufficiently resisted the G-suit's pressure and did not puke all over myself.

While at Roosevelt Roads, I learned that UDTB training took place near the airstrip. When I heard that, I knew that this was my chance to learn what was going on and just who these people were.

Arriving at the training area after work one evening, I went into the old wooden barracks. Everyone was asleep! It was only twenty hundred hours. I couldn't believe it. Were these mama's boys? A time would come when I would understand. As one of Rogers's Rangers rules states, "Eat and sleep anytime you can. You never know when you will have the chance again."

My first impression had been mistaken—there was one man awake, sitting at a small table near the door. To this day I don't know his name, but he sure impressed me. The son of a gun had this little, tiny girl waist and then arms and shoulders that were enormous. I thought I was a pretty big boy, what with my wrestling and weight lifting. I even held a few records at Penn State, for a very short period of time, but this guy was strong, unbelievable.

As the junior—very junior—midshipman that I was, I quickly stated the purpose of my visit. Treating me with all the respect and disdain the Navy usually reserves for the lesser services, the man grunted at me and directed me to see another man nearby. That was how I met Chief Tom Blais.

What a great guy, Tom Blais. A barrel-chested chief who had gone through UDTB twice! After being in the Teams for some time, Blais had gotten out to go to Central America to search for gold or something. After getting enough to make a pair of earrings for his lovely wife, Florence, Tom returned to the Navy only to have to go back through UTDB again. Not only was he required to complete UDTB training again, but some of his instructors were his previous students and he had been known as a real hard-ass instructor.

But that is probably a whole story in itself. Tom Blais knew UDTB training, and he took the time to tell me about it and what I could expect. Without sugar-coating anything, Tom Blais convinced me that the Frogmen and, if possible, the SEALs was where I wanted to be in the Navy. At that time Chief Blais was probably not too impressed with the young midshipman in front of him. I hadn't even graduated from college yet. But I told that man that I would see him in four years, and I meant it.

For the cruise, my destroyer had berthed the midshipmen all of the way forward under the fo'c'sle, next to the bosun's locker. In these lovely accommodations, all of the midshipmen could get a full appreciation for the enlisted berthing spaces and enjoy the maximum movement of the ship. The bow went up and down as the hull rolled left and right as she cut her way through the seas toward home. Late summer is hurricane season in the Atlantic, and we soon found ourselves in one. Everybody aboard seemed to be getting seasick, even some of the old chiefs.

There I was walking about, cocky and arrogant, without a twinge of sickness, making fun of all of my suffering fellow sailors. And it was a very rough time! Men who were off duty were strapped in their racks, and the weather decks were secured, meaning no one was allowed outside the skin of the ship. It was a dangerous situation. I remember the ship taking thirty-eight-degree rolls. After a day or two of bad seas, I realized that if I became ill at any stage, I would really pay a price. "You have really given a lot of people a hard time, McCombie," I said to myself. "You had better not get seasick!"

As an eighteen-year-old kid, my incontrovertible logic said that if I didn't eat anything, I couldn't get sick, right? Wrong! Never had I been so wrong! Not eating is almost a guaranteed way of getting seasick. I became so ill that I just wanted to die—crawl out on a weather deck and roll over the side, let the sea have me or at least what was left of a retching, quivering, mortified eighteen-year-old kid. You really haven't been miserable until you have been seasick for days, until the ship docks and your feet are on dry land.

In spite of the ride and my condition, I wrote Chief Blais a letter. My handwriting probably wasn't as impressive as it might have been, but I got the letter finished. In any case, Chief Blais probably never dreamed that what I said would happen. Four years later it was a proud young officer who walked across the quarterdeck of SEAL Team and asked, "Where's Chief Blais? Please inform the Chief that Ensign McCombie is aboard." As the years went by, Tom Blais and I became fast and good friends.

When the OWENS finally returned to port in Norfolk and I was back on land and my stomach had stopped turning over, I decided that never again would I be seasick. The answer was my new discovery—to be a SEAL. By my becoming a SEAL, my career hasn't put me aboard ship as much as other sailors. In any case, I have never again been sea- or airsick. Well, once or twice with Combat Talon low-level flights when I was encouraged by the puke of a half-dozen other people. Anyway, if I was ever in another hurricane, meals were not something I would be skipping.

As graduation from Penn State approached, I found that high school basketball where we were told to "run off" ankle sprains had managed to do a number on my ankle. I had torn the ligaments in my ankle to the point where I was classified 4-F. I didn't have to go into the service at all, even though the draft was very much a reality. In Ohio, I found a doctor who was impressed by my plans. "If you're crazy enough to try this," he said, "I'm crazy enough to sign it," and he signed my application for the UDT/SEAL program as physically able.

Yet another hurdle confronted me before graduation. The Marine officer of my NROTC battalion wanted me to enter the Corps. I had a 4.0 in four years of physical training tests and had come back from the Marine portion of our summer ROTC program the number one midshipman in the country. At least that was what I was told. If there was such a rating, I've never seen it.

One day I was called into the director of naval science's office. He told me that my shenanigans had caught up with me and that he wasn't going to commission me in the Navy! I had been my normal self and hadn't followed all of the rules properly, amongst other venial sins. Something about taking the other midshipmen down to the bar where I worked and getting them loaded up prior to class. Sitting in the back of the room later, I would just watch the show as my classmates made fools of themselves.

Every Thursday, the class went out on the drill field and marched around for three hours with rifles on their shoulders. This was not what I wanted to do in the Navy, and I used every excuse possible to avoid this marionette drill. I guess they got suspicious the day I called in and said I had diarrhea. The consequences of my actions were that my individual ratings weren't very high, and that was the stick my Commanding Officer was holding over me. "If, on the other hand, you wanted to go into the Marine Corps, perhaps some agreement could be reached," he told me. I knew that this was just a setup to get me into the Marine Corps. Maybe the Marine Corps wanted me (Vietnam?), maybe the ROTC unit had a quota to meet. Whatever the reason, I didn't buy the ruse.

The number two officer of the ROTC unit, a Marine lieutenant colonel, wanted to know why I didn't have enthusiasm for the Corps. My answer was that I wanted to be a SEAL. "Well," he said, "why don't you go Force Recon?" I had done my homework. "If you go into Force Recon," I countered, "you may get jump school when you go in. Some years later, as an officer, you may get dive school. Later still, you may get demolition school. But if I go into the SEALs, I get all of those schools before I even report to the Team. The first thing that happens is that I get dive, demo, and jump school. It seems to me that the better deal for me is to be a SEAL." Little did I know what those schools would cost in physical demands.

The colonel more or less excused me from his office soon after that. Once I had called their bluff, they went ahead and commissioned me. After all, Vietnam wasn't over yet, and all of the services needed officers, especially combat arms "cannon fodder." Very near the time of my graduation from Penn State, I received orders from the Navy to report to COMNAVSPECWARGRULANT (Commander Navy Special Warfare Group–Atlantic, better known as Nosegroup). Talk about acronyms. I couldn't even say this one. Truth was, I was not much more than a trained civilian wearing a uniform. The Navy's way of talking was just one of the things I was going to learn very rapidly.

My car was an old Chevrolet Impala that I packed up and drove to Norfolk, where I checked in in the early summer of 1970. Norm Olson was the Chief of Staff at the time, with Wendy Webber being the Commodore of the Special Warfare Group at Little Creek. The death of my uncle had delayed my arrival, so I had missed the beginning of a class by two weeks. Another class was going to start in mid-August. Until my class started, I spent my time as the junior officer at the group staff. There were no real duties for me.

One day Norm Olson asked me if I played golf. Time on the links during my college days had made me a pretty good golfer, and I soon found myself on Commander Olson's team in the intramural golf league. Things got off to an inauspicious start. On the very first hole, Norm missed his putt and got more than a little angry. In his anger, Norm threw his putter straight at this young ensign—me.

"Yeow, Mama!" I exclaimed, ducking the spinning club. It was quickly explained that there was nothing personal in the incident, but I now understood why Commander Olson's nickname was Stormin' Norman. All the same, I shot ten strokes higher than I had shot in over a year. Consequently, we lost the match and Norm really got mad. Maybe he was just getting me ready for UDTB?

After the golf game we went to the officers' club. It stood where the base day care center is now. We stayed at the club until we were thrown out. Then we proceeded to the Duck Inn, where we stayed until we were thrown out. Now all of this was going on with a brand-new ensign, just an 0-1, being led around by his new bosses, the most senior guys in Naval Special Warfare, an 0-5 and an 0-6, during his first week of active duty. Finally, we ended up at Norm's house, where his lovely wife, Bobby, soon threw us out. Welcome to the fun-filled world of Naval Special Warfare.

During my time with the staff, I didn't do any real training. Norm Olson would take us out on a run now and then, but no real PT or anything very strenuous. My understanding at the time was that there was a lot of pressure from the Navy Training Command through the NAV-PHIBSCOL [Navy amphibious school] to raise the percentage of graduates from UDTB. Historically, about 18 to 22 percent of the applicants would complete the course. That percentage did not indicate efficiency to a bean-counting Navy. They wanted the cost of training held down, with more graduates for their bucks.

Fred Sabine, a truly great naval officer, and Rick Woolard came up with a way to increase the percentage of graduates in a classic SEAL fashion. What Rick suggested, and Fred agreed to, was that the school hold pretraining in order to get the students in shape for the actual course. That way, fewer would fall out because of poor physical conditioning. At least that's the story they sold the Navy. Actually, training was extended by six weeks, and the UDTB staff started kicking the students' everlovin' butts long before class began.

Starting class early, the staff ran us through the ringer. PT and all of the usual entertainment of UDT training was wreaked upon us with real enthusiasm. Consequently, half of the trainees quit before we even officially started class. It was only after the class had officially started that an on-the-record count of the students was made. With half of the "quitters" already gone at the beginning of class, the graduation percentage nearly doubled the historical norm. Yeah! Right! I was to learn over the years that Rick Woolard always kept his eye on the real objective whether it be the enemy or quality in UDTB graduates.

Some of the better athletes quit early. I remember that the best athlete in our group quit Friday before class officially "started." His logic was that pretraining was so hard that he didn't even want to try the real thing on Monday. On that Monday, the 17th of August, training began in earnest. I found that I wasn't having a hard time of it. My time in wrestling and other sports had hardened me mentally, and muscles had memory. I was able to stand up to what the instructors threw at us. It wasn't easy. I was tired and hurting most of the time, but I had become accustomed to that when I was wrestling. I managed to stay in the front group on most of the evolutions. Training, I initially believed, was no cakewalk, but it wasn't something I was willing to quit over either. Then came Hell Week.

Hell Week was just that, a solid week of hell. It was

tough, long, grueling hours of intense physical activity and little sleep to recover. Several things helped get me through the week. The instructors allowed the student officers to pick their boat crews. Lining up all of the other officer students, we would go down the line, first one officer picking and then the next, around and around until we each had a full crew. All of the other students were picking the big, strong horses for their crews. I picked all five-foot-eight-inch wrestlers.

Everyone in my boat crew was between five-seven and five-ten and had been a wrestler sometime in school. Every crewman would carry his share of the boat. Each man, Frank Walters, Gary Stillman, Jack Hatton, Chuck Steffy, Ron Caron, and "Little" MacDonald, knew what it was to go on automatic and just keep going. Our boat crew won every evolution in Hell Week. It really didn't matter what we were doing, we would come out ahead of the others. It pays to be a winner, and we would win, getting ourselves that blessed few additional moments of rest before the next evolution.

As the week progressed and people quit from the other boat crews, our ability to win continued to increase, as we had a full complement from the beginning of Hell Week until the end. It worked. I had picked my team for spirit, not size, and it held true. They had the spirit and gave it all. I never thought of quitting during Hell Week, at least not at first. Then came the boat twenty-mile paddle, and training changed for me.

I had gotten the G-2 [information] on the evolution and prepared according to my intelligence. First thing, I put an extra floor mat in the IBS [Inflatable Boat, small], giving us a flatter bottom and thus a cleaner hull with less resistance to the water. The new smooth bottom lines would let us paddle faster. Second, I had gotten the skinny on a trick the instructors would pull. Once the crews would arrive at Lynnhaven Inlet, the instructors would tell them to rest and eat lunch, C rations. It was timed so that none of the crews crossed the inlet until the incoming tide was at its strongest.

After hearing the instructors' intent, I got the tide tables for the area and knew precisely when the tides would change and how much time we could waste on the bank of the river. When our instructor left us to eat our rations, I had everyone back in the boat and paddling for home. We arrived over three hours ahead of the next crew. It looked like three hours of rest for the good guys—that's as much sleep as we had gotten all week. But an instructor we had nicknamed Mr. Banana had other ideas. He had us duck-walking in a crouch along the road. When that grew tiresome for him, there were IBS races up and down the beach for my men and me. We were too tired to protest that this treatment flew in the face of the credo that it pays to be a winner.

It was incredible—we were working harder than the losers who were still paddling. When the next boat crew finally came in, three hours later, Mr. Banana had another version of an IBS race for us. Instead of running along carrying our four hundred pounds of boat, we would have a ram race and run directly into each other. Although I protested the stupidity of this, one hundred push-ups convinced me that it probably wasn't really that bad an idea. Of course, we would collide together and go down in a pile, one big crumpled mass, much to the amusement of Mr. Banana.

After several iterations of this "jousting," and Mr. Banana fairly rolling with laughter, in the middle of one pile was me. In the confusion someone stepped squarely on my ankle, the bad one already messed up from high school basketball. The one that had gotten me listed as 4-F. I had been able to deal with it and was right up there with the front runners. That was over now. Training would become painful, very painful, and it stayed that way right up until the end. Now I learned what training was really all about. Never quitting. Never giving up, regardless of the difficulty or pain.

Hell Week ended on a Friday, and I had never been so tired in all of my life. I went to bed Friday night, woke up Saturday afternoon, took a leak, and went back to bed. I didn't wake up again until hunger got me up on Sunday afternoon.

All the way through Hell Week I kept telling myself, "As soon as this is over I am going to quit." Screw these guys, I thought, they are not going to make me quit. Only after I had proven I could do it would I tell these guys they could take their program and shove it up where the sun doesn't shine. I don't know how many times I told myself that during the week. It must have passed out of my consciousness during my long sleep, because on Monday after Hell Week, I reported with the rest of the sick, lame, and lazy to sick call and would soon be given an honorable excuse to leave training as well as the Navy.

The doctor examined me and said, "You're going to Portsmouth Naval Hospital for evaluation for retention in the Navy."

"Retention in the Navy!" I had just completed Hell Week! I was stunned. The doctor had written a chit for me to go to the hospital and be checked out. Not to fix my ankle, or even to drop me from the program, but to see if I should be kicked out of the Navy altogether.

"I've just finished Hell Week. I want to stay in UDT," I said.

"Forget that," the doctor responded decisively. "You're not staying in this training program," and with that he had finished with me.

Crushed, I limped back over to the unit and went into Lieutenant Rick Woolard's office. Sitting down, I watched him work on his papers. Rick was a consummate actor, as most good leaders are. He finally looked up at me and asked, "Yes, Mr. McCombie, what can we do for you?"

Being too brokenhearted to speak, I just pushed the doctor's chit across the desk to him. "Ha!" he guffawed. "We finally got rid of you, didn't we, Mr. McCombie?"

I didn't trust myself to speak right then, so I just sat there dejectedly. "So, what are you going to do?" Rick asked.

"I just want to finish training," I finally blurted out.

Rick picked up the chit, crumpled it into a ball, and threw it into the wastebasket. "Then I don't want to hear another word from you. Dismissed!" And he went back to studying his papers.

By afternoon I was back in the training I had been so determined to quit.

Rick is one of the special ones. An officer who can see the big picture but also has the instinct and the courage to do what is best for the Teams. It is hard to imagine an officer doing that today. There are a few who can still make the right decisions that also put them at risk, but not many. Our system has become too bureaucratically unforgiving. It doesn't forgive any wrong decisions, and the only way to never make a wrong decision is to never make a decision. Hell, sometimes I think it doesn't forgive right decisions.

Now things were different for me. No longer did I run at the head of the pack. I was at the rear with those I had thought were lazy wimps and gimps. I had never understood why those men couldn't put out and be up at the head of the group. I didn't understand why they were seemingly content to be in the back of the pack. Now I was one of them, and none of us were very content, believe me.

There is nothing more painful than everybody else seeming to breeze along and no matter how much you put out, how hard you bust your ass, the best you can do is just keep up. Then you are subjected to the "circus" or "Extra Military Instruction" [EMI]. These sessions were designed to get a student who the instructors didn't want in "their" Teams to quit. Nobody was thrown out of training. The only way out was to quit! A circus was conducted to eliminate people.

When a circus was "awarded," a group of students, including the unknowing target, would be kept at the conclusion of the training day. The instructor would announce that remedial training would be over when one or two or whatever number of students they had decided quit. Then we would begin PT. Without rest or respite, the session would continue into the night until the requisite number of students quit. Then and only then could we go rest for the following training day. Our goon squad participated in these sessions as extras and as targets.

Understand that in any other group of men, these guys

would be worlds ahead. They were accustomed to being the superstars back in high school, college, or even the fleet. If you take the level of a national-class athlete and move down just one small notch, that is where you find most of the active-duty SEALs, then and today. Some SEALs are active Olympians even in the Teams.

So these guys had to deal with this enormous psychological weight day in and day out. My opinion of the men in the back of the pack changed considerably. They were assuredly to become good operators. The men who would really put out when the chips were down were those men with the intestinal fortitude to continue day after long day eating the psychological and physical dust of those in front, but never quitting. These were the men who just wouldn't stop. With both legs broken and one arm wounded, they would still crawl forward to get the mission done. And that isn't just talk. During World War Two, the beaches at Normandy bore witness to actions just like that. This was without doubt the biggest lesson I took from UDTB.

Running and swimming were excruciating now. The swim from Vieques back to Roosey Roads, a straight distance of over seven and one-half miles between the islands, is one of the big evolutions of the Puerto Rico phase of training. The instructors put you in the water on the beach of Vieques at dawn and say, "See you for supper." The strong currents always move swimmers far off course, and you end up swimming ten to fourteen miles on the average. It took me nine and one-half hours, in pain all the way. But I did complete the swim, and in the top third of my class at that. Guys I couldn't beat on the one-mile Saturday swims I beat out on the Vieques swim. Some of them were still swimming late that night. I couldn't sprint with my ankle the way it was, but I could dog it out.

Going from being the hot dog of the class to the shitbird is a tremendous psychological trauma. I went from being the second-best swimmer to the second-worst. Being an officer and a leader of men just made the situation that much worse. I never got back to my position up front.

The good news is I never forgot the lessons the rat pack taught me.

There were other parts of training I could still handle pretty well, even excel at. My time in the Scouts and especially out in the woods with my dad and brothers paid off. This proved especially true on one evolution we had during demolition training.

The evolution took place on Pineros Island. Pineros is a small piece of land sticking up from the Caribbean near Puerto Rico. Parts of the island had been built up for the British fleet during World War Two. The SEALs and UDT had been spending part of their training time blowing up bits and pieces of the landscape. Our demolition problem this particular night was to insert on the island, work our way to the peak of a hill, and destroy the lookout tower there. This was, in part, a form of graduation exercise for the demolition and land warfare part of our training.

Rick Woolard was the instructor in charge for that evolution. Jim Redman was the point man, and I was the squad officer. Going in at night, Jim led us up to the tower but kept getting slightly off track on the way. I didn't think anything of it, but continued to correct our path to head for the target. I had been on the island a few days earlier and had climbed the hill. I had no compass, but with my youthful training in woodcraft, I simply always knew which way to go.

Rick had been noticing what I was doing. Once on target, we loaded our demolition according to the plan we had made and took cover nearby. There was a tunnel, more likely an old bomb shelter, close under the tower where we could safely hide. While we stood in the tunnel waiting for the explosion, signaling a successful mission, a small gecko kept biting at Rick's foot. Geckos are small, harmless, but sometimes aggressive lizards found in the tropics. Moving quickly, Rick reached down and snatched the lizard up.

Holding the lizard in front of him, Rick reached up with his free hand and turned down the ends of his handlebar mustache, giving a kind of Genghis Khan look. With a frown that matched his mustache, Rick squeezed the gecko and popped the head off the little reptile. Dropping the carcass, Rick turned back up the ends of his mustache as if to say the blood letting is over, we can party now. Needless to say, I never tried biting Rick on the boot.

After the charges went off and we had checked the target, I took the lead for the return trip to our rubber boats, with the skills my father had helped to build in me. When we stepped onto the beach, we were within a few feet of the IBS. Rick and the other members of our team were astounded that in pitch dark of the night, without map or compass, I had arrived to within four feet of our IBS. I knew we were close, but I must admit, even I was surprised that we were that close. Of course, I took credit for the success, as I needed the morale boost.

Graduating from UDTB is something of a blur. Perhaps it had something to do with the fact that liquor was very cheap in Puerto Rico and the class came back with CO-NEX boxes [secured steel shipping boxes] full of booze. In fact, the winter training time became a kind of traditional holiday-stock-up-the-household-bar for the coming year. A quart of Bacardi rum was eighty-five cents and two-gallon glass carboys of rum wrapped in woven bamboo went for three seventy-five. Until the drug trade forced an end to our unofficial importation, the yearly booze run was something to look forward to.

Graduation did come, and I was going to be assigned to a Team. In fact, I was going to Seal Team TWO instead of first going through initiation with a UDT Team. It was really rare on the East Coast for a trainee to report directly to Seal Team TWO. Lieutenant John C. Brewton had been killed in Vietnam in January of 1970, and the Team wanted to bring in two new officers. Rick Woolard stood in front of the officers of my class and asked for volunteers for SEAL Team TWO. I immediately raised my hand.

Volunteering wasn't the easiest thing to do just then. A platoon of SEALs had been caught in a claymore ambush and had been rehabilitating from serious wounds in the whirlpool bath of our training unit. Deep gouging wounds covered their bodies. Every day we were able to see the gaping wounds that modern warfare and a claymore had inflicted on those men's bodies. The image was a great motivator to train hard and according to the unit's motto, "The more you sweat in peace, the less you bleed in war." Either these guys hadn't sweated much in peace, or an element of chance was intrinsic to guerrilla war. In any case, volunteers for SEAL Team were not as prolific as before that platoon's return from Vietnam. Mark Waterman and I volunteered and were accepted.

It was after UDTB graduation that the class went down to Fort Benning for jump school, where we all learned how to fall out of the sky and become paratroopers. The black hats at Benning were good, but we had been had by professionals, and the black hats really didn't have the time in three weeks to hurt us. Plus the Army had a lot of regulations to protect the trooper that the UDTB instructor did not have. Consequently, the only ways to get in trouble at Benning were to miss muster because you had been out in town all night or to fall prey to Army Regulations.

That was a situation one of our men found out about, as Smiley Welch nearly got kicked out of training for living up to his nickname. A black hat accused Smiley of silent insubordination. We couldn't believe it. All he was doing is smiling! We climbed the flagpole and hung a life-size Mickey Mouse balloon on it over that one.

Our class is one of the ones that stole the wind socks off the jump tower. What can I say? The boys liked to climb high things when they were drinking. I later found that many of the Army schools were somewhat of a pain in the ass. After you have passed Hell Week and proven yourself, any other training where they intentionally limit your sleep is just a bother. Even some of the schools considered more difficult, such as SERE (survival, evasion, resistance, and escape), I went through with something of a stupid attitude. After all, I thought, no matter how these guys act, they're still Americans and they can't kill me or maim me, though they could inflict a lot of pain. Without the specter of serious injury or death facing you, if you can handle pain (because they will hurt you), fear goes away. Thank goodness, I didn't learn that they had buried alive a few guys at the Pickle Meadows SERE school before I went through. My attitude might have been a little different.

After jump school came dive school in Key West, Florida. Key West was not a bad place to be when you compared it to Little Creek, Virginia, in January. It was a good time to be young, a bachelor, and in the best of shape of your life. We were diving open-circuit with twin ninety-cubic-foot tanks, and I can remember flipping those tanks on over my head as if they didn't weigh anything. The whole class would run over the beach to the water with those twin steel cylinders on our backs, along with a lead weight belt and our other diving gear.

Uniforms for the school were casual at best. We would wear whatever felt right for the day's training. Well, this one instructor decided to put a stop to our eclectic outfits. Standing out one day for PT, we were told that we would learn a lesson in wearing the proper uniform of the day. While we performed the exercise, that man counted us through 2,500 four-count jumping jacks. After around one thousand repetitions we were barely able to move our arms and legs in a stumbling, jerky manner. Nevertheless, he kept counting and we kept jerking. We completed the exercise and learned forever that uniform means ''all the same.''

What had originally been planned for us was a marathon session of log PT. But the night before, we had sneaked in and stolen all of the telephone poles used for log PT and hidden them. Now they were mad, and the instructors were going to run us into the ground by their running in relays. One instructor would run us until he slowed down, then another fresh instructor would take over to keep us going.

Well, dive school wasn't UDTB, and we weren't going to take this on graduation day. At the start of the run, when the instructor went out on the road and turned left, the entire class turned right and kept right on going through all of his screeching to get our asses back there.

I think that was the only mutiny I ever led in the Navy. After the run, we threw all of the instructors into one of the water tanks, and then we graduated. That was dive school, and a good time was had by all.

After dive school, I finally walked across the quarter-deck at Team TWO. However, I still had a long way to go before I was accepted by the others as a SEAL. There were five schools you had to complete after UDTB, jump school, and dive school. Until you had also completed SERE school, either the Army Ranger school, Raider/LRRP [Long Range Reconnaissance Patrol] school, or the Special Forces officer course, two additional schools, and SEAL Basic (actually predeployment training), you were not considered ready to integrate into a platoon, participate in its operations, or go to Vietnam, my ultimate objective.

The schools were not always immediately available. No matter how good you were, you waited. It was a hard rule for a young hard charger to be subjected to, but the rules had been developed over the years the Teams had been in existence. Some of the unlearned lessons had cost men their lives, so the rules were obeyed. Nobody whined that this was not fair. The other officer out of UDTB, Mark Waterman, and I were the only people in SEAL Team TWO who did not have at least one tour in-country. Most everyone had two or three, and some had five or six.

After eight months, and completion of my schools, I was finally a qualified SEAL. The 1130 designator had been authorized in 1969 to indicate an individual was a fully trained SEAL. I now had my designator, but I was far from fully trained or fully accepted.

For a long time, there was no outward sign that an individual was a SEAL or even a UDT man. Now a new uniform device was authorized for the SEALs to be worn on the chest above any ribbons and jump wings. It would be several months yet after I had qualified before we would receive the new Special Warfare Trident device to wear on our uniforms. I was on the team when we voted on the design of the insignia. Only one member, Dennis "Zipper-Gut" Drady of SEAL Team TWO, voted to accept a device, and even he did not vote for the gaudy eagle holding a musket and a trident. It didn't matter— the West Coast liked the idea, and so did Washington. We got the "Budweiser" whether we wanted it or not.

The first Tridents were gold for officers and silver for enlisted men. UDT had a similar device, only minus the eagle. Soon the color difference was eliminated and both officers and enlisted wore gold tridents. It was, and is, a large rather garish affair having an eagle with outspread wings behind and above an anchor. In the eagle's claws are a trident and a flintlock pistol. The symbolism was for the three environments that the SEALs operated in, the sea, air, and land.

Over the years we have become accustomed to the appearance of the device and now wear it with pride. At the time, it seemed to fly in the face of our low-profile operating style. But long before the Trident showed up, I was struggling to qualify as an operator, and those were long months. I was ready for a symbol of accomplishment, or at least recognition.

For the longest time I would walk through the passageways of Team TWO and nobody would even speak to me. People just didn't come over to the Team directly from UDTB. Here I was, a cheery, happy young ensign, and nobody would talk to me except for official business. Then they spoke with as few words as possible. It would be tough walking down the passageways calling out, "Good morning, so-and-so. Good morning, so-and-so," over and over and receiving only stony silence and stares in return.

Back then, just because you were assigned to a SEAL Team didn't make you a member. First you had to prove your mettle, preferably in Vietnam. Mike Boynton would pass me and I would call out, "Good morning, Petty Officer Boynton." Nothing would come back, no response at all.

This went on for weeks, long weeks. The one exception was Lou Boink. Lou was a legitimate hero from his Vietnam tours and must have felt sorry for this lonely ensign. He was setting up a detachment to go to Crete in April.

I would help him where I could with the paperwork and anything else I could do. He reciprocated by recognizing my existence. At least he would talk to me about the Team and what I should be doing.

One morning I called out my usual greeting to Mike Boynton as I passed him in the passageway. Much to my surprise, he answered me! Looking directly in my eyes, Mike said, "Good morning, Enswine," and he continued on his way. Boy, even being called an enswine made me feel good. Maybe I wasn't accepted, but my existence was recognized.

The best manner to be accepted, I found, was good work. EXOTIC DANCER was an annual joint special operation exercise. SEAL Team TWO participated in it every year. Lieutenant Aubrey Davis had several members of his platoon chopped up pretty bad in Vietnam. They were on their way to recovery by now. Dave Strong, Aubrey's assistant officer in charge [AOIC], had moved on, so I was put in this combat-hardened, combat-wounded platoon as the AOIC for Lieutenant Davis. Bobby Schamberger, leading petty officer, led a motley crew of individuals whose wounds still burned red and whose memories of real war were fresh and vivid.

Evidently I performed satisfactorily during this exercise, because by the end of EXOTIC DANCER I was pretty well integrated into the platoon. The Team now would admit I existed, however reluctantly. There was still the problem of my being the only one in the command who had not been to Vietnam. There was little more obvious indicator of who hadn't been in-country than the Team's most junior officer standing in formation with an expert rifle, expert pistol, and National Defense Ribbon next to Teammates with five and six rows of medals.

On 23 July 1971, eleven officers and seventeen enlisted men from SEAL Team TWO went on two days' TAD [temporary additional duty] to the Naval Air Station in New Orleans for the launching of the USS BREWTON DE-1084. The ship was named after Lieutenant (jg) John Cooke Brewton, who was killed in Vietnam while in SEAL Detachment Alfa, Tenth Platoon, January 1970. On

Friday evening the SEALs attended a reception sponsored by Admiral and Mrs. Zumwalt, then viewed the launching on Saturday morning, the 24th of July.

That is how the event reads in the official command history for SEAL Team TWO, 1972. The reality has a few more details than that. Almost every SEAL in TWO who could attend the ceremony did. I was one of those eleven officers there. This was the first time I went TAD with the Team for a party! Our flight was not a normal military flight, although we did restrain ourselves from jumping from the aircraft over Bourbon Street. We'd soon have plenty of time there. At the reception, I seem to remember only admirals, their wives, and SEALs. At the reception, Admiral Zumwalt, the CNO, who has always been a strong SEAL supporter, made the mistake of asking Jerry Waters how everything was going.

"Shitty," Jerry replied.

"Really? What's the matter?"

"Admiral," Jerry responded, "you're the guy that says he knows about SEALs and you're always dealing with SEALs and you always want to have SEALs around and la-de-da-de-dah SEALs. Well then, you know that the only thing we drink is rum and Cokes, and there's no rum in this place."

Of course, there was Jack Daniel's Black, Chivas Regal, and some of the finest drinks in the world at the open bar. But there was no Bacardi rum. Literally within minutes, we saw several stewards running up the ladder-well with a case of Bacardi rum on each one's shoulder. I'm not sure the rum lasted the evening.

The next morning at the launching, the Team was a sight to behold. We had visited the town, most of us staying out the entire night, and came to the commissioning still strongly feeling the effects of the night before. Rich Kuhn was still buttoning his summer dress whites as we were lining up.

There is an expression, the "zactlies," that is where your mouth smells "zactly" like your ass, and we were all suffering from a bad case of the zactlies this particular morning. And Mrs. Zumwalt, God bless her soul, came down and kissed every one of us. That woman must be a saint and have the strongest stomach in the civilized world. I'm pretty sure one of the men tongued her, and I know I saw one of the men grab her by the buttocks in the only manner he knew how to kiss.

Mrs. Zumwalt moved through the line with the grace and aplomb of a queen, never showing the slightest reaction to these improprieties. It was the most unbelievable thing I had ever been associated with, at least by that time in my young career. This was my introduction to the SEAL Team at an official Navy function.

The Team didn't have patches or car decals, and we had only just gotten the Tridents for our uniforms. Some of the guys were upset about having to wear the Trident. Now we could be seen for who we were, not necessarily a good thing. I had been instructed that the right answer for "What do you do in the Navy?" was to say "I'm a Navy diver." Nobody ever said SEAL. Sometimes I wondered why. What with our physical condition and overwhelming self-confidence, it was pretty obvious who we were. Suffice it to say, a group of us could sure be noticed if you looked.

I should not have been surprised that the team partied hard on liberty. Since we all lived under a partly self-imposed strict security blanket, when we let our hair down and relaxed, we did it with as much gusto as we attacked our work.

One of my first assignments after coming to the Team was to be the officer in charge on a demolition job in New Jersey. Bud Thrift, a warrant officer at the time, was my assistant. Along with Mikey Boynton, Joe Hulse, and a couple of other guys, we went up to New Jersey in January. Our job was to blow up a bunch of old pilings and piers in the harbor of Bayonne, New Jersey.

Here I was, brand new to the Teams, Ensign McCombie, and I was in charge of guys like Bud Thrift, Mike Boynton, and Joe Hulse? Yeah, right. It soon became apparent what the trip would be like. Bud Thrift was driving the official car and I was riding in the passenger seat when we came up to the toll taker's booth at the Chesapeake Bay Bridge tunnel. At that time the All-state "Good Hands" people were being talked about a lot, and Bud played it up.

"Do they keep that booth warm for you in the winter?" Bud asked the attendant.

Looking at Bud as if he were completely out of his mind, the man answered, "Yeah."

"Do they keep it air-conditioned in the summer?"

Even more puzzled, the attendant answered, "Yeah."

"Well, if you have any trouble, you just contact me. I'm with the Good Hands people," Bud said, cupping his hands in the manner of the people on the TV commercial. With that, we drove off.

The job went easily enough. The C-4 had come up in a truck convoy with the men, and we all met in Bayonne. The job was rapidly completed, and we went out to have some liberty. While we were in a local bar, I was enjoying my bachelor status and working on picking up this particular girl. I thought I was doing rather well until a local guy came in.

Coming up to me, the man insisted that the girl I was talking to was his. "Well, if that's true, it's not obvious to her," was my answer to him. That didn't sit too well with the guy. He wasn't quite sure what he wanted to do, so he continued blustering about some Mafia connection and that it would be a good idea if I backed off.

That guy may very well have been in the Mafia for all I knew, but I couldn't back down in front of my Team-mates. Not being quite sure what to do, I went to the head. Evidently, my mafioso chum decided to try and come into the head after me. That was not the right thing to do with Mike Boynton in the bar. I may have been a brand-new SEAL and still quite wet behind the ears, but I was a SEAL and a Teammate.

When I got out of the head, Mikey had picked the guy up and thrown him through the air ten or fifteen feet to-wards the door. Mike must have been drunk just a bit, because he missed the door. After the guy got up from where he had impacted against the wall, he staggered out of the bar. I think I bought Mike a drink. The Mafia apparently doesn't impress the SEALs very much.

The old SEALs were much that way. We didn't make any kind of announcement about who we were, nothing showed on our uniforms, and except amongst ourselves we didn't talk about work much. If you "pushed the envelope," you could quickly find out what a SEAL was capable of doing. Most importantly, nobody ever did get the number of the truck that hit you, i.e., they didn't even know they had just met a SEAL.

We took our time off seriously, and we took our jobs seriously. There was a reason we received extra pay for hazardous duty. Jerry Waters was not lost in combat. And the hazards could continue into our family life as well. I was married in March of 1971, and one of the things I had to tell my wife, Denise, was not easy to live with.

"Honey," I said. "if I don't come home from work someday, don't call anyone. Somebody will be in touch with you and tell you what you need to know. And I'll be home as soon as I am able." To her lasting credit, Denise had the strength to live with the situation, though many other SEAL wives couldn't.

Later on, when I was the Commanding Officer of Team TWO, Denise would try to help the new generation of SEAL wives cope with the stresses of marriage to a Team member. If the woman didn't find something to keep herself busy and interested, it would be a very strong indicator that another SEAL family was heading for the reefs. It takes a special man to be a SEAL, but there is no doubt that it takes an even more special woman to stand by these madmen throughout their career.

The largest pressure that could be put on a SEAL family was knowing that the man of the house was going to war, and I was doing everything in my power to go. I had put in my chit for duty in Vietnam practically on my first day at the Team. I renewed the request every chance I got. Platoons were returning from deployments to Vietnam without being replaced. It was obvious that the war was winding down and Vietnamization was the future. I was not going to get to play.

It looked like my chance was slipping away. If you

were going to be a SEAL and train your ass off, you had to test your mettle in the ultimate arena, combat. As a young, highly trained SEAL officer, I knew I was immortal and couldn't be hurt by anyone. Nobody was as good as the SEALs. I was as patriotic as any man in the Teams, but the real reason for going into the crucible of combat was to see just how really good you were.

Vietnam was ending, finally, for some. At long last, I had made it through the rank structure far enough that my name was coming up on the rotation list. But nobody else was deploying. I had made lieutenant (jg) in September 1971. With the ending of the Vietnam commitment, a number of officers who had been over in UDT came back to the SEAL Team. Suddenly, I'm back on the bottom of the rotation list, and no new billets were coming up. It really looked as if I would never go.

Out of the blue, it seemed, an officer's billet for duty in Vietnam showed up. Lieutenant Commander John Ferruggiaro was the CO of Team TWO at the time. Ron Yeaw was ops officer, with Tom Blais his assistant. Calling me into his office, Ron told me that I was slated to go to Ranger school. "Ron," I said, "when is that billet for Vietnam opening up?"

"During your second phase of Ranger school," he answered.

"God, I have got to go to Vietnam!" I exclaimed. "Is there anything I can do?"

Tom Blais gave me a suggestion that sounded pretty good. The only trouble was that I would have to talk to the CO himself to get the okay. Back then, the CO was the "Old Man"; you just didn't walk in and bother him with the questions of one of his most junior officers. But going into his office, I took my shot.

"Captain," I said, "I want to go to Vietnam and I'm going to miss my only opportunity to go. The war's just about over. If I go to Ranger school, everything will be done before I get out. Here is what I want to do." The words tumbled out almost incomprehensibly. "I will go to the Raider/LRRP school down at the 82nd Airborne instead. If I don't come back the Honor Man from Raider/

LRRP school, then you can turn me around and send me off to Ranger school. But if I do graduate as the Honor Man of the class, I get the billet to Vietnam, okay?''

Ferruggiaro, forewarned by a good Ops boss, chuckled a bit, then agreed to my suggestion. He knew that there was no way the Army was going to let a Navy man be the honor graduate of their school.

Radioman Third Class Fletcher and Lieutenant (jg) McCombie left Little Creek on 5 September 1971 for four weeks of Raider/LRRP school at the 82nd Airborne, Fort Bragg, North Carolina, Class 4-71. The school itself was something like a short version of Ranger school, only four weeks long instead of Ranger school's sixteen weeks. You really had to bust your hump to make it through the school. But after UDTB—it was now called BUD/S, for Basic Underwater Demolition/SEAL—other schools just seemed an inconvenience.

Long before I had gotten down to Fort Bragg, I had been had by professionals who complied with few constraints; more lack of sleep and lack of food didn't make for any good training for a SEAL. We had proved our fitness during Hell Week. But there was something else I was working for now, so I kept my nose clean. The classroom and practical fieldwork were of use, and good lessons were learned. The Army put out some good schools, but LRRP school was just something that I could eat up, with my background in the woods.

Some of the training at the school did have its humorous moments. With all my time hunting, I had been taught how to field-dress game before I was out of grade school. As an Eagle Scout, my woodcraft included becoming a pretty good rough camp cook. One night, the instructors gave us a goat to eat. That was all we had, just this goat. Almost none of the Army guys knew what to do with the animal. A black sergeant from Georgia and I had that goat dressed out and roasting while the other soldiers were still trying to figure out how we killed it.

It was second nature for me to take out a knife and butcher the carcass. Some of those Army guys would have sat there and starved. To them, meat was something that you got out of a plastic bag at the supermarket. Well, that class the Raider/LRRP school had two top graduates, Distinguished Honor Man (an Army man) and Honor Man (me). That was good enough for me.

Returning from Raider/LRRP school, I immediately was nicknamed "Raider Ryan." Rick Woolard had been known for years as "Ranger Rick," and he was my hero in the Teams, so there now was a Ranger and a Raider from Team TWO. After I had fulfilled my part of the bargain, the billet I had been hoping to get had disappeared. It seemed Vietnam just wasn't going to happen for me. Oh well, I thought, here we go again, and I carried on.

My next work assignment was with Warrant Officer Roger Moscone to set up a detachment at Roosevelt Roads in Puerto Rico. Moscone was something of a character at the Team. He certainly was an impressive person at first glance, with his six-foot-two-inch height, 285 pounds, with twenty-two-inch arms and a fifty-five-inch chest. Just an enormous man. He drove a little Volkswagen bug.

Moscone had a devious sense of humor along with a creative mind. Roger would invite the newest ensign out to lunch. Being really quite honored and pleased to be accepted this early in his stint at SEAL Team TWO, the officer would agree with enthusiasm. That was his mistake.

Lunch with Moscone usually consisted of getting into his little Volkswagen and driving off-post, straight to the nearest school. Moscone would leer and make comments about the girls walking by. That is, third-grade girls. The comments wouldn't be loud enough to be heard by anyone but the helpless officer in Moscone's front seat.

With a high-pitched tittering voice, Moscone would comment, "Whoo, look at that one! Ohh, whoo whooo, just look at that one!" The poor ensign would be absolutely mortified and trying to crawl under the dashboard, anything to get away from this madman. Moscone's size would keep any thoughts of getting him mad well under control.

All of this was a great laugh to Moscone and was his part in the indoctrination of new Team members. In truth, if anything ever happened to a child with Moscone nearby, there wouldn't be enough left of the perpetrator to bother prosecuting. Nevertheless, the young officers didn't know this. The next day, Moscone would call out the young officer's name about lunchtime. Junior officers, especially ensigns, would be hiding in closets and going out for sudden beach runs—anything to get out of Moscone's reach.

The practical jokes at SEAL Team were classic. They ranged from "Fingers" Fellers (a demolition man, obviously) taking a bite and only a single bite out of "Fly" Fallon's lunch sandwich every day to stripping and shaving all of the body hair, then dyeing all of the body except the face and hands of the "groom to be" with indelible black ink and gentian violet. At the wedding the groom would look fine. The first night of the honeymoon, the bride was in for quite a surprise. One of the SEALs in particular enjoyed exhorting the men to exact a toll on the others. When this particular SEAL left the command, retribution was swift and exacting. He was stripped and hung by his ankles from the chin-up bar. Then at regular intervals the corpsman would give him an enema. As his bowels reacted, dripping his own excrement over him, he was asked to remember all of the times he had played jokes on others.

In any case, Roger Moscone and I went to Puerto Rico. We went to the old Chiefs' Club out on the point to set it up for the incoming men. Trading a bunch of Ka-bar knives to the local Seabees, we got them to paint the building for us and generally fix it up. Going diving we got some lobster and fish. We then would throw barbecues for all of the workers and soon had the old Chiefs' Club shipshape awaiting the first platoon.

Ferruggiaro called me at Roosey Roads with stunning news late in February. "Do you still want to go to Vietnam?" he asked.

Without hesitation I answered, "Yes!"

"Then get back here [Little Creek] and get your gear

together," he said. "You have twenty-four hours to get back here and twenty-four hours after that to leave for Vietnam."

"Aye-aye, I'm on my way, sir," I answered and was practically out the door before the phone landed on the hook. I managed to grab a flight to Guantanamo Bay in Cuba almost immediately. Then I got stuck overnight. There was no question in my mind that I was going to lose the job again. The next morning, I managed to grab a flight up to Norfolk and just screamed up to Team TWO. Arriving there, I found out that everything had changed again.

This time for the better. There was time for me to spend some leave with my wife. The billet was waiting for me, but the powers that be wanted me to attend Vietnamese language school before I shipped over. That was how Denise and I ended up in Coronado in April of 1972, in time to see Tom Norris on TV.

To prepare for duty in Vietnam, I was sent to Vietnamese language school in Coronado. My wife and I were staying in a little efficiency apartment at the Glorietta Bay Hotel. One day, while watching the TV news, I saw Tom Norris on the set. Tom Norris had been my roommate back in Virginia Beach before I married Denise. He had gone on his second assignment to Vietnam. I had unhappily stayed home and happily married Denise.

Calling out, "Denise, there's Tom!" I paid close attention to the story. Norris had just rescued a downed pilot in Quang Tri Province, going deep behind enemy lines with only his interpreter, Kit. Kit [Nguyen Van Kiet] was awarded the Navy Cross for this operation. In fact, he was the only Vietnamese to be awarded the Navy Cross during the entire war.

Because it was a classfied operation, Tom was only written up for the Silver Star. Much later, when I returned from Vietnam myself, I rewrote the citation for the Medal of Honor. The CO of the Team at the time did not forward the Medal of Honor recommendation up through channels. Later, when Dick Marcinko took command of the Team, he ran it through, and Tom deservedly received the

Congressional Medal of Honor. I was in France with the French Swimmer/Commandos when the award ceremony took place. Thanks to a lengthy French mail strike, I received the letter telling me about the award the day the ceremony took place in the White House.

Back to Coronado now, by the end of July, I was on my way to Vietnam. Denise, pregnant with our first child, was going to Pennsylvania to stay with my family. During my flight to Vietnam, a panoply of thoughts were going through my head. My feelings ran from excitement to trepidation. This was not only my first time going to war, it was my first major trip out of the country, my first time overseas. Except for Puerto Rico, I hadn't been out of North America.

At the time I had no fear of my own mortality. My thoughts were that other people had gone before me, and what others had done, I could certainly do. The guys who had gone before and didn't come back had screwed up. I truly believed that. It was neither bravery nor courage. It was not arrogance on my part, but the confidence of youth. The Teams had trained me and I could face whatever came my way.

All of that was waiting ahead of me in Vietnam. Flying in to Tan Son Nhut airport, I was expecting Tom Nelson to meet me. Getting off the plane, surprise, no Tom. After I'd waited a while, still nobody arrived to pick me up. Not knowing where I had to report, I did the next best thing—I played golf.

Next to the airport was a regulation golf course. Walking over, I rented a set of clubs, got the mandatory Ba for a caddy, and began a game. That should indicate the attitude I had for being in a combat zone. By the time I had gotten to the seventeenth hole, this Navy commander came screaming and yelling up to where I was playing. It was Tom Nelson voicing his displeasure about what the hell I thought I was doing.

Telling him straight out, I said that I had waited over an hour without knowing where to go. No one had showed up, so I had just occupied my time. "Are we going to the war now?"

As I remember it, Tom Nelson was so dumbfounded he actually allowed me to finish my game. Gathering my gear, we climbed aboard his vehicle and drove off to Cat Lai. At Cat Lai was Commander Dave Schaible, the officer in charge of the Naval Advisory Unit. Schaible was one of the best officers I have ever had the pleasure to serve with. If there was anyone I can point to and say he was my "sea daddy," it would be Dave Schaible. Before graduating from high school the man joined the Navy back in World War Two as an enlisted man aboard submarines. After the war, Schaible completed high school and attended a year of school at the University of Buffalo before he reenlisted in the Navy at the outbreak of the Korean War.

Schaible seemed to have done everything, joined the UDT in 1951, serving with UDT 5 and Underwater Demolition Unit 1. During his career as an officer, Dave commanded ships, was the CO of the underwater swimmers school in Key West, CO of UDT 22, CO of SEAL Team ONE, CO of the EOD school at Indian Head, and finally Commodore of Naval Special Warfare Group ONE. The man had more leadership in his little finger than most officers could dream of having. This was someone worth serving under.

Sometimes, after duty, Dave would tell submariner stories about sitting on the bottom off of Japan during the war. He and the crew would listen to grappling hooks scraping along their hull. The Japanese would throw the hooks over hoping to snag a suspected submarine. If they caught something, a depth charge would slide down the cable. Something hard to imagine sitting in an Officers' Club with a cold beer, but Dave would make us feel the long, tense hours on the bottom.

Commander Schaible assigned me to be the officer in charge of Detachment Charlie, where I was the SEAL advisor to an LDNN platoon. I was only a lieutenant junior grade (0-2) but had been frocked as a full lieutenant (0-3) for my duty in-country. As far as the folks back home knew, all of the operational SEAL units had been returned to the United States. The men over in Vietnam, such as myself, were not on deployment. We were assigned to Vietnam for a full year as a PCS, permanent change of station.

The next morning after my arrival in-country, I was sent up to Thuan An in I Corps to join my LDNN platoon. The very next night I found myself out in the field on an op with my platoon. I wanted to get the reputation of a go-getter, but this was a little ridiculous. I hadn't been in the country seventy-two hours yet!

On the operation, we were off the coast in a ferroconcrete junk waiting to insert behind enemy lines while still in South Vietnam. While lying there on the deck, looking at the millions of stars in the southern hemisphere, I was suddenly hit with the immediacy of my situation. Here I was brand new to combat advising a group of men, some of whom had been fighting their entire lives. What in God's name was I doing here? What in the world could I teach these men who had fought most of their adult lives? Less than a week before, I had been up in San Francisco with Denise. Now I was lying on a gently rocking boat in the South China Sea awaiting the time to go ashore where people wanted to kill me.

My feelings must have been pretty obvious, though I don't think I spoke out loud. One of my SEAL Teammates, Chamberlain, was with us, and he looked over at me. "Hey, Mr. Mac," Chamberlain called out quietly.

"Yeah," I rasped whisperingly. My mouth was suddenly as dry as the desert back near San Diego.

"This is your first op, isn't it, *Trung-uy* [Vietnamese for lieutenant junior grade]?"

"Yeah, it is," I answered a little more firmly.

"Well, don't worry about it," he said. "We'll be all right,"

I had only been in the platoon a day and they had fully accepted me. Quite a change from my first months at Team TWO. A year and a half before, I had volunteered for the duty I had right now. Actually, the duty I had volunteered for so long ago wasn't exactly what I was doing now, because now we had very little support and no medical evacuation. I remember the guys talking about when the medevac time had gone from an eight-to-ten-minute response to a twenty-minute or longer response time. They had flatly stated that they wouldn't go back to Vietnam under these conditions.

Here I was without any medevac at all. Did they know something I didn't?

We also didn't have any artillery support. Occasionally, we would be given naval gunfire support if it was available. Mostly we operated on our own nickel, without a squad or platoon of fellow SEALs either. Just one SEAL enlisted man and one officer was the usual complement. The rest of the unit was made up of LDNNs. This was a different concept of operating than I had been prepared for with my predeployment training.

Most of our missions would be going in behind the lines to chart base camps and identify enemy positions for naval gunfire and B-52 air strikes. On some occasions, we would remain within sight of the objective during the attack to be forward observers (FOs) and direct the placement of fire. One night one of the teams did call in immediate fire on a tank, but that was just a target of opportunity.

We could be armed with anything we wished for the operations. I had an SKS, an AK-47, and a CAR-15 for my own use, and I would take whatever felt right. Doug Huth was over six feet in height and hard to miss. When we could be seen by silhouette at night, the enemy could easily spot Doug as an American, and then they would really try to get us. Finally, there was an advantage to being under six foot tall. I had to remember this one to tell my high school basketball coach. One thing was, the big SEALs could carry big guns, and sometimes that felt mighty good.

I had been on three or four ops and had pretty well calmed down. The operations went well and as planned. We had little or no enemy contact. But the first time I had enemy fire coming my way it put a whole new light on things. It's mostly amazement that you feel when you realize that somebody is shooting at you. Not just random fire in your direction. But somebody is actually shooting at *you*! The buzzing snap of bullets would go on for a moment before the idea hit home that these people wanted to kill you. They're shooting at *me*!

The kind of operations we went on, it would be rare for someone to detect us, let alone fire directly at us. As rare as it would be for us to be shot at, it would be even more rare for us to return fire. With no support, we just didn't let ourselves be seen. With the few men we had, we just didn't have the firepower to take on an enemy unit. This situation greatly affected our choice of weapons. The AK-47 and SKS had the same sound signature, muzzle flash, and tracer color as the enemy's own weapons. An M16, M60, and especially a Stoner would stand out to the VC and NVA, telling them where and possibly who we were.

With most of our operations being passive in nature, avoiding contact and observing, I began to get a little itchy. I wanted to do an active operation. We needed intel. So I decided we were going to go out and get a prisoner for interrogation. After I had stated my intention to the other SEALs, Chamberlain spoke up. "You son of a bitch, sir," he said. "You've only been here a couple of months—now you want to go out and be a hero."

But the operation was a go, and off we went. We inserted from a junk in an area where bunkers had been seen earlier. On board the junk was another SEAL officer who would bring in the boat when we needed extraction. I had the radio on my back to be sure of communications. My call sign was Rubber Duck.

The plan was to go up to one bunker we had spotted, pile in the door, grab one guy, and hose down everything else in the room. We were not nearly as sophisticated in technique as close quarter combat is today. A little more of an active plan than we had been using up till then. Being that it was my plan, I was going to be the first through the door of the bunker. I had just crept up to the door and was preparing to go in when it happened.

The radio on my back broke squelch and the voice of the officer back on the junk came through clearly:

"Rubber Duck, Rubber Duck, this is Mother Duck. Over."

Well, that was it—anybody in the bunker would have heard that. Blam—we slammed into the bunker and faced nothing.

It was empty, and the whole mission turned out to be a dry hole. But if there had been someone in that bunker, things could have been a lot different. With the warning from the radio, we could have gone through that door and had our asses handed back to us.

I hadn't checked in with Mother Duck for a while, and he had become worried. Later on, the officer told me that he wanted to be sure everything was okay. "Well, it was," I answered. "At least until you started asking about it." Another lesson learned.

Another time, we went against a group of VC tax collectors we knew were coming into an area. The tax collectors had a good enough intel network of their own that we just could not get at them. Every time we would lie in wait for them, they would know we were there and bypass us. Finally, we boarded the junks in the Vietnamese village that was being taxed by these collectors. Every morning, these junks would go out to sea to fish, returning in the evening. We hid aboard a junk during the day while it was out fishing. Coming in late in the day from the sea would not be something the VC would expect. When they tried to tax the boats and the village, we could nail them.

The reason nobody would expect us to be hiding on the junks is that we would have to be completely nuts to attempt such a thing. We didn't know these fishermen; they could have done almost anything with us. What they did do was lead a bunch of us, Mike Thornton, Chamberlain, Brooks, Wanous, Woodruff, Kaneakua, and me, down into the hold of one of the boats. We spent the entire day in the stinking hold of a Vietnamese fishing junk. Inside the hold was like an oven. What little air there was to breathe was polluted with fish stink. But while the men fished all day long, we stayed out of sight in the hold.

The payoff came that night when the junks came back into port. As the fishermen went to their families for chow, we slipped up and hid on deck of a nearby junk, not taking chances of a compromise. When the tax collectors came swimming across the canal, we had them.

Our intent was to capture the collectors. The best way to develop another operation is to gather the information during the operation you're on. But one of the LDNNs opened up on the VC tax collectors too soon. One concussion grenade into the water and that ended the incident. We didn't find the bodies until the next day, and there was no interrogation.

Looking back on it, I realize that we were incredibly lucky. Here we had allowed ourselves to be bottled up in the hold of this boat, where the men on deck could have signaled anyone. When the men went off to have chow with their families we did change boats, in case they ratted on us at that time. Oh well, I guess it's better to be lucky than only good.

Other things went well right from the start. SEALs tried to pick free-fire zones in which to stalk the NVA and Viet Cong, while the other forces often worked under very strict rules of engagement. We also had our own living quarters and facilities. The average soldier in Vietnam would spend a year in the field eating C rations day after day, getting a shower perhaps every six weeks, and wearing uniforms until the boots literally rotted off his feet. R&R for the soldier would be getting permission to hitchhike down Highway One to Vung Tau or Saigon for five days.

On the other hand, we had fairly good quarters, a refrigerator that stayed full of beer, a hooch maid who came in and kept our quarters squared away. Our hooch maid even made fresh French bread for us every few days. I really liked this bread, a little like pumpernickel with all these little black flecks in it, lots and lots of these little black spots. Then one day I saw it being made.

As the dough was being kneaded, flies were buzzing all around the baker and her wares. Any flies that would land on it were just kneaded in. After a short time, the flies had just become a part of the dough. Then it was baked. That's where my pumpernickel came from. Oh man, I thought, it's a good thing I've been eating this stuff for a few months before I saw this.

The situation was like the story about the newbie in Vietnam. When he first arrives, he goes to a restaurant and orders a beer and sends it back because there is a fly in it. After several months in-country, he merely takes the fly out of his beer and drinks it. About time to rotate back to CONUS, if he ever gets a beer without a fly, he sends it back wanting to know where his fly is.

In September, I had something quite different for me going on. Denise was due early that month to deliver our first child. I had made a bet with my teammates that it would be a boy. Coming from a family of five boys, I figured the situation was a fairly safe bet. Commander Schaible refused to take me up on my bet. "Peas, Ryan," Schaible said to me. "Peas, peas, Mendel's peas. No, I won't bet with you."

Commander Schaible remembered his genetics and the monk Mendel's heredity studies with peas. As always, Commander Schaible was right. My son, Ryan T. Mc-Combie, was born on 6 September 1972. The night I found out he was born, a group of us went out to the neighborhood "club." There was a landing craft that would ferry back and forth across a small inland waterway that separated Thuan An from an Air Force B-52 LORAN station across the water.

Over at the station, the Air Force had done themselves well. The E-2s and E-3s [privates and PFCs] had half an air-conditioned trailer with shower and toilet facilities to themselves. In another double-wide trailer they had constructed a bar and had a pool table. That was the "club" we would often go to when we were on liberty in the area.

Next to the trailer was a local establishment up on stilts in the manner of some Vietnamese buildings. The monsoon would flood the area and the stilts kept the main part of the building up out of the mud. The architecture resulted in a single-story building starting a story in the air. To cross over from the Air Force area, there were a series of planks across the deep mud that you would walk across to reach the ladder leading up to the Vietnamese place.

On that night, I had gotten shit-faced with the guys on nickel beers. Going over to the local establishment, we became considerably more rowdy. Actually, the party turned into a Wild West show as a number of us took turns shooting bottles off the wall with our sidearms. All the locals just took off on us and hid. A group of Special Forces troopers came into the place while we were still there.

The soldiers were pissed at us in no small way because we had chased everybody away. The officer in charge, a major, was seriously angry and pulled a .45 pistol on me, intending to drive me and my rowdies out. This was not a good idea.

Mike Thornton was with us, and Mikey is a big and extremely quick boy. While the trooper was dealing with me, Mike came up next to him and just knocked the pistol out of the man's hand. Grabbing the soldier by his chest and crotch, Mike picked the man up over his head, walked out the door, and threw him over the balcony into the mud.

"Somebody better get out there and rescue your boss before he drowns," we told the soldiers. "That mud's pretty deep." The Army decided that the Navy had won the day that time and left the playing field to us. My son's coming into the world had been celebrated in proper SEAL fashion.

Actually, my boy had been born a week or ten days before I found out about it. Tom Norris had gotten the news from the Red Cross and told me. I sent my wife twelve dozen roses to celebrate. Tom sent her a dozen himself. On a late show I had picked up a line from Humphrey Bogart or someone and sent my wife a note with the flowers: "Each petal is a thought of you." Not bad for a mud-crawling SEAL.

But AFEES [Armed Forces Exchange Service] screwed things up as only they can. Instead of the twelve dozen roses I had paid for, they delivered one dozen. The note "Every petal a thought of you" was with the flowers. Denise got them, read the note, and thought it was nice.

Not even SEAL plans always work when you get non-quals involved.

One notable operation was a successful diversion of the enemy forces. Back in May, the NVA had captured the provincial capital, Quang Tri City, during their spring offensive. Now the ARVN Rangers were trying to take the city back. The idea for our mission was to create a diversion so the NVA would turn their artillery east toward the coast, giving the Rangers an opportunity to retake the city. The diversion would be to make the enemy think there was going to be an amphibious landing by Marines on the shores of the Gulf of Tonkin, east of Quang Tri.

The operation was much like what SEALs did in Desert Storm but on a smaller scale. Our job was to go in and do a hydrographic recon of landing beaches. The enemy knew that a recon of the beaches was always done before a landing. The main problem was that for the diversion to work, the enemy had to have indicators that a reconnaissance was being conducted.

This became a real cat-and-mouse operation for us, walking a thin line of being seen yet still not allowing ourselves to be caught. There was a destroyer just offshore to provide fire support, but splashing around in the waters off enemy beaches was not the thing I most wanted to do. If something happened, nobody would be coming along to help bail us out.

We did a straight-out, lead-line hydrographic recon of the target beach. I remember Jack Brooks doing swims in and out half the night. By the numbers, we measured the water's depth and the bottom's contour lines, just like in training. Only this time, the "judges" watching from beyond the surf zone were armed enemy troops. Failing here would be permanent.

The diversion did work. Enemy artillery was turned toward the beaches to cover any landing forces. The ARVN Rangers were able to take the city for a while, before the NVA took it back permanently. It wasn't a week before the same beach saw more action.

As the war wound down for U.S. forces, we were getting fewer and fewer operations. One op came up and,

even though we were the best of friends, Tom Norris
pulled rank on me to take it. Tom was scheduled to go
back to the States within a few weeks, and he wanted to
go out a few more times before he left for the last time.
I had wanted to go, but Norris was the senior officer and
won out. I would soon know that I was the lucky one.

The operation began on October 31, Halloween. Tom
Norris was the officer in charge, and Mike Thornton, a
SEAL from Team ONE, was his assistant. Three Vietnamese LDNNs made up the balance of the five-man
team. The mission was to gather intel on the Cua Viet
Naval River Base. The base had been captured earlier in
the year. Because of his large size, Mike Thornton was
going to be rear security for the op. Inserting from a junk,
the team moved ashore to an area where it was very hard
to get your bearings, a few klicks from North Vietnam.

If I had been on the op, I would have recognized the
area almost immediately. It was the same beach where we
had done our recon only a week earlier. Tom said later
that he knew they had inserted into the wrong area, but
continued with the operation to teach the LDNNs a lesson.
The object was for us to completely turn over operations
to the LDNNs very soon. If you live through them, the
best way to learn is from your mistakes. Though Tom
knew they were in the wrong location, he didn't know the
enemy was still riled up from the week before and prepared to repel invaders.

Tom's team finally realized they were in the wrong
place and that the operation was compromised. Two
NVAs were walking down the beach, and Tom decided
to try and capture them. The team only captured one of
the men and the other took off across the sand dunes.
Almost immediately, fire started coming from a nearby
NVA camp. It was time to leave.

The team was heavily outnumbered, and they called for
naval gunfire. While leapfrogging back to the water, one
LDNN broke ranks and ran, leaving one flank open. With
only a few dunes between the team and the open beach,
Norris ordered the rest of the men to pull back while he
and one LDNN put out covering fire. Within five minutes,

the incoming naval gunfire support would obliterate the beach right where the men were lying.

We had always carried M72A2 LAW rockets with us on ops to simulate artillery. Firing a rocket at the enemy would make them think more rounds were on the way and they would take cover, giving us a chance to get away. Standing up slightly to fire his last M72A2 LAW rocket, Norris was hit right between the eyes with a 7.62 round. The round tore in above his left eye and exited the side of his head, causing a massive wound and almost immediate unconsciousness. The LDNN ran away from what he thought was the lieutenant's dead body.

The LDNN reported that the lieutenant was dead to Mike Thornton. "Bullshit!" was all Mike said, and he headed back to Norris's last position. As a few NVA soldiers ran up where Norris lay, Mike blew them away with his AK. A grenade exploded, and Mike took some fragments in his legs. When he reached Norris, he thought Tom really was dead. The bullet had opened up Tom's skull on the left side and brain tissue could be seen. But Mike wasn't going to leave the body behind. Amazingly enough, Tom came around enough to speak to Mike.

Picking up the wounded SEAL, Mike ran to the relative safety of the water, firing back at the enemy as he went. The last LDNN, who had stayed behind to provide cover, went into the water with Tom and Mike. Swimming out to sea, Mike had to tow Tom along. They were in the water for hours before being picked up by the U.S. Navy.

Some of the Vietnamese LDNNs made it back to the base and reported that Tom had been left back on the beach. I was in Thuan An when the news came in. With the word being that Tom had been left on the beach, I immediately started to mount an operation to go in and get him out. Even though we had been specifically ordered not to go in after Tom, I knew speed was essential, so I ignored the order and proceeded to mount a rescue operation. Long before things had gone very far, Mike showed up and told us what was left of Tom was out of enemy hands.

I stayed with Tom down in Hue City all night while

awaiting medical evacuation availability to the Philippines. The doctors were worried that if Tom went unconscious, he would go comatose. I did everything I could to keep him awake that night, talking, joking, and telling stories. Norris made it through the night and every night since.

The one LDNN who had stayed with Mike and Tom hadn't gotten away untouched. The man had been shot right across the cheeks of his ass. When everything was over, the man, Kuan, went up to Mike and said, "Mikey, I'm not going on any operations with you ever again. I've been on three operations with you and I've been shot three times. No more." We all laughed. And if Kuan didn't want to go with Mike anymore, he didn't have to.

Later on, when Mike was telling us the details of the operation, I took the time to pinch out the grenade fragments he had in his thighs. There weren't very many, and they hadn't gone in much more than the thickness of the skin. Mike jokingly asked me if he was going to get a Purple Heart, and I said no. The only medal Tom Norris was going to get on that op, with his head blown off, was the Purple Heart. I told Mike that he sure wasn't going to get the same medal for fragments I dug out with my fingernails. Mike did eventually receive a Purple Heart for his wounds, slight as they were, and deservedly so. He was also awarded the Medal of Honor.

When Christmas came along, I spent my R&R time going back to the States to see Denise and my new son. I did miss on going to Thailand or Australia, but I needed to see my firstborn son.

When I returned to Vietnam after my R&R, Tom Nelson had a new assignment for me. "McCombie," Tom said, "you're going down to Nam Can and get yourself killed." Welcome back to Vietnam! While I stared at him, he continued, "You're going because I need you there. You'll get killed because you don't listen and take too many chances."

"Commander," I said, "I am the junior officer in-country." By this time, Tom Norris had been replaced by Mike Slattery. "If I'm going to go down there and just get killed, why don't you send one of the other guys?''

"Because," Nelson said, "they'll get killed quicker than you will."

How can you argue with logic like that? "Oh, okay," I said, and that was the end of it. So off I went to the opposite end of South Vietnam, the Ca Mau Peninsula and Nam Can on the Cua Lon River. Up in MR 1 [I Corps] I had been the advisor to an LDNN platoon, and I would be doing the same job down at Nam Can in MR 4 [the old IV Corps]. But the jobs were the same only in title.

Up in MR 1, it had been a constant struggle to keep my LDNNs in the field. Getting them, and keeping them, operational was a continuous fight. When I went over the beach on a recon mission, there would be seven of us, two SEALs and five LDNNs. We would be carrying upwards of three radios. The number of radios was to ensure that at least one worked. After a number of missions, I realized that if I carried the radio myself, there would be one operational.

The LDNNs would intentionally damage the radio or be sure it wasn't waterproofed properly or otherwise sabotage it. Without a working radio, the op would be immediately scrubbed, which is exactly what the LDNNs wanted.

When I arrived in Nam Can, the situation was completely different. This platoon was a pack of fighting tigers. They wanted to fight everybody all the time. They had tattooed *Sat Cong* ["Kill the Communists"] on their chests to ensure none would be traitors or think about losing the war.

The ops with my Nam Can LDNNs went well—they would follow advice and recognized the difference in training between themselves and the Navy SEALs. There was only one op I didn't go on with my platoon, because I had been called away up to Vung Tau for two days in January 1973. The LDNNs had put the op together themselves with fresh intel. Everything went wrong. When I returned, half my men were either wounded or dead. It probably wouldn't have made any difference if I was there, but I felt responsible. The results were pretty final.

Without a platoon to lead, it was time for me to go home. Every day I would go out and shoot targets with my .38 caliber Combat Masterpiece, but that palled quickly. At home I had a wife and a new baby. Shooting targets and inspecting claymore mines around the perimeter is not why I had volunteered for Vietnam. I wanted to be back in the field conducting combat operations. I was ordered home and left Vietnam on 9 February 1973. I may not have been the last SEAL officer to be sent to Vietnam, but I was the last one to operate in combat.

I left my platoon of Vietnamese with mixed feelings, glad to go home but feeling I was deserting them. All of my personal weapons, a Chicom Type 54 pistol, an SKS, an AK-47, my .38 Combat Masterpiece, and my M1 Garand, I left with my LDNN platoon commander.

My arrival in the States was a lot different than my arrival in Vietnam. No golf game this time. I walked through the mass of antiwar protesters at Travis Air Force Base. There were police lines on either side of us, holding back the protesters. I was treated with more respect by the Vietnamese than my own people. The police held the crowds back, but they couldn't stop all the thrown objects that were coming our way.

I had been out of touch with the States and forgotten how vociferous the protests could become. I remember distinctly being struck by an object thrown from the mob and going after the thrower. A policeman pushed me back into line, keeping me from my assailant. I certainly didn't think I was a hero, but I had made a sacrifice for my country and did what my country asked. It didn't matter who was right or wrong about the war. I, as a soldier, did not deserve what was waiting for me. Screaming mobs were not what I expected for my arrival home. And yet that's what I and many other soldiers got.

Thoughts of the war have never particularly bothered me. I guess I've been lucky that the aftermath of Vietnam has never come back to haunt me. No flashbacks or PTSD [post-traumatic stress disorder]. SEALs were different. When we fought, it was on the same level as the enemy.

We went to Vietnam with the intention of fighting. We were the aggressors, not the victims. We did a good job of it.

My last Officer's Fitness Report from my duty in Vietnam, from November 9, 1972, to February 9, 1973, when Commander William Earley was my senior advisor and filled out my report, stated what I did during my time there. I was listed as having been the OIC of SEAL Det C and Advisor to an LDNN (SEAL) Platoon as an 0-3. Where the report really gets interesting is in the comments section. It read:

> *Lt McCOMBIE is a decidedly capable and competent officer whose sedulous vigor for difficult assignments is ever prevalent. His courage and presence of mind during exceptional stress combat situations is readily apparent in the cool serene manner in which he executes his extremely hazardous missions. During his Vietnam tour, Lt McCOMBIE was Officer-in-Charge of SEAL Detachment "Charlie" and advised an LDNN (SEAL) platoon in proper methods and techniques of planning, coordination, and execution of clandestine SEAL combat operations. On several occasions this advisor role necessitated his arrangement and utilization of American naval gunfire as the only available means of support for perilous missions in heavily fortified NVA-held areas. His administrative skill has shown significant improvement and it is felt he will continue to ameliorate these efforts and strive for preferable administrative performance with greater attention to detail. In numerous instances he has demonstrated trenchant articulation in his verbal expression of ideas. Lt McCOMBIE's finest quality is by far his natural leadership propensity and intrinsic charisma which inspires his subordinates to their utmost efforts. The com-*

mendable proclivity of this quality, coupled with his continued growth and maturity, will assuredly reap sustaining benefits for both himself and the United States Navy. He is recommended for promotion when due. The total absence of racial or intercultural incidents at this command is indicative of his concern for the equal opportunity aspects of leadership. 9FEB73 William L. Earley

A SEAL with a book of synonyms and a thesaurus is a dangerous thing indeed.

Returning to the Team, I became training officer and soon went to France as an exchange officer to the French frogmen. Upon my return to the States, I became operations officer for UDT 21. In 1978 I went down to Florida to be the operations officer for the predecessor of today's JSOC [Joint Special Operations Command], the Joint Special Operations Support Element [JSOSE]. Then I was the Executive Officer of SEAL Team TWO, followed by duty in Congo, Africa, as well as time spent in other countries on SEAL duties. But in July of 1986, I became the Commanding Officer of SEAL Team Two.

Arriving on the quarterdeck and hearing the words "SEAL Team TWO arriving," was wonderful. When I was an Ensign, I had sworn that I would stay in the Navy until I could command a SEAL Team. At the time, the commanding officer had changed from Lieutenant to Lieutenant Commander. I never dreamed that required rank would continue to rise from Lieutenant Commander to Commander, or that it would take sixteen years before I took command.

AFTERWORD

The end of the SEALs' tours in Vietnam came during the early 1970s. By March of 1972, the last SEAL units had left Vietnam without reliefs. Only a few SEAL-qualified officers may have spent any significant time in South Vietnam before the final fall of the country in July 1975.

For over ten years, there had been a SEAL presence in Vietnam. From the original small numbers of men in the Mobile Training Teams of 1962 and 1963 to their peak years in 1968 and 1969, the SEALs had left their mark on the pages of modern warfare.

Though numbering less than 150 men in-country at any one time, the SEALs had an effect on the enemy far out of proportion to their numbers. Using the most conservative numbers, the SEALs accounted for 50 enemy dead for each SEAL lost. Including probable kills and other factors, that ratio can be easily expanded to over 200 enemy losses for each SEAL loss.

Starting from two small units of 55 men each, SEAL Teams ONE and TWO grew until they numbered 23 officers and 115 men in their platoons.

These numbers dropped after the war, with older SEALs leaving the Teams and financial cutbacks affecting the Teams' operations. By the mid-1970s, the SEAL Teams were at their lowest postwar strength, with their numbers being less than their authorized strengths. By the late 1970s and into the 1980s, the value of the Teams was recognized more and more as one of the forces to use in today's limited warfare situations. When the situation is too delicate for the hammer approach of most conventional forces, the scalpel precision of the SEALs can be called on. Today there are seven full SEAL Teams and two SEAL Delivery Vehicle Teams made up of fully qualified operators. SEALs have seen action in Central and South America, Africa, the Middle East, and elsewhere, including the actions in Grenada, Panama, the Persian Gulf, and Somalia.

The full limits of the SEALs may never be reached. Today there is even a SEAL in space, as a member of one of the Space Shuttle crews was an active officer in SEAL Team TWO before entering the shuttle program.

Though the accomplishments of today's SEALs are numerous, to a man they look back at the Vietnam War–era SEALs with no little awe. And well they might. Measuring by decorations alone, a system the SEALs don't fully approve of, the Teams are the most decorated units of their kind ever in the U.S. military. The SEAL Teams' decorations include 3 Medals of Honor, 5 Navy Crosses, 42 Silver Stars, 402 Bronze Stars, 2 Legions of Merit, 352 Navy Commendation Medals, 51 Navy Achievement Medals, 3 Presidential Unit Citations, and uncounted Purple Hearts and foreign decorations—over 860 medals for two combat units never measuring more than three hundred men total at any time during the war.

UDT/SEAL MEMORIAL PARK, INC.

Beginning with operations in North Africa in November 1942, the U.S. Navy hastily organized a detachment of special volunteers to spearhead an invasion. In the summer of 1943, formalized training of Naval Combat Demolition Units (NCDUs) commenced at Fort Pierce, Florida. The Navy Frogman was born.

In July 1943, Naval Combat Demolition Unit One responded to an urgent requirement to open the channel through the Sicily beaches. NCDUs were also among the first to land on Omaha and Utah beaches. Sustaining casualties in excess of 40 percent, the surviving Omaha force returned to Fort Pierce, while the Utah force deployed to participate in the invasion of southern France.

In the Pacific, Saipan was invaded with UDTs paving the way. From this point on, UDTs participated in every Pacific island campaign from Borneo to Okinawa. By the war's end, there were thirty-four Teams deployed or in training, totaling over 3,500 men. Following demobilization, four Teams remained, two on each coast.

During the Korean conflict, UDTs again played a key role by reconnaissance and raids north of the DMZ against enemy railroads, bridges, and tunnels.

In 1962, the Navy responded to an expanding role in counterinsurgency and unconventional warfare by forming two SEAL Teams. The two small Teams amassed an impressive combat record. They became the most highly decorated units in the Vietnam War. These numerous awards include three Congressional Medals of Honor.

Today the UDTs have been incorporated into the Navy's six SEAL and two SDV Teams. These highly trained teams have been used continuously in every military campaign since Vietnam. Many missions have been successfully completed, but because of their sensitive nature, they remain classified.

The UDT/SEAL Memorial Park, Inc., has been founded to ensure that the efforts of these brave men do not go unnoticed. This group of concerned citizens is raising donations (tax-exempt) to build a statue memorializing the heroism of these great Americans. Please send a tax-deductible donation to:

UDT/SEAL Memorial Park, Inc.
Mr. Joseph Dearing
2352 Great Neck Circle
Virginia Beach, VA 23454

BOOKS BY
BILL FAWCETT

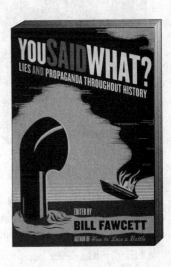

YOU SAID WHAT?
Lies and Propaganda Throughout History
ISBN 978-0-06-113050-2 (paperback)

From the dawn of man to the War on Terror, Fawcett chronicles the vast history of frauds, deceptions, propaganda, and trickery from governments, corporations, historians, and everyone in between.

OVAL OFFICE ODDITIES
An Irreverent Collection of Presidential Facts, Follies, and Foibles
ISBN 978-0-06-134617-0 (paperback)

Featuring hundreds of strange and wonderful facts about past American presidents, first ladies, and veeps, readers will learn all about presidential gaffes, love lives, and odd habits.

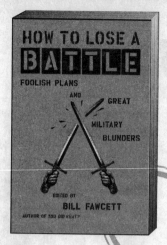

HOW TO LOSE A BATTLE
Foolish Plans and Great Military Blunders
ISBN 978-0-06-076024-3 (paperback)

Whether a result of lack of planning, miscalculation, a leader's ego, or spy infiltration, this compendium chronicles the worst military defeats and looks at what caused each battlefield blunder.

YOU DID WHAT?
Mad Plans and Great Historical Disasters
ISBN 978-0-06-053250-5 (paperback)

History has never been more fun than it is in this fact-filled compendium of historical catastrophes and embarrassingly bad ideas.

HUNTERS & SHOOTERS
An Oral History of the U.S. Navy SEALs in Vietnam
ISBN 978-0-06-137566-8 (paperback)

Fifteen former SEALs share their vivid, first-person remembrances of action in Vietnam—brutal, honest, and thrilling stories revealing astonishing truths that will only add strength to the SEAL legacy.